Enhanced A+ CoursePrep
StudyGuide/ExamGuide
for Core Exam and OS Exam

**COURSE
TECHNOLOGY**™

THOMSON LEARNING

Australia • Canada • Mexico • Singapore • Spain • United Kingdom • United States

COURSE TECHNOLOGY
™
THOMSON LEARNING

Enhanced A+ CoursePrep StudyGuide and CoursePrep ExamGuide for Core Exam and OS Exam

by Jean Andrews is published by
Course Technology

Senior Product Manager:
Lisa Egan

Managing Editor:
Stephen Solomon

Development Editor:
Lisa Ruffolo, The Software
Resource

Marketing Manager:
Toby Shelton

Editorial Assistant:
Janet Aras

Manufacturing Manager:
Denise Sandler

Production:
Karen Jacot

Internal Design:
Dianne Schaefer, Books By Design

Cover Design:
Betsy Young and Abby Scholz

Compositor:
GEX Publishing Services

Disclaimer
Course Technology reserves the right to revise this publication and make changes from time to time in its content without notice.

ISBN 0-619-03438-6
ISBN 0-619-03524-2

TABLE OF CONTENTS

PREFACE

The Enhanced A+ CoursePrep ExamGuide and A+ CoursePrep StudyGuide are the very best tools to use to prepare for exam day. Both products provide thorough preparation for the newly revised A+ certification exams created by CompTIA. These products are intended to be used with a core "Guide to" textbook, like *Enhanced A+ Guide to Managing and Maintaining Your PC*, (0-619-03433-5), also by Jean Andrews. CoursePrep ExamGuide and CoursePrep StudyGuide provide you ample opportunity to practice, drill, and rehearse for the exam!

COURSEPREP EXAMGUIDE

The Enhanced A+ CoursePrep ExamGuide, ISBN 0-619-03524-2, provides the essential information you need to master each exam objective. The ExamGuide devotes an entire two-page spread to each certification objective for the newly revised A+ exams, helping you to understand the objective, and giving you the bottom line information—what you *really* need to know. Memorize these facts and bulleted points before heading into the exam. In addition, there are seven practice test question for each objective on the right-hand page: that's 700 questions total! CoursePrep ExamGuide provides the exam fundamentals and gets you up to speed quickly. If you are seeking even more opportunity to practice and prepare, we recommend that you consider our most complete solution, CoursePrep StudyGuide, which is described below.

COURSEPREP STUDYGUIDE

For those really serious about certification, we offer an even more robust solution—the Enhanced A+ CoursePrep StudyGuide, ISBN 0-619-03438-6. This offering includes all of the same great features you get with the CoursePrep ExamGuide, including the unique two-page spread, bulleted memorization points, and practice questions. In addition, you receive a password valid for six months of practice on CoursePrep, a dynamic test preparation tool. The password is found in an envelope in the back cover of the CoursePrep StudyGuide. CoursePrep is a Web-based pool of hundreds of sample test questions. CoursePrep exam simulation software mimics the exact exam environment. The CoursePrep software is flexible, and allows you to practice in several ways as you master the material. Choose from Certification Mode to experience actual exam-day conditions or Study Mode to request answers and explanations to practice questions. Custom Mode lets you set the options for the practice test, including number of questions, content coverage, and ability to request answers and explanation. Follow the instructions on the inside back cover to access the exam simulation software. To see a demo of this dynamic test preparation tool, go to *www.courseprep.com*.

FEATURES

The *Enhanced A+ CoursePrep ExamGuide* and *A+ CoursePrep StudyGuide* books include the following features:

List of domains and objectives taken directly from the CompTIA Web site The book is divided into two sections: one section is devoted to the Core exam, and one section is devoted to the OS exam. Each section begins with a description of the domains covered on the exam. The objectives under each domain are found within the sections. For more information about the A+ Exams, visit CompTIA's Web site at **www.comptia.org**.

Detailed coverage of the certification objectives in a unique two-page spread Study strategically by really focusing on the A+ certification objectives. To enable you to do this, a two-page spread is devoted to each certification objective. The left-hand page provides the critical facts you need, while the right-hand page features practice questions relating to that objective. You'll find that the certification objective(s) and sub-objectives(s) are clearly listed in the upper left-hand corner of each spread.

 Software Icon: This icon appears to the left of certification objectives that are software related.

 Hardware Icon: This icon appears to the left of the certification objectives that are hardware related.

An overview of the objective is provided in the **Understanding the Objective** section. Next, **What you Really Need to Know** lists bulleted, succinct facts, skills, and concepts about the objective. Memorizing these facts will be important for your success when taking the exam. **Objectives on the Job** places the objective in an industry perspective, and tells you how you can expect to use the objective on the job. This section also provides troubleshooting information.

Practice Test Questions: Each right-hand page contains seven practice test questions designed to help you prepare for the exam by testing your skills, identifying your strengths and weaknesses, and demonstrating the subject matter you will face on the exams and how it will be tested. These questions are written in a similar fashion to real A+ Exam questions. The questions test your knowledge of the objectives described on the left-hand page and also the information in the *Enhanced A+ Guide to Managing and Maintaining Your PC, Comprehensive, Enhanced Third Edition* (ISBN 0-619-03433-5). You can find answers to the practice test questions on the CoursePrep Web site, **www.courseprep.com**, along with the Web-based exam preparation questions.

Answer Boxes: You can use the boxes to the right of the practice test questions to mark your answers, grade yourself, or write down the correct answer.

Glossary: Boldfaced terms used in the book and other terms that you need to know for the exams are listed and defined in the glossary.

For more information: This book evolved from *Enhanced A+ Guide to Managing and Maintaining Your PC, Third Edition Comprehensive* (ISBN 0-619-03433-5). Please refer to that book for more in-depth explanation of concepts or procedures presented here. Course Technology publishes a full series of PC Repair and A+ products which provide thorough preparation for the newly-revised A+ Exams. For more information, visit our Web site at **www.course.com/pcrepair** or contact your sales representative.

How to use this Book

The *Enhanced A+ CoursePrep ExamGuide and CoursePrep StudyGuide* are all you need to successfully prepare for the A+ Certification exams if you have some experience and working knowledge of supporting and maintaining personal computers. This book is intended to be used with a core text, such as *Enhanced A+ Guide to Managing and Maintaining Your PC, Third Edition Comprehensive*, (ISBN 0-619-03433-5), also published by Course Technology. If you are new to this field, use this book as a roadmap for where you need to go to prepare for certification—use the *Enhanced A+ Guide to Managing and Maintaining Your PC* to give you the knowledge and understanding that you need to reach your goal. Course Technology publishes a full series of PC Repair and A+ products. For more information, visit our Web site at **www.course.com/pcrepair** or contact your sales representative.

Acknowledgments

It's always a pleasure working with the Course Technology team. Thank you, Lisa Egan, Product Manager, for your continuing support, and thanks to Lisa Ruffolo, the Developmental Editor. Also, thanks to Karen Jacot, Production Editor.

Studying for exam day can be stressful, but the rewards are well worth the efforts. This book is dedicated to the people who are using it to get certified. Best to you!

A+ Core Objectives

The following descriptions of the A+ Core objective domains are taken from the CompTIA Web site at *www.comptia.org/index.asp?ContentPage=/certification/aplus/aplus.asp*.

% OF EXAM

DOMAIN 1.0 INSTALLATION, CONFIGURATION, AND UPGRADING   30%

This domain requires the knowledge and skills to identify, install, configure, and upgrade microcomputer modules and peripherals, following established basic procedures for system assembly and disassembly of field replaceable modules.

DOMAIN 2.0 DIAGNOSING AND TROUBLESHOOTING   30%

This domain requires the ability to apply knowledge relating to diagnosing and troubleshooting common module problems and system malfunctions. This includes knowledge of the symptoms relating to common problems.

DOMAIN 3.0 PREVENTIVE MAINTENANCE   5%

This domain requires the knowledge of safety and preventive maintenance. With regard to safety, it includes the potential hazards to personnel and equipment when working with lasers, high voltage equipment, ESD, and items that require special disposal procedures that comply with environmental guidelines. With regard to preventive maintenance, this includes knowledge of preventive maintenance products, procedures, environmental hazards, and precautions when working on microcomputer systems.

DOMAIN 4.0 MOTHERBOARD/PROCESSORS/MEMORY   15%

This domain requires knowledge of specific terminology, facts, ways and means of dealing with classifications, categories and principles of motherboards, processors, and memory in microcomputer systems.

DOMAIN 5.0 PRINTERS   10%

This domain requires knowledge of basic types of printers, basic concepts, and printer components, how they work, how they print onto a page, paper path, care and service techniques, and common problems.

DOMAIN 6.0 BASIC NETWORKING   10%

This domain requires knowledge of basic network concepts and terminology, ability to determine whether a computer is networked, knowledge of procedures for swapping and configuring network interface cards, and knowledge of the ramifications or repairs when a computer is networked. The scope of this topic is specific to hardware issues on the desktop and connecting it to a network.

1.1 Identify basic terms, concepts, and functions of system modules, including how each module should work during normal operation and during the boot process

SYSTEM BOARD • PORTS

UNDERSTANDING THE OBJECTIVE

The system board is the most important and largest circuit board inside the computer case. All hardware components must connect to the system board because on it is the central processing unit (CPU), the most important integrated circuit (IC) of the computer, through which all data and instructions must pass for processing.

WHAT YOU **REALLY** NEED TO KNOW

◆ There are two kinds of ICs on a system board and other circuit boards: complementary metal-oxide semiconductor (CMOS) chips and transistor-transistor logic (TTL) chips.

◆ CMOS chips require less electricity, hold data longer after the electricity is turned off, are slower, and produce less heat than TTL chips do.

◆ Names for the system board include main board, main logic board, motherboard, and planar board.

◆ System board components can include a slot or socket for the CPU, a chip set, **RAM**, **ISA**, **PCI**, accelerated graphics port (**AGP**), and Video Electronics Standards Association (**VESA**) expansion slots, a ROM BIOS chip, power connections, a keyboard port, and so forth. You should be able to recognize these on a diagram.

◆ The **CPU** is installed on the system board in a socket or slot and sometimes requires a **voltage regulator** to step down the voltage from the system board before it is used by the CPU.

◆ Some CPUs have a fan or temperature sensor connected to the CPU housing that requires a voltage connection to the system board.

◆ The boot process and many basic I/O operations are controlled by the system BIOS stored on the ROM BIOS on the system board.

◆ Communication of control information, timing of activities, data, address information, and electrical power for components on the system board take place over a **bus**.

◆ Configuration information about hardware and user preferences is stored on a system board in the CMOS RAM chip, **DIP switches**, and **jumpers**. Many system boards today use JumperFree mode whereby configuration is done primarily in CMOS setup.

◆ The **system clock** is responsible for timing activities on the system board.

◆ A system board normally has several built-in, on-board ports including one or more serial, parallel, keyboard, mouse, and USB ports.

◆ On-board ports can be enabled, disabled, and configured in CMOS setup. Sometimes an unused, on-board port must be disabled if it is using an IRQ needed by another device. When troubleshooting a problem with an on-board port, verify the port is enabled in CMOS setup.

OBJECTIVES ON THE JOB

When replacing a system board, use the same size board that was removed and one that accommodates the CPU, memory, and circuit boards. Jumpers and DIP switches are set when the system board is first installed and should not need to be changed after that.

PRACTICE TEST QUESTIONS

1. **Which statement about the system board is false?**
   a. The system board is sometimes called the motherboard, planar board, or main logic board.
   b. The system board is a field replaceable unit.
   c. The system board contains the CPU.
   d. The system board requires 115 volts of power.

2. **In the drawing at the right, item 6 is a(n):**
   a. floppy drive connector
   b. PCI bus slot
   c. CPU socket
   d. cache memory chip

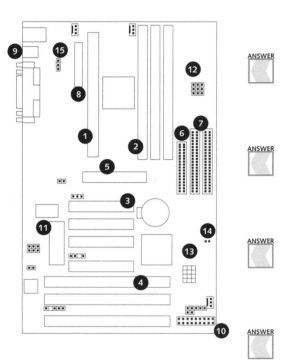

3. **In the drawing at the right, item 15 is a(n):**
   a. IDE connection
   b. keyboard connection
   c. bank of jumpers
   d. sound card connection

4. **In the drawing at the right, item 3 is a(n):**
   a. IDE connection
   b. ISA expansion slot
   c. PCI expansion slot
   d. CPU socket

5. **In the drawing at the right, item 11 is a(n):**
   a. ROM BIOS chip
   b. keyboard port
   c. jumper bank
   d. DIMM slot

6. **A FRU that is installed on the system board is:**
   a. the CPU
   b. a PCI expansion slot
   c. the CPU Socket 7
   d. the system board chipset

7. **Timing on the system board is controlled by the:**
   a. CPU
   b. system BIOS
   c. real-time clock
   d. system clock

1.1
cont.

Identify basic terms, concepts, and functions of system modules, including how each module should work during normal operation and during the boot process

POWER SUPPLY

UNDERSTANDING THE OBJECTIVE

The power supply provides power to all components inside the computer case (for example, the system board, circuit boards, hard drive, and so forth) and some outside the case (for example, the keyboard).

WHAT YOU **REALLY** NEED TO KNOW

◆ Power to the system board comes from the power supply by way of power cords connected to a P1 connection for **ATX** system boards and P8 and P9 connections for **AT** system boards.

◆ A power supply converts 115-volt alternating current (**AC**) to distinct direct current (**DC**) outputs.

◆ The AT power supply provides the system with +12 v, -12 v, +5 v, and -5 v.

◆ The ATX power supply provides the above four voltages and also +3.3 volts.

◆ Most ATX power supplies have a wire that runs from the front of the computer case to the ATX system board lead. This wire must be connected and the power on the front of the case turned on before the system receives power.

◆ A **resistor, capacitor, diode, transistor**, and **ground** all are electrical components. You should be able to define and recognize their symbols.

◆ Hot, neutral, and **ground** have to do with house circuit, and you should understand these terms and recognize the symbol for ground.

◆ **Amperes, ohms, farads, volts**, and **watts** are electrical measurements that you should be able to define and identify the relationships between them.

OBJECTIVES ON THE JOB

The power supply is an essential PC component. Understanding how it works and knowing about the different types of power supplies are essential pieces of knowledge for a PC technician.

A power supply contains a fan that helps cool the inside of the computer case. The fan runs on regular AC house current, and sometimes fails, requiring that the entire power supply be replaced. Never allow a PC to run without a working fan because it can overheat; instead, replace the power supply. If the fan on the new power supply quickly fails, the problem might not be caused by a faulty fan, but rather by a short somewhere else in the system that draws too much power. Try disconnecting other components inside the computer case such as the hard drive, floppy drive, or circuit boards connected to the system board. If disconnecting one of these components causes the fan to start working, then the disconnected component most likely has a short and should be replaced.

When a system board fails, always consider that a faulty power supply might have damaged the system board. Check the voltage output of the power supply before installing a new system board to ensure that the power supply will not immediately damage the new system board.

When replacing a power supply, use the same type of power supply—either an AT or ATX. Also consider the total wattage requirement of the system and use a new power supply that is rated at a wattage to run at about 60 percent capacity.

PRACTICE TEST QUESTIONS

1. **Which power supply provides 3 volts of DC current to a system board?**
    a. the AT power supply
    b. the CPU power supply
    c. the ATX power supply
    d. Only AC current is supplied to a system board.

    ANSWER

2. **What is the symbol for a diode?**

    ANSWER

    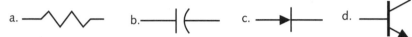

3. **What is the unit of measure for the capacitance of a capacitor?**
    a. volts
    b. ohms
    c. coulombs
    d. microfarads

    ANSWER

4. **Which statement is true about the power from an ATX power supply to a system board?**
    a. There are two power connections named P8 and P9.
    b. There is a single power connection named P1.
    c. The power goes to the system board by way of the CPU voltage regulator.
    d. The system board does not get its power from an ATX power supply.

    ANSWER

5. **Which statement is true about a power supply?**
    a. A power supply converts AC to DC.
    b. A power supply converts DC to AC.
    c. A power supply is a large transistor.
    d. A power supply can supply power to the system for 30 seconds after a power outage.

    ANSWER

6. **The voltage used by a floppy disk drive is:**
    a. +3 volts
    b. -12 volts
    c. +5 volts
    d. 0 volts

    ANSWER

7. **An AT system board uses which voltages?**
    a. +12, -12, +5, and -5 volts
    b. +12 and -12 volts
    c. +3.3 volts
    d. +12, -12, +5, -5, and +3.3 volts

    ANSWER

1.1
cont. Identify basic terms, concepts, and functions of system modules, including how each module should work during normal operation and during the boot process

PROCESSOR/CPU

UNDERSTANDING THE OBJECTIVE

The CPU is the most important IC in a computer system. All data and instructions pass through the CPU for processing.

WHAT YOU **REALLY** NEED TO KNOW

- Names for the CPU include central processing unit, microprocessor, and processor.
- CPUs are rated by internal and external speeds in MHz, special functionality such as MMX technology, size of internal and external data paths, the amount of memory cache included inside the CPU housing or on the CPU chip itself, and the voltage requirements.
- A CPU can run in either **real mode** or **protected mode**.
- When a CPU runs in protected mode, two programs can run without interfering with each other's memory space.
- **MMX** is a CPU technology that is used by multimedia software to improve performance.
- SSE (Streaming SIMD Extensions) further improves CPU multimedia performance. SIMD stands for single instruction, multiple data, and is a method used by MMX. AMD has a competing technology to SSE called 3DNow!
- Memory cache included on the CPU microchip is called internal cache, primary cache, Level 1 or L1 cache. Cache outside the CPU microchip is called external cache, secondary cache, Level 2 or L2 cache.
- Pentium III L2 cache stored on a separate microchip within the CPU housing is called discrete L2 cache.

Table of Intel Pentium CPUs

CPU	Speed (MHz)	Primary L1 Cache	Secondary L2 Cache	System Bus Speeds (MHz)
Classic Pentium	60 to 200	16K	None	66
Pentium MMX	133 to 266	32K	None	66
Pentium Pro	150 to 200	16K	256K, 512K, or 1 MB	60, 66
Pentium II	233 to 450	32K	256K, 512K	66, 100
Celeron	266 to 600	32K	Some have 128K	66, 100
Pentium II Xeon	400, 450	32K	512K, 1 MB, or 2 MB	100
Pentium III	400 and up	32K	256K, 512K	100, 133
Pentium III Xeon	500 and up	32K	256K to 2 MB	100, 133
Pentium IV	1.3 GHz and up	12K	256K	400

OBJECTIVES ON THE JOB

A PC technician must understand what a CPU does, know how to select the best CPU for a system and be able to troubleshoot problems with the CPU.

PRACTICE TEST QUESTIONS

1. **Running a system board at a higher speed than that suggested by the manufacturer is called:**
    a. turbo mode
    b. overclocking
    c. MMX technology
    d. cache mode

2. **What does the CPU do?**
    a. controls the power to the other components on the system board
    b. executes program instructions
    c. controls which keys can be pressed on the keyboard
    d. all of the above

3. **Which CPU technology is appropriate to improve performance in a multimedia computer system?**
    a. MMX
    b. SSE
    c. 3DNow!
    d. all the above

4. **If the CPU is running at 300 MHz and the system bus is running at 100 MHz, then the multiplier is:**
    a. 1/3
    b. 100
    c. 3
    d. 300

5. **Typical speeds for today's system bus are:**
    a. 60, 66, and 100 MHz
    b. 100, 133, and 200 MHz
    c. 400, 500, and 1,000,000 MHz
    d. 20, 40, and 80 MHz

6. **RISC stands for:**
    a. reduced instruction set computer
    b. random instruction set computing
    c. RAM increasing storage container
    d. random instruction system computer

7. **A memory cache stored on the CPU microchip is called:**
    a. L1 cache
    b. L2 cache
    c. CPU cache
    d. Discrete cache

1.1
cont.
Identify basic terms, concepts, and functions of system modules, including how each module should work during normal operation and during the boot process

MEMORY • MONITOR

UNDERSTANDING THE OBJECTIVE

Data and instructions (programs) are permanently stored in secondary storage devices (hard drive, floppy disk, CD-ROM, and so forth) even when the PC is turned off, but must be moved to memory on the system board before the CPU processes them (this memory is called primary storage). A monitor is the primary output device of a PC.

WHAT YOU **REALLY** NEED TO KNOW

On memory:

◆ Memory or RAM is stored on the system board in a memory module called a SIMM, DIMM, or RIMM. In addition to RAM, a memory cache to speed up memory access is contained on older system boards in microchips or memory modules, or inside the CPU housing as L1 or L2 cache.

◆ Know the definitions of these terms that apply to DOS and Windows 9x memory management (not Windows 2000 memory management): **high memory area (HMA), conventional** or **base memory, upper memory, extended memory**, and **expanded memory**.

◆ HMA is between 1024K and 1088K and is used to load part of DOS away from conventional memory, thus allowing for more program/data space in conventional memory.

◆ Conventional or base memory is between 0K and 640K and is used to load legacy device drivers, part of the operating system kernel, user-configurable parameters, and program/data files.

◆ Upper memory (also called reserved memory) is between 640K and 1 MB, and is used to load real mode device drivers and system BIOS.

◆ Extended memory is all memory above 1024K.

◆ In Windows 9x and Windows 2000, **virtual memory** is space on the hard drive that is used as if it were RAM.

◆ Windows 2000 manages memory and virtual memory as one continuous memory space that is made available to applications.

◆ HIMEM.SYS is a DOS memory manager that acts like a **device driver** (managing the "device" memory) making memory above 1024K available to programs.

On monitors:

◆ **Dot pitch** is the distance between dots of color on a monitor screen and is measured in millimeters.

◆ A **pixel** is a group of dots and is the smallest addressable spot on the screen.

◆ Common screen **resolutions** are 800 × 600 pixels and 1024 × 768 pixels.

◆ **Interlaced** monitors compensate for a slow **refresh rate**.

OBJECTIVES ON THE JOB

Monitors are considered "black boxes" by a PC technician who is not trained to service one. Don't open them in the field as they can contain high electrical charges even after the power is off. Upgrading memory is a common task for PC technicians. Generally, adding memory to a sluggish system can improve performance.

PRACTICE TEST QUESTIONS

1. **Another name for reserved memory is:**
   a. base memory
   b. extended memory
   c. expanded memory
   d. upper memory

   ANSWER

2. **Which type of monitor provides the highest quality performance?**
   a. VGA
   b. CGA
   c. SVGA
   d. HGA

   ANSWER

3. **A parity error is most likely caused by what device?**
   a. a hard drive
   b. RAM
   c. ROM
   d. a CPU

   ANSWER

4. **Which device is not considered a field replaceable unit?**
   a. RAM
   b. a CPU
   c. a system board
   d. a soldered cache IC

   ANSWER

5. **Which DOS device driver is used to gain access to extended memory?**
   a. EMM386.EXE
   b. HIMEM.SYS
   c. COMMAND.COM
   d. RAMDRIVE.SYS

   ANSWER

6. **Space on the hard drive that is used as though it were RAM is called:**
   a. RAM space
   b. drive memory
   c. RamDrive
   d. virtual memory

   ANSWER

7. **Which memory module is used to hold memory cache on the system board?**
   a. SIMM
   b. DIMM
   c. COAST
   d. RIMM

   ANSWER

1.1 Identify basic terms, concepts, and functions of system modules, including how
cont. each module should work during normal operation and during the boot process

STORAGE DEVICES

UNDERSTANDING THE OBJECTIVE

Data and instructions (programs) are permanently stored in secondary storage devices (hard drive, floppy disk, CD-ROM, and so forth) even when the PC is turned off. Before this data or programs can be used or executed, they must be copied from secondary storage into memory.

WHAT YOU **REALLY** NEED TO KNOW

◆ Most hard drives use **IDE** technology in which the hard drive controller is permanently attached to the hard drive and controls where data is physically stored on the drive without interference from system BIOS or the OS.

◆ **SCSI** is another type of hard drive technology that uses a SCSI bus that can be connected to other SCSI devices.

◆ A PC must boot from an operating system stored on a secondary storage device, called the bootable device. Examples of bootable devices are floppy disks, hard drives, CD-ROM drives, and removable drives.

◆ Boot priority or boot sequence is determined in CMOS setup and is the order that the system BIOS uses to attempt to boot from a bootable secondary storage device.

◆ A SCSI hard drive cannot be the bootable device unless this feature is supported by the system BIOS.

◆ Some examples of external removable drives are Iomega Zip drives, Iomega Jaz drives, Imation SuperDisk, tape backup drives, writeable CD-ROM drives (CD-R), and rewriteable CD-ROM drives (CD-RW).

◆ An Imation SuperDisk can use a floppy disk or a 120 MB disk. An Iomega Zip drive can use a 100 MB or 250 MB disk.

◆ Initially, only hard drives used IDE technology. New standards mean that other secondary storage devices such as Zip and CD-ROM drives can use an IDE connection to the system board. These **ATAPI** standards have to do with the interface protocol between the device and the CPU, which must be supported by the OS.

OBJECTIVES ON THE JOB

PC technicians are expected to install, support, and troubleshoot secondary storage devices.

The operating system is loaded from a secondary storage device such as a floppy disk, hard drive, CD-ROM drive, or Zip drive. For DOS or Windows 9x, a FAT file system is installed on the storage device that includes track and sector markings on the storage media, a master boot program, a FAT, a root directory, and system files. When the PC boots, BIOS checks a specified device to see if it contains the operating system. If the device does not contain the file system and the system files, BIOS displays an error message similar to the one below:

Non–system disk or disk error…Replace and strike any key when ready…Disk boot failure. When you get this error, replace the floppy disk with a good system disk or boot from the hard drive.

PRACTICE TEST QUESTIONS

1. **What is the purpose of ATAPI standards?**
   a. They determine how data is stored on a hard drive.
   b. They provide protocol standards that are used when a device using an IDE interface communicates with the CPU.
   c. They determine how data is stored on a CD.
   d. They control how the CPU communicates with a hard drive.

2. **What is a Jaz drive?**
   a. a removable secondary storage device
   b. a very fast hard drive
   c. a drive used to store music files
   d. a floppy disk drive designed for extra high density disks

3. **Which statement is true about an IDE hard drive and a SCSI hard drive?**
   a. A SCSI drive is generally faster than an IDE drive because of the way data is stored on the drive.
   b. A SCSI drive is generally faster than an IDE drive because of the bus used by the drive.
   c. An IDE drive is always faster than a SCSI drive.
   d. An IDE drive is generally faster than a SCSI drive because of the way data is stored on the drive.

4. **How can you change the boot priority of a system?**
   a. change a parameter in the Windows 9x registry
   b. make the change using a jumper on the hard drive
   c. make the change in CMOS setup
   d. change the way the data cable is connected to the hard drive

5. **What is boot priority?**
   a. the most important task for the user to do after the PC boots up
   b. the order that system BIOS uses to find a boot device
   c. the first task BIOS performs when the PC is turned on
   d. the order of operating systems stored on the hard drive

6. **Which statement is true about Zip drives and Jaz drives?**
   a. Zip drives hold more data than Jaz drives.
   b. A Zip drive is an internal drive and a Jaz drive is an external drive.
   c. A Jaz drive holds more data than a Zip drive.
   d. Zip drives and Jaz drives always use a parallel cable connection.

7. **Which statement is true about secondary storage?**
   a. Secondary storage always uses magnetic media.
   b. Secondary storage can use magnetic media or optical media.
   c. Secondary storage is not permanent storage.
   d. There is always more primary storage in a system than there is secondary storage.

1.1
cont.
Identify basic terms, concepts, and functions of system modules, including how each module should work during normal operation and during the boot process

STORAGE DEVICES • HARD DRIVES

UNDERSTANDING THE OBJECTIVE

Most hard drives today use IDE technology, which has to do with how data is stored on the drive and how the drive is controlled. SCSI hard drives are connected to a SCSI bus.

WHAT YOU **REALLY** NEED TO KNOW

◆ A hard drive can be an internal or external device. An internal drive connects to a data cable and power supply cord. An external drive connects to the system by way of a SCSI or IEEE 1394 port and has its own power supply.

◆ Hard drives contain several platters with data written on both the top and bottom of each platter. Each surface is called a head.

◆ Logically, each hard drive platter surface is divided into concentric circles called **tracks**. The surface is also divided into pie-shaped wedges called **sectors**.

◆ Each track is divided into sectors and each of these sectors can hold 512 bytes of data.

◆ A hard drive can be logically viewed as a series of sectors, each 512 bytes long. **File systems** depend on this fact when logically organizing data on the hard drive.

◆ A **cluster** is a group of sectors that is the smallest unit that can be assigned to a file (also called a **file allocation unit**).

◆ Know the definitions for these terms, which have to do with hard drives: **latency period**, **seek time**, **data transfer rate**, and **access time**.

◆ A hard drive is divided into partitions using FDISK or similar software. The partition table at the beginning of the hard drive gives the location of each partition and contains a program called the **master boot program** (MBR) that the BIOS executes during the boot process.

◆ The master boot program looks to the beginning of the **active partition** (the partition that is designated to contain the OS) for an OS boot program and then executes it.

◆ Under DOS and Windows 9x, a hard drive can be divided into one primary partition and one extended partition. The primary partition contains one **logical drive** or volume (usually drive C), and the extended partition can contain several logical drives.

◆ If there are two hard drives in a system, the primary partition of the first hard drive contains drive C and the primary partition of the second hard drive contains drive D.

◆ Each logical drive must be formatted (in DOS, use the FORMAT command), which creates a file system on the logical drive including the OS boot record, two copies of the FAT, and a root directory.

◆ Windows 2000 can support up to four hard drive partitions

OBJECTIVES ON THE JOB

Understanding how a hard drive is physically and logically structured is essential to installing and troubleshooting one.

PRACTICE TEST QUESTIONS

1. **A hard disk is divided into concentric circles called:**
   a. sectors
   b. tracks
   c. clusters
   d. heads

   ANSWER

2. **One sector on most hard drives contains:**
   a. 64 bits
   b. 1024 bytes
   c. 2 clusters
   d. 512 bytes

   ANSWER

3. **The program that writes sector and track markings to a hard drive is:**
   a. HIMEM.SYS
   b. FDISK
   c. FORMAT
   d. none of the above

   ANSWER

4. **Which file is not necessary in order for the DOS operating system to load?**
   a. IO.SYS
   b. COMMAND.COM
   c. MSDOS.SYS
   d. FDISK

   ANSWER

5. **If a system has two hard drives and the first drive contains two logical drives, which drive letter will be assigned to the first logical drive on the second hard drive?**
   a. drive C
   b. drive D
   c. drive E
   d. drive F

   ANSWER

6. **Which port can be used for an external hard drive?**
   a. serial port
   b. mouse port
   c. IEEE 1394
   d. network port

   ANSWER

7. **How many partitions on a hard drive can Windows 98 support?**
   a. 1
   b. 2
   c. 3
   d. 4

   ANSWER

1.1
cont.

Identify basic terms, concepts, and functions of system modules, including how each module should work during normal operation and during the boot process

MODEM

UNDERSTANDING THE OBJECTIVE

A modem is a device that allows a PC using digital data to connect to a phone line using analog communication. A modem can be either an external device (most likely connected to the PC using a serial port) or an internal circuit board installed in an expansion slot.

WHAT YOU **REALLY** NEED TO KNOW

◆ A data-terminal-equipment **(DTE)** device (for example, a computer or printer) is dependent on a data-communications-equipment **(DCE)** device (for example, a modem) for communication to another DTE device.

◆ Know the common AT commands used to control a modem. Precede a command line with AT, which stands for "attention."

AT Command	Description
ATA	A=Answer the phone
ATDT 5551212	D=Dial the given number
	T=Use tone dialing
AT &F1DT 5551212	&F=Reset the modem using factory defaults
	DT=Dial using tone dialing
ATM2L2	M2=Speaker always on (M0 is speaker always off)
	L2=Loudness at level 2
ATH	H=Hang up modem
ATI3	I=Identify the modem
	3=Return the ROM version of modem
ATZ0	Z0=Reset the modem and use user profile 0
ATDT	Connect modem to phone line (hear dial tone with no phone number sent)

◆ Know the following communication signals for serial communication used by modems:

Signal	Description
Carrier detect (CD or DCD)	Connection with remote is made
Data terminal ready (DTR)	Computer is ready to control modem
Data set ready (MR or DSR)	Modem is able to talk
Clear to send (CTS)	Modem is ready to talk
Request to send (RTS)	Computer wants to talk
Transmit data (SD or TXD)	Sending data
Receive data (RD or RXD)	Receiving data
Ring indicator (AA or RI)	Someone is calling

OBJECTIVES ON THE JOB

A modem is a field replaceable unit. PC technicians are responsible for installing modems and troubleshooting problems with them. Problems with modems can be caused by the hardware, the OS, the application using the modem, or the way the modem and its device drivers are configured.

PRACTICE TEST QUESTIONS

1. **A 33.6 modem should transmit data at _____ bits per second.**
   a. 33.6
   b. 33,600
   c. .0336
   d. 33,600,000

ANSWER

2. **What does the acronym CTS mean?**
   a. content to sit
   b. clear to send
   c. cluster to sector
   d. clear to start

ANSWER

3. **Which modem command is part of the handshaking process?**
   a. TXD
   b. RXD
   c. HELLO
   d. DTR

ANSWER

4. **The command to reset a modem is:**
   a. ATDT
   b. ATZ
   c. ATH
   d. RESET

ANSWER

5. **An external modem connects to:**
   a. the parallel port
   b. a game port
   c. a serial port
   d. a special adapter card made for modem interfaces

ANSWER

6. **When data is being sent by a modem, the _____ signal is raised.**
   a. RTS
   b. TXD
   c. RXD
   d. AA

ANSWER

7. **The modem command to hang up the phone is:**
   a. ATD
   b. ATH
   c. ATM
   d. ATZ

ANSWER

1.1
cont.
Identify basic terms, concepts, and functions of system modules, including how each module should work during normal operation and during the boot process

FIRMWARE • BIOS • CMOS

UNDERSTANDING THE OBJECTIVE

Firmware is software stored on microchips on the system board and other circuit boards and devices. It contains instructions used to control basic input and output operations of the PC and includes the system BIOS (basic input output system). One CMOS chip on the system board holds configuration information about the PC even when power is off, and is commonly known as CMOS setup or simply CMOS.

WHAT YOU **REALLY** NEED TO KNOW

- ◆ The (BIOS) is the set of programs called firmware that performs many fundamental input and output operations.
- ◆ BIOS on the system board can be permanently etched onto a ROM microchip or can be changed electronically.
- ◆ ROM chips that can be changed electronically are called **Flash ROM** or electronically erasable programmable read-only memory **(EEPROM)**.
- ◆ Flash ROM allows you to upgrade the programs in ROM without replacing the chip.
- ◆ The CMOS chip is a type of RAM storage for configuration information about the computer system.
- ◆ BIOS contains the CMOS setup programs to alter CMOS.
- ◆ Startup BIOS performs **Power on self test (POST)** and includes programs to access CMOS setup.
- ◆ The system board contains the system BIOS or on-board BIOS, but expansion boards can also contain BIOS, which provides software to perform the most fundamental or basic instructions to hardware and sometimes serves as the interface between higher-level software and hardware.

OBJECTIVES ON THE JOB

Verifying, changing, and optimizing settings in CMOS setup is an essential skill of a PC technician. Upgrading BIOS is sometimes necessary, especially on older systems.

When upgrading BIOS, be certain to use the BIOS upgrade compatible with your computer. You can download the upgrade from the Web site of the BIOS or computer manufacturer. You often copy these files to a floppy disk, which makes the disk bootable. Next, boot from the floppy disk to display a menu allowing you to select the option to complete the upgrade.

The BIOS is responsible for the boot process until it loads the operating system. During startup, the BIOS performs POST, a check of essential hardware devices, and communicates problems encountered by error messages displayed on the screen. If errors occur early in the boot process before video is available, errors are communicated as a series of beeps. These beep codes are different for each BIOS manufacturer; some computer manufacturers alter these beep codes as well. Interpreting the BIOS beep codes is an essential skill in troubleshooting problems with a PC during the boot process. The best source of information about beep codes and BIOS error messages and their meaning is the Web site of the BIOS or computer manufacturer.

PRACTICE TEST QUESTIONS

1. **When the PC loses setup information each time it is booted, a possible cause of this problem is:**
   a. the BIOS is Plug and Play
   b. the CMOS battery is weak and needs replacing
   c. the CPU is loose in its slot or socket
   d. BIOS is corrupted and needs to be refreshed or upgraded

2. **The system date and time can be set using:**
   a. DOS commands
   b. jumpers on the system board
   c. CMOS setup
   d. either a or c

3. **One reason you might flash ROM is to:**
   a. install a larger hard drive
   b. change the system clock frequency
   c. install a second floppy drive
   d. install Windows 95

4. **Plug and Play is a feature of:**
   a. ROM BIOS
   b. Windows 95
   c. some hardware devices
   d. all of the above

5. **How do you access CMOS to view settings and make changes?**
   a. Press a certain key combination during booting.
   b. Press a certain key combination after the OS loads.
   c. Press the Esc key as you turn off the power to the system.
   d. Use a setup CD that comes with the operating system.

6. **The program to change CMOS can be stored:**
   a. on the hard drive in a special partition
   b. on the ROM BIOS
   c. on floppy disk
   d. all of the above

7. **The type of ROM BIOS that can be changed without exchanging the chip is called:**
   a. Change BIOS
   b. ROM BIOS
   c. Flash ROM
   d. EPROM

ANSWER

ANSWER

ANSWER

ANSWER

ANSWER

ANSWER

ANSWER

1.1
cont. Identify basic terms, concepts, and functions of system modules, including how each module should work during normal operation and during the boot process

LCD PORTABLE SYSTEMS • PDA (PERSONAL DIGITAL ASSISTANT)

UNDERSTANDING THE OBJECTIVE

Notebook computers use a LCD (liquid crystal display) panel for display. There are two kinds of LCD panels on the market today: active-matrix (sometimes called thin film transistor or TFT) and dual-scan passive matrix display. Active-matrix or TFT is more expensive and provides better viewing quality than does dual scan display. A personal digital assistant (PDA) such as a Palm Pilot or a Pocket PC is a hand-held computer that has its own operating system and applications. You can use a PDA to store addresses and phone numbers, manage a calendar, run word processing, send e-mail, access web sites, play music, and exchange information with a desktop computer.

WHAT YOU **REALLY** NEED TO KNOW

◆ An LCD panel is made up of several layers that are illuminated by backlighting.

◆ The liquid crystal layer is sandwiched between column and row electrode layers, glass, and polarized layers. The electrode layers create a column and row grid, and each intersection of a column and row creates one pixel on the LCD panel.

◆ With dual-scan display, two columns of electrodes are activated at the same time. With active-matrix display, a transistor that amplifies the signal is placed at the intersection of each electrode in the grid, which further enhances the pixel quality.

◆ A PDA most likely uses either the Palm operating system for Palm Pilot devices or Windows CE.

◆ Some PDAs come with all application software preinstalled and others require the user to download applications at additional cost.

◆ Some PDAs allow you to download e-mail and Web site content from a desktop computer or notebook, and others can access e-mail and the Internet by a modem or wireless connection.

◆ Additional hardware (for example, a modem) and software (for example, a Web browser) might be required for a PDA to access the Internet.

◆ Not all Web sites are designed to be accessed by a PDA, and the Web content readable by a PDA is more limited than that readable by a desktop computer.

◆ Typically, a PDA comes with a cable to connect to a desktop or notebook computer by way of a serial or USB port, or a PDA might use an infrared connection. Special software such as ActiveSync by Microsoft might be needed to perform the synchronization.

◆ Similar to a notebook, a PDA is battery powered, uses either a grayscale or color active matrix or dual scan passive matrix display, and can sometimes benefit from additional memory.

OBJECTIVES ON THE JOB

LCD panels on notebooks are fragile and can be damaged. Take precautions against damaging the notebook's LCD panel from rough use. Video drivers for a notebook are vendor specific and usually come preloaded from the factory. Use only drivers recommended by the notebook manufacturer and be careful not to invalidate a factory warranty when servicing a notebook computer. Supporting a PDA requires knowledge specific to the manufacturer of the hardware and software.

PRACTICE TEST QUESTIONS

1. **Which type of LCD panel gives the best quality?**
   a. active matrix
   b. dual scan matrix
   c. VGA
   d. Super VGA

   ANSWER

2. **One pixel on a LCD panel is created by:**
   a. an electronic beam hitting a screen
   b. a triad of dots made of three colors: red, green, and blue
   c. the intersection of a column and row electrode
   d. a resolution setting configured at the back of the LCD panel

   ANSWER

3. **What is *not* advisable when supporting a notebook?**
   a. only use video drivers recommended by the notebook manufacturer
   b. update the notebook video drivers whenever a new driver appears on the market
   c. be aware of the notebook warranty agreement and how you might
      invalidate the warranty
   d. be aware that the LCD panel can be easily damaged

   ANSWER

4. **What operating system is typically used by a PDA?**
   a. Palm
   b. Windows CE
   c. Windows 2000
   d. either a or b

   ANSWER

5. **Which statement is *not* true concerning a PDA?**
   a. a PDA can use Windows CE
   b. a PDA is likely to have a method to upload files from a notebook computer
   c. a PDA might use an infrared connection to communicate with a desktop computer
   d. Windows 98 is the most common OS for a PDA

   ANSWER

6. **Which is true concerning dual scan display?**
   a. two electrode columns are activated at the same time
   b. a transistor is located at the intersection of each column and row of the electrode grid
   c. this technology yields the highest quality display on the market today
   d. all of the above

   ANSWER

7. **Which statement is true concerning using a PDA to access the Internet?**
   a. a Web site must be designed to provide data to a PDA
   b. the PDA must have hardware to access the Internet such as a modem
   c. the PDA must have software to access the Internet such as a Web browser
   d. all of the above

   ANSWER

1.2 Identify basic procedures for adding and removing field replaceable modules for both desktop and portable systems

SYSTEM BOARD

UNDERSTANDING THE OBJECTIVE

When installing a new system board in a PC, memory and the CPU are installed on the board, jumpers are set to communicate how the system board is configured, the system board is installed inside the case, and power, circuit boards, and LED wires are connected to it.

WHAT YOU **REALLY** NEED TO KNOW

- The **field replaceable units (FRUs)** on the system board are the CPU, cache memory modules (on older boards only), RAM modules, CMOS battery, and ROM BIOS chip.
- When selecting the system board, use an AT board with an AT power supply and an ATX board with an ATX power supply.
- Connect Pin 1 on the system board IDE or floppy drive connection with the colored edge of the ribbon cable.
- An IDE connection has 40 pins and a floppy drive connection has 34 pins.
- When replacing a damaged system board, verify the power supply is good because it might be the source of the problem and thus damage the new board.
- Steps to install a system board:
  1. Carefully read the documentation that comes with the system board. If you have questions, get answers before you begin the installation.
  2. Prepare a work place and take precautions to protect against electrostatic discharge (ESD).
  3. Set the jumpers on the system board. Jumpers may be used for the type of CPU, the speed of the CPU or its multiplier, how much memory cache is installed, what voltage the CPU will use, and other power features.
  4. Install the CPU and fan or heat sink.
  5. Install DIMMs, SIMMs or RIMMs.
  6. An optional memory test can be performed at this point to verify that the system board is good.
  7. Install the system board in the computer case.
  8. Use spacers or **standoffs** to insulate the system board from the computer case, but make sure that the system board is properly grounded to the case by a metallic connection and firmly connected to the case.
  9. Attach the power cords and front panel connectors to the system board.

OBJECTIVES ON THE JOB

The system board is considered a field replaceable unit, so a PC technician should know how to recognize a failed system board and replace it. A system board needs replacing when the power supply, memory, CPU, ROM BIOS chip, hard drive, and floppy drive have all been eliminated as the source of a hardware failure that prevents the system from booting. Replace a system board with one that can use the same CPU and memory modules as the old board and has the same form factor as the old board.

PRACTICE TEST QUESTIONS

1. **The purpose of a standoff is to:**
    a. prevent components on the system board from contacting the computer case
    b. ground the system board to the computer case
    c. hold the power supply connections to the system board
    d. provide a ground for the CPU

ANSWER

2. **Which of the following devices are considered FRUs?**
    a. a system board
    b. a video card
    c. a power supply
    d. all of the above

ANSWER

3. **Before replacing a dead system board, one thing you should do is:**
    a. back up all the data on the hard drive
    b. boot the system and verify all is working
    c. verify that the printer is working
    d. measure the voltage output of the power supply

ANSWER

4. **What is one thing that might cause damage to a system board as you service a PC?**
    a. not using an ESD bracelet
    b. not backing up critical data on the hard drive
    c. not backing up CMOS
    d. not verifying that the hard drive power cord is connected properly

ANSWER

5. **When installing AT power supply connections to a system board, what should you remember?**
    a. The power connections will only connect in one direction, so you can't go wrong.
    b. the black-to-black rule
    c. the red-to-red rule
    d. the P1 connection aligns with Pin 1 on the system board

ANSWER

6. **When installing a system board, which is installed first?**
    a. the power lead from the front panel
    b. the CPU
    c. the hard drive
    d. the case cover

ANSWER

7. **When exchanging a system board, why is it important to remove other components?**
    a. It's dangerous to leave other components inside the case while the system board is not present.
    b. The speaker might be damaged when the system board is removed.
    c. Removing them protects the power supply from damage.
    d. It is not important; remove other components only as necessary to expose the system board.

ANSWER

1.2
cont.

Identify basic procedures for adding and removing field replaceable modules for both desktop and portable systems

STORAGE DEVICE • HARD DRIVE

UNDERSTANDING THE OBJECTIVE

A storage device can be an internal or external device. When storage devices are installed inside a PC, the resources needed by the device and available system resources (IRQ, DMA channels, and I/O addresses) must be determined. The device must be physically installed and logically configured. External storage devices can connect by way of a serial, parallel, USB, IEEE 1394 or infrared port. A hard drive can be either an IDE or SCSI device.

WHAT YOU **REALLY** NEED TO KNOW

◆ To write protect a 3-1/2 inch floppy disk, uncover the hole in the corner of the disk.

◆ Hard drives, CD-ROM drives, floppy drives, controller cards, and data cables are all considered field replaceable units.

◆ The BIOS on older systems may not support large hard drives and might need upgrading.

◆ When installing a hard drive, today's drives do not need **low-level formatting**.

◆ To install an IDE hard drive:

1. Step through the entire installation before you begin working to make sure you have everything you need and know the answers to any questions that might arise as you work.

2. If you are removing an existing hard drive, back up the data on the drive.

3. Turn off the power and remove the computer case cover.

4. Set the IDE master/slave/CSEL jumpers on the drive.

5. Fit the drive into the bay and install screws to secure the drive to the bay.

6. Connect the data cable to the IDE connection on the back of the hard drive and to the IDE adapter card or connection on the system board, connecting Pin 1 on the connections to the edge color on the data cable.

7. Connect the power cord from the power supply to the power connection on the drive.

8. Replace the computer case cover and turn on the power. If CMOS supports auto detection, then verify that CMOS detected the drive correctly.

9. If CMOS does not support auto detection, then record the drive parameters in CMOS setup.

10. After the drive is physically installed, use FDISK to create partitions on the drive, format each partition, and install the OS.

11. Verify that the drive is working.

OBJECTIVES ON THE JOB

Installing storage devices is a common task for a computer repair technician. Most storage devices use an IDE interface with the system board, although SCSI is sometimes used for hard drives in high-end systems to improve speed and performance.

PRACTICE TEST QUESTIONS

1. **If a system has two IDE hard drives that each have primary and extended partitions with one logical drive in each partition, what is the drive letter assigned to the primary partition of the second hard drive?**
    a. C
    b. D
    c. E
    d. F

2. **After performing a low-level format of a hard drive, what is the next step in the installation process?**
    a. format the drive
    b. partition the drive using FDISK
    c. install the operating system
    d. enter the drive parameters in CMOS

3. **What kind of cable is a 34-pin data cable?**
    a. IDE hard drive cable
    b. SCSI hard drive cable
    c. IDE CD-ROM cable
    d. floppy drive cable

4. **How many pins does an IDE data cable have?**
    a. 25
    b. 34
    c. 40
    d. 50

5. **When a CD-ROM drive and an IDE hard drive are sharing the same data cable:**
    a. set the hard drive to master and the CD-ROM drive to slave
    b. set the CD-ROM drive to master and the hard drive to slave
    c. set both drives to master
    d. set both drives to slave

6. **A port on the back of a PC has 50 pins. What type port is it?**
    a. IDE port for an external hard drive
    b. SCSI port
    c. Parallel port
    d. IEEE 1394

ANSWER

7. **Which IRQ does the primary IDE channel use?**
    a. IRQ 5
    b. IRQ 7
    c. IRQ 14
    d. IRQ 15

ANSWER

1.2 cont. Identify basic procedures for adding and removing field replaceable modules for both desktop and portable systems

POWER SUPPLY • INPUT DEVICES • KEYBOARD • MOUSE

UNDERSTANDING THE OBJECTIVE

When installing a power supply, match the power supply type to the system board and its case. Input devices are connected to the system board by way of ports (serial, parallel, IEEE 1394, USB, DIN, mini–DIN, and so forth) connected directly to the system board or to ports on the circuit boards.

WHAT YOU **REALLY** NEED TO KNOW

◆ The power supply is a field replaceable unit. If there is a problem with the fan or any other component inside the power supply, replace the entire power supply.

◆ When removing a power supply from a computer case, look on the bottom of the case for slots that are holding the power supply in position. Often the power supply must be shifted in one direction to free it from the slots.

◆ Unless you have the proper training, never open a power supply; it can shock you even after the electrical power is disconnected.

◆ If you install a new input device and it does not work, check the following:

   - Verify that the port it is using is enabled in CMOS setup.

   - Verify that there are no conflicts with the system resources that the port is using.

   - For a mouse using a serial port, test the port using diagnostic software and loop-back plugs.

◆ A mouse is powered by current received from the power supply by way of the system board, mouse port, and mouse cable.

◆ DOS requires loading a device driver for a mouse, but Windows 9x and Windows 2000 have internal support for a mouse.

◆ When a key is first pressed on a keyboard, a **make code** is produced. When the key is released, a **break code** is generated. The chip in the keyboard processes these actions to produce a scan code that is sent to the CPU.

◆ One pin in a keyboard cable carries +5 volts of current that comes from the power supply by way of the system board and is used to power the keyboard. Other pins in the keyboard cable are used for grounding, the keyboard clock, and keyboard data.

OBJECTIVES ON THE JOB

Installing a keyboard and a mouse are simple jobs for a PC technician. Installing a power supply is more complex because often the entire computer must be disassembled to access the power supply. If a key on a keyboard does not work, after making a reasonable effort to clean the key, replace the keyboard. A mouse often gets dirt inside the ball mechanism and needs cleaning. A mouse can wear out over time and need replacing.

PRACTICE TEST QUESTIONS

1. **The ESD bracelet is designed to protect:**
   a. the hardware from damage
   b. the PC technician from harm
   c. both the hardware and the technician
   d. neither the hardware nor the technician

2. **What might you need to upgrade after installing a new hard drive in a system?**
   a. CMOS
   b. ROM BIOS
   c. an operating system
   d. a CD-ROM drive

3. **Before exchanging a power supply, you should:**
   a. measure the voltage output of the old power supply
   b. measure the capacitance of the old power supply
   c. back up critical data on the hard drive
   d. both a and c

4. **If the cable connector on a keyboard does not fit the keyboard port on the system board, then:**
   a. the keyboard cannot be used on this system
   b. use a DIN/min-DIN adapter to make the connection
   c. connect the keyboard using a serial port
   d. change the keyboard port in CMOS

5. **If the mouse port on a system board does not work, then:**
   a. check CMOS to see that the port is enabled
   b. try using a serial port mouse
   c. reboot the computer and try again
   d. all of the above

6. **What ports can a mouse use?**
   a. DIN
   b. mini-DIN
   c. serial port
   d. all of the above

7. **How does a keyboard get its power?**
   a. from the system board by way of the keyboard port
   b. from an AC adapter connected to the keyboard
   c. the keyboard does not need power
   d. from a battery inside the keyboard

1.2 Identify basic procedures for adding and removing field replaceable modules for
cont. both desktop and portable systems

PROCESSOR/CPU • MEMORY

UNDERSTANDING THE OBJECTIVE

Both the CPU and memory are installed on the system board. Both must match the type and size that the system board supports, and both are very susceptible to ESD, so caution must be taken as you work.

WHAT YOU **REALLY** NEED TO KNOW

◆ Protect memory modules and the CPU against ESD as you perform the installation; always use an anti-static **ground bracelet** as you work.

◆ When installing a CPU:
- Install the **heat sink** or CPU fan on the CPU housing, following the directions accompanying the heat sink or fan.
- For a socket, before inserting the CPU, open the socket by lifting the **ZIF** handle, and, for Slot 1, open the side braces on both ends of the slot.
- For a fan, attach the power lead from the fan to the pins on the system board.
- After installing the CPU, if the system appears dead or sounds beep codes, suspect that the CPU is not securely seated. Turn off the PC and reseat the CPU.

◆ When installing memory:
- For RIMM memory, all memory sockets must be filled. If the socket does not hold a RIMM, install a C-RIMM (continuity RIMM). The C-RIMM serves as a placeholder to achieve continuity throughout all sockets.
- Memory modules have spring catches on both ends of the memory slot.
- Look for notches on the memory module to exactly fit notches on the slot that indicate the correct orientation as well as the type of memory the slot can accommodate.
- Don't force modules into a memory slot; they are probably the wrong type of module if they don't fit easily into the slot.
- After installation, if the count is not correct for the new memory, turn off the PC, reseat the memory, or for a DIMM, move the module to a new slot.
- To remove a module, release the latches on each side and, for a SIMM, gently rotate the module out of the socket at an angle. For a DIMM, lift the module straight up and out of the slot.
- For some older systems, you must tell CMOS setup how much memory is installed.

OBJECTIVES ON THE JOB

A CPU might be replaced if the old CPU is bad or you are attempting to improve performance with an upgraded CPU. Upgrading memory is a more common task for a PC technician than upgrading a CPU. Before upgrading either a CPU or memory, verify that the new component is compatible with the system board and the other components already installed.

PRACTICE TEST QUESTIONS

1. **A system has two SIMMs installed and two SIMM slots are still open. Which is correct?**
   a. You can install a third SIMM in one of the available slots.
   b. You must remove the two SIMMs and replace them with two larger SIMMs.
   c. You can install two more SIMMs in the empty slots, but they must match the already installed SIMMs.
   d. You can install two more SIMMs without matching the other SIMMs in any way.

2. **A system has four DIMM slots and one DIMM installed. Which statement is correct?**
   a. You can install one, two, or three more DIMMs of any memory size supported by the system board.
   b. You can install only one or three more DIMMs, but not two more.
   c. The additional DIMMs you install must match in memory size to the one DIMM already installed.
   d. The total amount of memory installed cannot exceed 64 MB.

3. **Which statement is true about RAM on a system board?**
   a. EDO and BEDO memory modules can exist together on a system board.
   b. SIMMs and DIMMs are protected against ESD by a coating on the tiny circuit boards.
   c. Most BIOS detect new RAM installed without manually changing CMOS settings.
   d. A single SIMM can be installed on a Pentium system board.

4. **After installing memory and booting the system, the memory does not count up correctly. The most likely problem is:**
   a. a memory module is bad
   b. the modules are not seated properly
   c. the CPU was damaged during the memory installation
   d. a circuit board became loose during the installation and needs reseating

5. **How many pins are there on a DIMM?**
   a. 30
   b. 64
   c. 72
   d. 168

6. **Without the system board documentation, how can you tell if a DIMM is the correct type of memory for a system board?**
   a. There is no way to tell; the documentation is the only source of that information.
   b. Match the notches on the DIMM to the notches in the memory slot.
   c. Look at the documentation that comes with the DIMM; it lists the system boards that the DIMM will work in.
   d. If the length of the DIMM and the DIMM slot, are the same, it will work.

7. **Why does a Pentium system require that SIMMs be installed in pairs?**
   a. It takes two 32-bit SIMMs to accommodate a 64-bit data path.
   b. It takes two SIMMs to yield 8 MB of memory, which is required for a Pentium to work.
   c. Pentium system boards are designed to require at least two SIMMs so that the system will have enough memory for normal operation.
   d. None of the above; a SIMM can work on a Pentium system board as an individual module.

O B J E C T I V E S

1.2 Identify basic procedures for adding and removing field replaceable modules for
cont. both desktop and portable systems

VIDEO BOARD • NETWORK INTERFACE CARD (NIC)

UNDERSTANDING THE OBJECTIVE

Video boards are the interface between the CPU and the monitor and are sometimes called video cards, graphic adapters, display cards, or graphic accelerators. Video boards contain some memory to hold display data before it is sent to the monitor. Video boards today are installed in AGP slots, although older systems used PCI, VESA, or ISA slots. Graphics accelerators have their own processors to manage video and graphics to improve performance.

WHAT YOU **REALLY** NEED TO KNOW

◆ Older systems used a local I/O bus slot for video cards called the VESA VL bus slot.

◆ The VESA bus slot was replaced with the PCI slot which has now been replaced with the AGP slot for video boards.

◆ The AGP bus connects directly to the CPU, running at the same speed as the system bus with a 32-bit data path.

◆ An AGP slot is a 132-pin slot, and the AGP Pro standard uses a wider 188-pin slot. The extra pins provide additional voltage to high-end graphics accelerators.

◆ Windows 98 and Windows 2000 support AGP. Windows 95 does not support AGP, causing Device Manager in Windows 95 to report a problem with the video board even though video is working properly.

◆ When installing a video card, once the card is physically installed in the video slot, install the video card drivers. Use the drivers recommended by the manufacturer, which are normally included on a CD bundled with the card.

◆ If you don't have the correct video drivers, download the drivers from the Web site of the video card manufacturer.

◆ For network cards, use the network card that matches the network protocol (for example, Ethernet) and cabling type (for example, RJ-45 port with CAT 5 cabling) of the network.

◆ Install the network card in a PCI or ISA slot (PCI is best) and then install the network card drivers. After the drivers are installed, turn off the PC, connect the network cable, and reboot the PC to connect to the network.

◆ Verify the network card is working by checking the lights on the card. One light stays lit when the PC is connected to the network, and another light flashes when data is being transmitted over the network.

◆ If a network card fails to work, try uninstalling and reinstalling the network card drivers. Verify with the network administrator that you are using the correct drivers.

OBJECTIVES ON THE JOB

If the video system fails, before exchanging the video card, check the simple things first including the on/off monitor switch, power to the monitor, monitor adjustments, video drivers and video cable. Only then exchange the video card for a known–good card. A network card sometimes fails and needs replacing, but first verify that the network cable is good and the network is working properly.

PRACTICE TEST QUESTIONS

1. **The fastest port used for video boards today is:**
   a. VESA
   b. PCI
   c. AGP
   d. IEEE 1394

2. **What is the difference in an AGP slot and an AGP Pro slot on a system board?**
   a. An AGP slot is wider than an AGP Pro slot.
   b. An AGP Pro slot is wider than an AGP slot.
   c. There is no difference; both slots are the same size and shape.
   d. The AGP slot has 188 pins and the AGP Pro slot has 132 pins.

3. **What is one thing you can do to speed up a sluggish system that is graphic intensive?**
   a. Add memory to the video board.
   b. Move the video board to a different slot on the system board.
   c. Buy a larger monitor.
   d. Upgrade the power supply.

4. **AGP 4X is defined by the AGP 2.0 specification. The 4x refers to:**
   a. data throughput that can be achieved by the video card
   b. the number of memory chips on an AGP video card
   c. the number of pins on the AGP slot
   d. the size of the video card

5. **What bus is no longer found on system boards today?**
   a. ISA
   b. PCI
   c. AGP
   d. VESA

6. **The video system does not work. What is the first thing you check?**
   a. Is the monitor turned on?
   b. Is the video cable good?
   c. Is the monitor adjusted correctly?
   d. Is the video card good?

7. **How can you tell that the network card is connected to and communicating with other network equipment on the network?**
   a. View resources in Network Neighborhood.
   b. View a shared printer in the Printer window.
   c. Check for a solid light on the network card.
   d. Check for a blinking light on the network card.

OBJECTIVES

1.2
cont. Identify basic procedures for adding and removing field replaceable modules for both desktop and portable systems

PORTABLE SYSTEM COMPONENTS: AC ADAPTER • DIGITAL CAMERA • DC CONTROLLER • LCD PANEL • PC CARD • POINTING DEVICES

UNDERSTANDING THE OBJECTIVE

Notebook computers are generally purchased as a whole unit, including hardware and software. You are less likely to upgrade a notebook's hardware or OS, than you would a PC's. A notebook likely has the standard ports that a PC has including serial, parallel, USB, infrared, and mouse ports. Also, a notebook can have a video-out port so that you can use a monitor as an alternative display device. External devices such as a modem or an external DVD drive are connected to the notebook by way of a PC Card.

WHAT YOU **REALLY** NEED TO KNOW

◆ Power on a notebook can be controlled by the Advanced Configuration and Power Interface (ACPI) standards developed by Intel, Microsoft, and Toshiba.

◆ Windows 98 offers several features to support notebooks that were not included with Windows 95.

◆ Multilink Channel Aggregation is a Windows 98 feature that allows a notebook to use two modem connections at the same time to speed up data throughput when connected over phone lines.

◆ You can download data from a digital camera to a notebook or PC using a serial or USB cable supplied by the digital camera manufacturer as well as software to manage the process.

◆ Windows 9x has Briefcase to keep files in sync between a notebook and PC. Windows 2000 uses Offline Files for a similar purpose.

◆ Windows 2000 offers the ability to hot swap an external IDE device or floppy disk drive.

◆ Notebooks have a pointing device such as a touchpad or trackball embedded on the notebook, but a user can install a mouse using a mouse or serial port as an alternate pointing device.

◆ Instead of a battery, you can use an AC adapter to power a notebook. The AC adapter recharges the battery. If you recharge the battery too often, the battery will not last as long been charges. Only recharge the battery when it is dead or almost dead.

◆ The LCD panel is delicate and should be protected against rough use.

OBJECTIVES ON THE JOB

Notebooks are very proprietary in design, which means the skills to support them are brand specific. Also be aware that a notebook's warranty can be voided if you open the notebook case or install memory, batteries, or a hard drive that was not made by, or at least authorized by, the notebook manufacturer. Almost all operating system installations on notebooks are customized by the manufacturer, and a floppy disk comes with the notebook that contains data and utilities specific to the configuration. Read the supporting documentation for the notebook before you consider upgrading or reinstalling the OS.

PRACTICE TEST QUESTIONS

1. **Which operating system uses a feature called Offline Files to synchronize files between a PC and notebook?**
   a. Windows 98
   b. Windows 95
   c. Windows 2000
   d. DOS

2. **To download data directly from a digital camera to a notebook, which statement must be true?**
   a. The notebook must have a USB port.
   b. The notebook must have Windows 2000 installed.
   c. The notebook must have software provided by the digital camera manufacturer installed.
   d. The notebook and the digital camera must be made by the same manufacturer.

3. **To hot swap an external storage device, which statement must be true?**
   a. The notebook must be rebooted in order for it to sense the newly installed device.
   b. The OS must support hot swapping.
   c. The external device must be an IDE device.
   d. all the above.

4. **If a notebook does not have an internal modem included in the hardware, how is a modem typically added to the system?**
   a. as an external IDE device
   b. connected to the notebook using the serial port
   c. as a PC Card
   d. connected to the notebook using the USB port

5. **What Windows 98 feature allows you to use two modems to speed up data throughput over phone lines?**
   a. ACPI
   b. Microsoft Exchange
   c. Multilink Channel Aggregation
   d. Virtual Phone Lines Aggregation

6. **What is the danger in using the AC adapter too much to power a notebook?**
   a. The AC adapter will burn out prematurely.
   b. The notebook will waste too much electricity.
   c. The change of damage from ESD is increased.
   d. The battery will not last as long between charges.

7. **What is important to first determine before servicing or upgrading a notebook computer?**
   a. What is the warranty agreement and under what conditions is the agreement voided?
   b. What are the latest updates to the OS installed on the notebook and is the OS the most current version?
   c. How long has it been since the battery was replaced or recharged?
   d. Is all software installed on the notebook properly registered with the software manufacturer?

1.3 Identify available IRQs, DMAs, and I/O addresses and procedures for device installation and configuration

STANDARD IRQ SETTINGS • MODEMS • FLOPPY DRIVE CONTROLLERS • HARD DRIVE CONTROLLERS • USB PORTS• INFRARED PORTS • HEXADECIMAL/ADDRESSES

UNDERSTANDING THE OBJECTIVE

Before installing a new device, determine what system resources (IRQ, DMA channel, or I/O address) are in use. For DOS, use MSD, and for Windows, use Device Manager. Older devices are configured to use these resources by DIP switches or jumpers on the devices themselves. Newer Plug-and-Play devices are automatically configured. Ports on a system board also use these same resources. To enable or disable a port or control its resources, use CMOS setup.

WHAT YOU **REALLY** NEED TO KNOW

◆ IRQs 8 through 15 cascade to IRQ2, which is not available for I/O devices. IRQ9 is wired to the pin on the ISA bus previously assigned to IRQ2.

◆ The 8-bit ISA bus only has wires for the first 8 IRQs. The 16-bit ISA bus has wires for all 16 IRQs.

◆ Floppy drive controllers use DMA channel 2.

◆ DMA channel 4 is not available for I/O because it cascades into the lower four DMA channels.

◆ An I/O address is expressed in hexadecimal form. You should understand the hexadecimal number system and be able to convert 4-digit hex numbers to decimal form.

◆ A SCSI bus system uses a single set of resources (an IRQ, I/O addresses and possibly a DMA channel). All SCSI devices on the bus share these resources. A USB bus system works the same way.

◆ An infrared transceiver can use the resources of a serial port and provide virtual ports for infrared devices. These virtual ports are assigned their own individual resources.

◆ Know the following IRQ and I/O addresses for devices:

IRQ	I/O Address	Device
0	040-05F	System timer
1	060-06F	Keyboard controller
2	0A0-0AF	Access to IRQs above 7
3	2F8-2FF	COM2
3	2E8-2EF	COM4
4	3F8-3FF	COM1
4	3E8-3EF	COM3
5	278-27F	Sound card or parallel port LPT2
6	3F0-3F7	Floppy drive controller
7	378-37F	Printer parallel port LPT1
8	070-07F	Real-time clock
9-10		Available
11		SCSI or available
12	238-23F	System-board PS/2 mouse
13	0F8-0FF	Math coprocessor
14	1F0-1F7	Primary IDE hard drive
15	170-170	Secondary IDE hard drive

OBJECTIVES ON THE JOB

Resolving resource conflicts is often a challenge for a PC technician. Determine which current resources are being used. You must then force conflicting devices to use a different resource.

PRACTICE TEST QUESTIONS

1. A disk drive can access primary memory without involving the CPU by using a(n):
    a. IRQ
    b. port address
    c. DMA channel
    d. I/O address

2. IRQ14 is reserved for:
    a. the coprocessor
    b. a mouse
    c. the secondary IDE controller
    d. the primary IDE controller

3. A jumper group has three positions on the block. What is the largest hex number that can be represented by this block?
    a. F
    b. 7
    c. 8
    d. 001

4. The purpose of an IRQ is to:
    a. give the CPU a way to communicate with a device
    b. give the device a way of interrupting the CPU for service
    c. pass data from the device to the CPU
    d. give a device a way to pass data to memory

5. The purpose of an I/O address is to:
    a. give the CPU a way of communicating with a device
    b. give a device a way of requesting service from the CPU
    c. give a device a way of sending data to the CPU
    d. allow a device to pass data to the CPU

6. Which IRQ can a device using an 8-bit ISA bus NOT use?
    a. 5
    b. 4
    c. 7
    d. 10

7. On the 16-bit ISA bus, IRQ2 is used to cascade to the higher IRQs, so its position on the ISA bus is taken by which IRQ?
    a. IRQ0
    b. IRQ7
    c. IRQ9
    d. IRQ15

1.4 Identify common peripheral ports, associated cabling, and their connectors

CABLE TYPES • CABLE ORIENTATION • SERIAL VERSUS PARALLEL • PIN CONNECTIONS INCLUDING DB-9, DB-25, PS2/MINI-DIN, RJ-11, RJ-45, BNC, USB, AND IEEE-1394

UNDERSTANDING THE OBJECTIVE

Common peripheral ports include parallel, 9-pin and 25-pin serial (DB-9 and DB-25), USB, game port, DIN, mini-DIN (PS/2), video port, wide and narrow SCSI, phone line (RJ-11 or RJ-12) connectors, and network connections. IEEE-1394 is used for fast data transmission such as that needed for video data.

WHAT YOU **REALLY** NEED TO KNOW

- ◆ Know how to identify all the above ports in a diagram.
- ◆ Parallel cables can be mono- and bi-directional and have a DB25-pin female connection at the computer end and a 36-pin Centronics connection at the printer end.
- ◆ Standards for parallel ports and parallel cables are covered under the **IEEE 1284** standards.
- ◆ A parallel port can be configured as bi-directional, **extended capabilities port (ECP)**, or **enhanced parallel port (EPP)**.
- ◆ An ECP parallel port uses a DMA channel to speed up data transmission.
- ◆ RS-232 is the standard for serial communication. A COM port is sometimes called an RS-232 port.
- ◆ Serial ports are 9- or 25-pin male, D connectors that transmit data 1 bit in series.
- ◆ **Null modem cables** use serial ports and connect two DTE devices, such as two PCs.
- ◆ The maximum length of a serial cable is 50 feet.
- ◆ The 5-pin DIN connection and the 6-pin min-DIN or PS/2 connection are both used for a mouse or a keyboard.
- ◆ A current video port (SVGA) is a 15-pin female port with 3 rows of pins.
- ◆ A phone line connection looks like a phone jack and can be type **RJ-11** or **RJ-12**.
- ◆ Cable lengths are limited because of communication interference.
- ◆ A USB port has four pins, two for power and two for communication.
- ◆ An IEEE-1394 port can have four or six pins. The extra two pins on a six-pin port are used to power the device.
- ◆ Common network connections are **BNC** and **RJ-45**.
  - A BNC network connector is used by **Ethernet** 10Base2 (Thinnet) and 10Base5 networks. A BNC connection is round, similar to a video jack.
  - A RJ-45 connection is used with twisted-pair cable by Ethernet 10BaseT (Twisted pair) and Ethernet 100BaseT (Fast Ethernet) networks and looks like a large phone jack. These connections are more common than BNC.

OBJECTIVES ON THE JOB

A PC technician should be able to identify different cables and ports and know how to use them. Ports require system resources and can be enabled and disabled in CMOS setup. To know what resources a port is using, for DOS use MSD; for Windows 9x use Device Manager.

PRACTICE TEST QUESTIONS

1. **A 25-pin female port on the back of your computer is most likely to be a:**
   a. parallel port
   b. serial port
   c. video port
   d. game port

ANSWER

2. **What component controls serial port communication?**
   a. the ISA bus
   b. the PCI bus
   c. UART
   d. BIOS

ANSWER

3. **When connecting a floppy drive data cable to a system board connection, how do you know the correction orientation of the cable to the connection?**
   a. The red color on the cable goes next to the power supply.
   b. The edge color on the cable goes next to pin 1 on the connection.
   c. The orientation does not matter.
   d. Use the black-to-black rule.

ANSWER

4. **Which port cannot support a printer?**
   a. COM1
   b. COM2
   c. LPT2
   d. the game port

ANSWER

5. **Which port provides the fastest data transmission rate for a printer?**
   a. RS-232
   b. parallel
   c. serial
   d. DIN

ANSWER

6. **Which device can use a DMA channel?**
   a. the serial port
   b. the parallel port
   c. the keyboard
   d. the mouse

ANSWER

7. **Which device uses a 9-pin data cable?**
   a. the parallel port
   b. the serial port
   c. the keyboard
   d. the SCSI port

ANSWER

MASTER/SLAVE • DEVICES PER CHANNEL • PRIMARY/SECONDARY

UNDERSTANDING THE OBJECTIVE

An Enhanced IDE (EIDE) system can support up to four devices. Older Integrated Drive Electronics or Integrated Device Electronics (IDE) systems could only support two devices. Sometimes people use the term IDE when they really mean EIDE.

WHAT YOU **REALLY** NEED TO KNOW

◆ Up to four IDE devices can be installed on an **EIDE** system using the two IDE channels (primary and secondary).

◆ Each IDE channel can have a master and a slave device.

◆ Earlier IDE/ATA standards only apply to hard drives, but newer extensions to these standards apply to many devices including CD-ROM and tape drives that use the ATAPI standard.

◆ Variations of the IDE/ATA standards developed by ANSI include ATA, ATA-2, Fast ATA, Ultra ATA, and Ultra DMA.

◆ Older hard drives using an ST-506/412 interface and RLL or MFM encoding schemes have two cables, one for data and one for control signals, and a controller card inserted in an expansion slot.

◆ RLL and MFM drives had to be low-level formatted as part of the installation process, but new IDE hard drives are low-level formatted at the factory.

◆ If an IDE hard drive gives the error message "Bad sector or sector not found," try using a low-level format program supplied by the hard drive manufacturer to refresh the track and sector markings on the drive.

◆ IDE hard drives don't use controller cards, but use a small adapter card or an IDE connection on the system board.

OBJECTIVES ON THE JOB

IDE is currently the most popular interface for storage devices in computer systems. A PC technician must be comfortable with installing and configuring IDE devices.

When installing an IDE drive, remember that the red stripe down the data cable aligns with Pin 1 on the drive and on the IDE connection. Pin 1 on the hard drive is usually next to the power connector.

An IDE hard drive can have jumper switch connections for master, slave, single, and cable select. If there is only one drive using a data cable, set the jumpers to single.

When two drives are sharing a single data cable, only one of these drives must control communication with the system. One way to determine which drive controls communication is to set one drive to master (the controller) and the other drive to slave. Another way to determine which drive controls communication is to use a special data cable called a Cable Select data cable. These special cables can be identified by a small hole somewhere on the cable. When using one of these cables, set both drive jumpers to Cable Select. Then install the drive that will be the master closest to the system board and the drive that will be the slave at the furthest distance from the system board on the data cable.

PRACTICE TEST QUESTIONS

1. **When installing a second IDE device on an IDE channel, you must:**
    a. use CMOS setup to set the second device as the slave
    b. use CMOS setup to set the second device as drive D:
    c. use jumpers on the device to set it to slave
    d. use software that comes with the device to set it to slave

2. **How many EIDE devices can be installed in a system?**
    a. 1
    b. 2
    c. 4
    d. 8

3. **A system has a single IDE device installed on the primary IDE channel, and a new IDE device is installed on the secondary IDE channel. The new device does not work. What might be a cause of the problem?**
    a. The secondary IDE channel cannot be used until at least two devices are installed on the primary IDE channel.
    b. The second device should be set to slave.
    c. The secondary IDE channel might be disabled in CMOS setup.
    d. Both IDE devices are using the same IRQ.

4. **What IRQ does the primary IDE channel use?**
    a. IRQ2
    b. IRQ10
    c. IRQ14
    d. IRQ15

5. **Two IDE devices share a data cable. Which statement is true?**
    a. One device is using the primary IDE channel and the other device is using the secondary IDE channel.
    b. The data cable has 34 pins.
    c. The devices are sharing an IRQ.
    d. Both devices are set to slave.

6. **What type of hard drive requires a low-level format as part of the installation process?**
    a. SCSI
    b. IDE
    c. MFM (ST-506/412)
    d. any hard drive whose drive capacity is less than 504 MB

7. **A CD-ROM drive that uses an IDE interface to the system board is following what specifications?**
    a. Ultra ATA
    b. ATAPI
    c. ANSI
    d. ATA-2

1.6 Identify proper procedures for installing and configuring SCSI devices

ADDRESS/TERMINATION CONFLICTS • CABLING • INTERNAL VERSUS EXTERNAL • EXPANSION SLOTS, EISA, ISA, PCI • JUMPER BLOCK SETTINGS (BINARY EQUIVALENTS)

UNDERSTANDING THE OBJECTIVE

Small Computer Systems Interface (SCSI) is a type of closed bus. SCSI devices are connected to a host adapter that connects to a system bus. Within a physical device, each virtual device or unit is assigned a logical unit number (LUN). Of the several SCSI standards, some are compatible with one another and others are not.

WHAT YOU **REALLY** NEED TO KNOW

◆ SCSI-1, SCSI-2, and Fast SCSI devices connect using a Centronics-50 or DB-25 male connector. All wide SCSI devices use a 68-pin connection.

◆ Both narrow and wide SCSI can use either single-ended or differential cables. A differential cable can be up to 25 meters long and a single-ended cable can be up to 6 meters long, depending on the SCSI standard used.

◆ Eight or 16 devices (including the host adapter) can be chained on a SCSI bus, depending on the standard used (SCSI IDs are 0 through 15).

◆ The SCSI host adapter is assigned SCSI ID 7 or 15, and a bootable SCSI hard drive is assigned SCSI ID 0.

◆ A SCSI device is assigned a single SCSI ID, but one physical device can have multiple units or virtual devices in it, each assigned a LUN. For example, a 12-tray CD changer or juke box is assigned a single SCSI ID, but each tray in the changer is assigned a LUN.

◆ A SCSI ID can be set for a device by setting jumpers or DIP switches on the device or by software.

◆ The SCSI chip on a hard drive that controls the transfer of data over the SCSI bus is a **SCSI bus adapter chip (SBAC)**.

◆ A SCSI device can be an internal device or an external device, and the host adapter can be anywhere in the SCSI daisy chain. The host adapter can be installed in a PCI, ISA or EISA expansion slot.

◆ DOS does not support SCSI devices, but SCSI device drivers from the manufacturer can be installed in CONFIG.SYS. Windows 9x and Windows 2000 support SCSI.

◆ Many computers have built in SCSI interface software in their system BIOS, and some allow a SCSI hard drive to be the boot device. See the CMOS setup screen for SCSI options.

◆ A SCSI bus requires **termination** at each end of the SCSI bus to eliminate electrical noise and reflected data at the ends of the SCSI daisy chain.

OBJECTIVES ON THE JOB

SCSI devices are popular because they are generally faster than similar devices that don't use SCSI technology, but SCSI installations can be more complex than other installations.

PRACTICE TEST QUESTIONS

1. **A SCSI ID is set on a SCSI device using three jumpers. If the ID is set to 6, what will be the jumper settings?**
   a. On, On, and Off
   b. On, On, and On
   c. Off, On, and On
   d. Off, Off, and On

ANSWER

2. **Which statement about a SCSI configuration is true?**
   a. The host adapter must be at one end of the SCSI chain.
   b. The host adapter must *always* be terminated.
   c. A SCSI chain cannot have both internal and external devices on the same chain.
   d. A SCSI chain can have both internal and external devices and the host adapter can be anywhere in the chain.

ANSWER

3. **Two SCSI hard drives are installed on the same SCSI bus. Which statement is true?**
   a. The two SCSI drives must have the same SCSI ID.
   b. The two SCSI drives must have different SCSI IDs and one must have SCSI ID 7.
   c. The two SCSI drives must have different SCSI IDs.
   d. It does not matter which SCSI IDs the drives have.

ANSWER

4. **How many devices can be used on a single SCSI bus, including the host adapter?**
   a. 6
   b. 8
   c. 14
   d. 10

ANSWER

5. **A SCSI CD-ROM drive is installed on an existing SCSI bus in a system. Which statement is true?**
   a. The CD-ROM SCSI ID must be different than any other SCSI ID already assigned.
   b. The CD-ROM SCSI ID must be set to zero.
   c. A new host adapter must be installed that supports CD-ROM drives.
   d. It does not matter which SCSI ID is assigned to the CD-ROM drive.

ANSWER

6. **How can a SCSI ID be set on a SCSI device?**
   a. by software
   b. by jumpers on the device
   c. by DIP switches on the device
   d. all of the above

ANSWER

7. **A SCSI bus has three SCSI devices and a host adapter. Which device(s) can communicate with the CPU?**
   a. Only the host adapter communicates with the CPU: all communication goes through it.
   b. Each device on the SCSI bus can communicate directly with the CPU.
   c. Hard drives can communicate with the CPU, but all other SCSI devices must communicate through the host adapter.
   d. Only two devices on a SCSI bus can communicate with the CPU: the host adapter and one other device.

ANSWER

TYPES (EXAMPLE: REGULAR, WIDE, ULTRA-WIDE)

UNDERSTANDING THE OBJECTIVE

Of the several SCSI standards, some are compatible with one another and others are not compatible.

WHAT YOU REALLY NEED TO KNOW

◆ Narrow SCSI uses an 8-bit data path and 50-pin cables.

◆ Wide SCSI uses a 16-bit data path and 68-pin cables.

◆ SCSI-1, SCSI-2, and SCSI-3 can have up to 8 devices on a bus.

◆ Fast Wide SCSI and Wide Ultra SCSI can have up to 16 devices on a bus.

◆ SCSI-1 is commonly know as Regular SCSI.

◆ SCSI-2 is also known as Fast SCSI or Fast Narrow SCSI.

◆ SCSI-3 is also known as Ultra SCSI, Ultra Narrow SCSI, or Fast-20 SCSI.

◆ The following table summarizes SCSI standards:

Names for the SCSI Interface Standard	Bus width Narrow=8 bits Wide=16 bits	Maximum Length of Single-ended Cable (meters)	Maximum Length of Differential Cable (meters)	Maximum Number of Devices
SCSI-1 (Regular SCSI)	Narrow	6	25	8
SCSI-2 (Fast SCSI)	Narrow	3	25	8
Fast Wide SCSI (Wide SCSI)	Wide	3	25	16
SCSI-3 (Ultra SCSI)	Narrow	1.5	25	8
Wide Ultra SCSI (Fast Wide 20)	Wide	1.5	25	16
Ultra2 SCSI	Narrow		12 LVD*	8
Wide Ultra2 SCSI	Wide			16
Ultra3 SCSI	Narrow		12 LVD*	8
Wide Ultra3 SCSI	Wide		12 LVD*	16

* LVD: Low voltage differential cable allows for lengths of up to 12 meters.

OBJECTIVES ON THE JOB

When purchasing and installing SCSI devices, a technician must know which SCSI standards are compatible with other SCSI standards and not mix standards on the same SCSI bus that are incompatible. These standards apply to device drivers, the host adapter, cabling, termination devices, and SCSI devices.

PRACTICE TEST QUESTIONS

1. **SCSI-2 can support how many devices?**
   - a. 1
   - b. up to 6
   - c. up to 8
   - d. up to 16

2. **The data path of Wide Ultra SCSI is:**
   - a. 4 bits
   - b. 8 bits
   - c. 16 bits
   - d. 32 bits

3. **Which is the fastest SCSI standard?**
   - a. Regular SCSI
   - b. Fast SCSI
   - c. Fast-20 SCSI
   - d. Wide Ultra3 SCSI

4. **Which of the following is a difference between a single-ended SCSI cable and a differential SCSI cable?**
   - a. The single-ended SCSI cable can be longer than the differential SCSI cable.
   - b. The single-ended SCSI cable can be used with Regular SCSI, but the differential SCSI cable cannot.
   - c. Differential SCSI cable is more popular than single-ended SCSI cable because it is less expensive.
   - d. Data integrity is greater for a differential SCSI cable than for single-ended SCSI cable.

5. **What is true about SCSI termination?**
   - a. Each end of the SCSI chain must be terminated.
   - b. Each SCSI device must be terminated.
   - c. The SCSI host adapter is always terminated.
   - d. Terminators will always be installed inside the computer case.

6. **Which major SCSI standard does not include a standard for 16-bit data transmission?**
   - a. SCSI-1
   - b. SCSI-2
   - c. SCSI-3
   - d. All SCSI standards can use 16-bit data transmission.

7. **How many pins does a Narrow SCSI data cable have?**
   - a. 50
   - b. 9
   - c. 68
   - d. none of the above

MONITOR/VIDEO CARD • MODEM

UNDERSTANDING THE OBJECTIVE

A video subsystem includes the video card, monitor, and monitor cable. Video drivers must be compatible with the OS and the video card. They can be included by the OS or provided by the video card manufacturer.

A modem can be installed as an external device or an internal circuit board. Installation includes assigning system resources, physically installing the hardware, and installing device drivers to interface with the device.

WHAT YOU **REALLY** NEED TO KNOW

◆ Older systems installed a video card in a VESA slot, but systems today use only a PCI or AGP slot for a video card.

◆ To install a video card:

1. After physically installing the video card in the slot, connect the monitor data cable to the port on the back of the card.

2. Turn on the power to the computer and the monitor.

3. Install the device drivers for the video card. For DOS, run the installation disk. For Windows 9x and Windows 2000, the OS recognizes a new device and automatically performs the installation. You can use the setup disk from the video card manufacturer in the installation process.

4. Set display properties for the monitor to user preferences.

◆ In Windows, know the menu path to the Display Properties dialog box.

◆ A modem can be an external device, which most commonly uses a serial port.

◆ An external modem using a serial port uses the IRQ and I/O addresses assigned to the serial port.

◆ An internal modem must be assigned an IRQ and I/O addresses by the system. Most modem cards are Plug and Play, so the system automatically assigns the resources.

◆ After physically installing the modem, install device drivers using the setup disk that comes with the modem.

◆ To test a newly installed modem in Windows, use HyperTerminal to make a phone call. Know the menu path to HyperTerminal.

OBJECTIVES ON THE JOB

Installing a video card, monitor, and modem are common tasks expected of PC technicians. Both a video card and a modem require device drivers to operate. Windows 9x has drivers for many video cards and modems, but, when given the option, you should use those provided by the device manufacturer.

PRACTICE TEST QUESTIONS

1. An external modem will most likely use which port on a PC?

    a. serial

    b. parallel

    c. SCSI

    d. DIN

2. Video cards are normally installed in which bus expansion slot?

    a. ISA

    b. PCI

    c. AGP

    d. either b or c

3. A VESA bus expansion slot:

    a. is never used for a video card

    b. is found on older systems but not used on newer systems

    c. is slower than an ISA expansion slot

    d. has a 16-bit data path

4. The AGP expansion slot:

    a. is used only for video cards

    b. has a data path of 64 bits

    c. is slower than a PCI expansion slot

    d. runs asynchronously with the system clock

5. What IRQ does an external modem use?

    a. the IRQ assigned to its serial port

    b. IRQ10

    c. An external modem does not need an IRQ because it is an external device.

    d. IRQ7

6. Which device does not require an IRQ?

    a. a modem

    b. a sound card

    c. a monitor

    d. a keyboard

7. Describe the port typically used by a monitor on today's systems.

    a. 9-pin female with two rows of pins

    b. 15-pin female with three rows of pins

    c. 15-pin male with three rows of pins

    d. 25-pin female with two rows of pins

USB PERIPHERALS AND HUBS • IEEE 1284 • IEEE 1394 • EXTERNAL STORAGE

UNDERSTANDING THE OBJECTIVE

Common storage devices are floppy disk drives, hard drives, DVD drives, and CD-ROM drives, which can be either internal or external devices. Installation includes assigning resources, configuring the drive and the system, and the physical installation. Installing device drivers can be either automatic or require an installation process. USB, IEEE 1284, and IEEE 1394 are standards that control various peripheral devices.

WHAT YOU **REALLY** NEED TO KNOW

- ◆ Floppy drives and hard drives don't normally require the manual installation of device drivers because the OS and/or BIOS interfaces directly with the drive.
- ◆ CMOS setup is configured to detect a floppy drive or hard drive. CMOS may need to be changed (as with floppy drive installation) or may automatically detect the new drive (as with hard drive auto detection, if available).
- ◆ Be able to identify the ports on the back of a sound card.
- ◆ When installing data cables for drives, connect pin 1 on the connection to the edge color on the data cable.
- ◆ For a CD-ROM installation, if the system has a sound card, connect the audio wire from the sound card to the CD-ROM drive.
- ◆ Up to 127 USB devices can be daisy-chained together off a single USB port. One USB device can provide a port for another device, or a device can serve as a hub, connecting several devices. The maximum length for a USB cable is five meters.
- ◆ Windows 95 with the USB update, Windows 98, and Windows 2000 support USB, but Windows NT does not.
- ◆ IEEE 1394, also known as FireWire or i.Link, is a peripheral bus standard. It uses serial transmission and is much faster than USB.
- ◆ EEE 1394 devices are daisy-chained together, and one host controller can support up to 63 devices.
- ◆ Windows 98, Windows NT, and Windows 2000 all support IEEE 1394.
- ◆ IEEE 1284 is a standard for parallel ports and cables, and includes specifications for EPP (enhanced parallel port) and ECP (extended capabilities port).
- ◆ ECP increases performance by using a DMA channel. Control the DMA channel used and enable and disable ECP using CMOS setup.
- ◆ EPP is a bi-directional parallel port standard.
- ◆ If a new external storage device does not work after an installation, verify the port is enabled in CMOS, and test the port using diagnostic software and loop-back plugs.

OBJECTIVES ON THE JOB

Installing peripheral devices on a PC is a common task for a PC technician.

PRACTICE TEST QUESTIONS

1. **After physically installing a floppy drive, the next step is to:**
   a. install the floppy drive device drivers
   b. inform CMOS setup of the new drive
   c. upgrade BIOS to support the drive
   d. disconnect the power cord to the hard drive

   ANSWER

2. **When does a parallel port require a DMA channel?**
   a. When the parallel cabled is bi-directional
   b. When ECP is enabled in CMOS setup
   c. When EPP is enabled in CMOS setup
   d. None of the above; a parallel port never uses a DMA channel

   ANSWER

3. **An IDE Zip drive data cable has how many pins?**
   a. 9
   b. 25
   c. 34
   d. 40

   ANSWER

4. **You install a printer, but the PC cannot communicate with the printer. What is one thing to check?**
   a. The parallel port does not have conflicting resources in Device Manager.
   b. The parallel port is enabled in CMOS setup.
   c. The printer is online.
   d. all of the above

   ANSWER

5. **You install a floppy drive and reboot the PC. The drive light on the floppy drive stays lit and the system hangs. What is the most likely source of the problem?**
   a. The floppy drive data cable is not connected correctly.
   b. The power cord to the floppy drive is not connected.
   c. The hard drive was damaged during the installation.
   d. The floppy drive is installed upside down.

   ANSWER

6. **You have installed an IDE CD-ROM drive as the only device using the secondary IDE channel, and the drive is not recognized by the system. What is likely to be wrong?**
   a. The jumper setting on the CD-ROM drive is set to master and should be set to slave.
   b. The secondary IDE channel is disabled in CMOS setup.
   c. There is an IRQ conflict with the keyboard.
   d. The drive was damaged by ESD during the installation.

   ANSWER

7. **You have installed an external Zip drive using a second parallel port in a system, and you cannot get the system to recognize the drive. What is likely to be wrong?**
   a. A Zip drive cannot use a parallel port but must be installed as a SCSI device.
   b. The parallel port has a resource conflict; check Device Manager.
   c. The parallel port is disabled in CMOS setup or configured wrong; check setup.
   d. either b or c

   ANSWER

PORTABLES: DOCKING STATIONS • PC CARDS • PORT REPLICATORS • INFRARED DEVICES

UNDERSTANDING THE OBJECTIVE

Most portable systems (notebook computers or laptops) are covered by strict warranty agreements and are generally serviced by the manufacturer; however, some service is possible and maintenance is also important.

WHAT YOU **REALLY** NEED TO KNOW

- ◆ A notebook computer uses an LCD panel as the main output device.
- ◆ A battery pack in a notebook computer provides power when the notebook is not connected to a power source.
- ◆ The battery is recharged when the notebook is connected to a power source by way of an AC adapter.
- ◆ A **docking station** is a device designed to allow a notebook to easily connect to a full-sized monitor, keyboard, and other peripheral devices.
- ◆ A **port replicator** makes it convenient to connect a notebook to a monitor, printer, external hard drives, and other external devices.
- ◆ A hard drive for a notebook computer is designed to work even when the notebook is being moved.
- ◆ An LCD panel is fragile and care should be taken to protect it.
- ◆ LCD panels are made of two polarized sheets of glass with a layer of liquid crystals between them. These layers are backlit with fluorescent light.
- ◆ When adding an infrared transceiver to a system, connect the transceiver to a port and reboot. Windows automatically detects and installs drivers.
- ◆ To activate an infrared transceiver, double-click the Infrared icon in Control Panel.
- ◆ Infrared devices are assigned virtual ports such as COM4 or LPT3.
- ◆ A PC Card requires two services from the OS, a socket service and a card service. The socket service manages the connection between the card and the PC and the card service is managed by the device drivers for the PC Card device.

OBJECTIVES ON THE JOB

As notebook computers become more popular, servicing and troubleshooting them is becoming a standard task for PC technicians.

A typical task is upgrading memory on a notebook computer. The most common memory modules on a notebook are single outline DIMMs (SO-DIMMs). They have 72 pins and support 32-bit data transfers. Another memory module for notebooks is a SO-RIMM, which has 160 pins and uses a 16-bit data path. Use only a brand of SO-DIMM or SO-RIMM recommended by the notebook manufacturer; using the wrong kind might void the notebook warranty. Be careful to protect against ESD as you work.

PRACTICE TEST QUESTIONS

1. What specification covers PC Cards?

    a. ISA

    b. EISA

    c. PCI

    d. PCMCIA

2. What device can a notebook computer use to make it convenient to connect to a LAN?

    a. a network printer

    b. a docking station

    c. a battery pack

    d. a network LCD panel

3. What notebook component is considered fragile?

    a. a PC Card

    b. the hard drive

    c. the battery pack

    d. the LCD panel

4. In Windows 98, how do you activate an infrared transceiver?

    a. Click Start, Accessories, System Tools, Infrared

    b. Click Start, Settings, Control Panel, and double-click the Infrared icon

    c. Click Start, Settings, Control Panel, System, Device Manager, Infrared device, Properties

    d. Use CMOS setup

5. In CMOS setup, if you enable the option named "UART2 Use Infrared", this setting causes the following to happen:

    a. Set UART2 to support an infrared transceiver and disable COM2

    b. Enable COM2 and enable an infrared transceiver

    c. Disable all serial ports and enable an infrared transceiver

    d. Disable COM1 and enable an infrared transceiver

6. What port on the back of a computer allows you to use a keyboard or other input device without a connecting cord to the computer?

    a. the USB port

    b. the remote serial port

    c. the PC Card port

    d. the infrared port

7. What type of PC Card can be used for a hard drive of a notebook computer?

    a. Type I

    b. Type II

    c. Type III

    d. Type IV

1.8 Identify hardware methods of upgrading system performance, procedures for replacing basic subsystem components, unique components and when to use them

MEMORY • HARD DRIVES • CPU

UNDERSTANDING THE OBJECTIVE

Memory is optimized when the system has a large amount of dynamic RAM (DRAM) and some static RAM (SRAM). Older systems store SRAM on the motherboard, which can be upgraded. Newer systems contain SRAM inside the CPU housing and, therefore, cannot be changed. For older systems, install enough SRAM to speed up memory access. For all systems, install additional DRAM so that software and data have enough room in RAM without having to rely too heavily on virtual memory. The optimum CPU for a system is determined by the system board, what CPUs it supports, and the intended purpose of the system. For optimal use of hard drive space, the cluster size should be small.

WHAT YOU **REALLY** NEED TO KNOW

- ◆ For Windows 9x, use at least 64 MB of RAM; 128 MB or 256 MB is optimal.
- ◆ When a system does not have enough RAM, disk thrashing can result as the OS shifts data in and out of virtual memory. The solution is to keep fewer applications open at a time or install more RAM.
- ◆ Upgrading memory means to add more RAM to a computer system. You can install DIMMs, SIMMs, and RIMMs in empty memory slots or you can exchange existing modules that hold small amounts of memory with those that hold more.
- ◆ The two kinds of SRAM are **primary cache** (L1 cache, internal cache) located on the CPU microchip and **secondary cache** (L2 cache, external cache) located on the system board or, for newer Pentium systems, on a tiny circuit board contained within the CPU housing.
- ◆ SRAM is installed in multiples of 256K. Optimal SRAM depends on the system, but 512K is commonly recognized as adequate for most systems.
- ◆ Defragment and back up data on a hard drive routinely.
- ◆ Protect hard drives from magnetic fields and extremely hot or cold temperatures.
- ◆ Windows 2000, Windows 98, and later versions of Windows 95 support FAT32, which can yield the optimal use of hard drive space because the cluster size is smaller than that of FAT16. Windows NT does not support FAT32.

OBJECTIVES ON THE JOB

Upgrading memory is a simple and relatively inexpensive method of improving the overall performance of a computer system. For a computer system to run at optimum performance under Windows 9x, use 128 MB of memory or more. Improving system performance is a task expected of PC technicians. Routinely defragment and scan a hard drive for errors.

PRACTICE TEST QUESTIONS

1. **Which storage device provides the fastest access time for large multimedia files?**
   a. the CD-ROM drive
   b. the IDE hard drive
   c. the SCSI hard drive
   d. the floppy drive

2. **Cache memory is usually installed on a system board in increments of:**
   a. 1K
   b. 256K
   c. 1 MB
   d. 4 MB

3. **What is a reasonable amount of cache memory on a system board?**
   a. 1K
   b. 1 MB
   c. 512K
   d. 16 MB

ANSWER

4. **L2 cache memory can exist in a system as:**
   a. individual chips on the system board
   b. in a COAST module installed on the system board
   c. inside the housing of a Pentium II or higher CPU
   d. all of the above

ANSWER

5. **What is the purpose of installing additional cache memory?**
   a. to give applications more room for their data
   b. to speed up data access time
   c. to allow more applications to be open at the same time
   d. all of the above

ANSWER

6. **Why do newer system boards not have cache memory installed?**
   a. It is contained inside the CPU housing.
   b. DRAM no longer needs SRAM to operate at fast speeds.
   c. Cache memory is so expensive.
   d. Newer CPUs cannot use cache memory.

ANSWER

7. **What can result if there is not enough RAM installed in a system?**
   a. disk thrashing
   b. The system is slow.
   c. Some applications might not be able to load.
   d. all of the above

OBJECTIVES

1.8
cont.

Identify hardware methods of upgrading system performance, procedures for replacing basic subsystem components, unique components and when to use them

UPGRADING BIOS • WHEN TO UPGRADE BIOS

UNDERSTANDING THE OBJECTIVE

Older ROM BIOS microchips could only be upgraded by replacing the chip. Newer BIOS chips (EEPROM chips) can be electronically upgraded. This technology is called Flash ROM, and the process is sometimes called flashing ROM.

WHAT YOU **REALLY** NEED TO KNOW

- ◆ Flash ROM allows you to upgrade BIOS without having to replace the chip.
- ◆ One reason to upgrade the BIOS is to install a hard drive with a capacity larger than the one supported by your current BIOS chip. Older BIOS only supported 504 MB or smaller drives.
- ◆ BIOS manufacturers often offer upgrades or fixes to their BIOS code. These upgrades can be downloaded from the manufacturer's web site on the Internet.
- ◆ The most popular manufacturers of BIOS software are Phoenix Software, Award Software, and American Megatrends (AMI).
- ◆ To identify the BIOS manufacturer of a BIOS chip, look for the manufacturer and model number written on top of the chip or look for the information written on the screen during booting.
- ◆ The ROM BIOS chip on the system board is larger than most chips and might have a shiny label on top.
- ◆ The BIOS on expansion cards written for 16-bit real mode DOS sometimes expects to use specific memory addresses in the upper memory address range from 640K to 1024K.
- ◆ Some real-mode device drivers will not work unless given specific memory addresses in upper memory.
- ◆ The BIOS for some devices only works when allowed to use specific IRQs, I/O addresses, DMA channels, or upper memory addresses.
- ◆ For standard devices, such as a floppy disk drive that uses IRQ6, using specific resources is not a problem, but for other devices, a resource conflict can result when two legacy devices attempt to use the same system resource.

OBJECTIVES ON THE JOB

Upgrading BIOS is most often appropriate when attempting to install a large hard drive in an older system. Sometimes a BIOS manufacturer will offer an upgrade when there are known problems with a particular BIOS model or in order to support new hardware or software. In most environments, you will not often be called on to perform this task.

PRACTICE TEST QUESTIONS

1. The major advantage of using Flash ROM is:
   a. upgrading BIOS without replacing the chip
   b. not having to reload the operating system
   c. protected hard drives
   d. increased memory capacity

2. One reason to upgrade a BIOS is to:
   a. install a larger hard drive
   b. install a second floppy drive
   c. cause the system to use less power
   d. perform routine maintenance on a system

3. You can find an upgrade for BIOS in:
   a. the CD that came with the system board
   b. files in the \Windows\System folder that contain BIOS upgrades
   c. the web site of the BIOS manufacturer
   d. the Microsoft web site, because they keep all BIOS upgrades in stock

ANSWER

4. How often does a PC technician perform a BIOS upgrade on a system?
   a. very seldom, maybe never
   b. at least once a year
   c. whenever new hardware is installed
   d. whenever routine maintenance is scheduled

ANSWER

5. To identify the BIOS manufacturer and model, look:
   a. on the top of the BIOS chip
   b. on the bottom of the system board
   c. on the power supply or the back of the computer case
   d. in the Word document stored in the root directory of the hard drive

ANSWER

6. When upgrading the BIOS, the most likely way to get the BIOS upgrade is to:
   a. read the upgrade file from the CD-ROM sent to you by the BIOS manufacturer
   b. download the upgrade from the Internet
   c. read the upgrade file from the system board setup CD-ROM
   d. type the code into a document on the screen

ANSWER

7. When upgrading BIOS, what should you remember?
   a. Be careful to not expose the ROM BIOS chip to light as you work; this can damage the chip.
   b. Be careful to not move the ROM BIOS chip in its socket, which can damage the chip.
   c. Be careful to upgrade using the correct upgrade from the manufacturer. Upgrading with the wrong file could make your system BIOS totally useless.
   d. Be careful to not type the wrong code into the BIOS program.

OBJECTIVES

1.8 Identify hardware methods of upgrading system performance, procedures for
cont. replacing basic subsystem components, unique components and when to use them

PORTABLE SYSTEMS: BATTERY • HARD DRIVE • TYPES I, II, III CARDS • MEMORY

UNDERSTANDING THE OBJECTIVE

Many add-on devices are installed in a notebook computer using PC Card slots (formally called PCMCIA slots). There are three sizes of PC Cards. Also, just as with personal computers, memory can be added to notebook computers.

WHAT YOU **REALLY** NEED TO KNOW

♦ Notebook computers commonly use small memory modules called **SO-DIMMs** that take up less space than a SIMM or DIMM. A SO-DIMM has 72 pins and a 32-bit data path.

♦ Another memory module for notebooks is a SO-RIMM, which uses a 16-bit data path and has 160 pins.

♦ When upgrading memory on a notebook, only use memory modules that are recommended by the notebook manufacturer.

♦ PC Cards of Type I, II, and III have different thicknesses.

♦ A notebook's BIOS must provide **socket service** and **card service** to PC Cards.

♦ PC Cards require little power to operate and are **hot swappable** (can be installed and removed without rebooting the computer).

♦ The first PC Cards used a 16-bit data path and followed the ISA bus standards. Newer PC Cards use CardBus technology, which offers a 32-bit data path and follows the PCI bus standards. Notebooks generally support both technologies.

♦ 16-bit and 32-bit PC Cards come in three sizes, rated Type I, II, and III cards.

PC Card Type	Thickness	Devices That Use This Type
Type I	3.3 mm	Memory cards (oldest type)
Type II	5 mm	Network cards, modem cards
Type III	10.5 mm	Hard disk cards

OBJECTIVES ON THE JOB

Two common tasks for a PC technician supporting a notebook computer are upgrading memory and verifying that a PC Card device is configured and working correctly on the notebook.

Another task is to help the user configure the power management features of a notebook computer. In Windows 98, click Start, Settings, Control Panel, and double-click the Power Management icon. In the Power Management Properties dialog box you can create, delete, and modify multiple power management schemes to customize how Windows 98 manages power consumption. For example, choose hibernation so that after a period of inactivity, the notebook computer stores information currently in memory and then shuts down. When it returns from hibernating, Windows 98 restores the computer to the way it was before the shutdown. When hibernating, the notebook is not using power. You can set the notebook to enable the hibernation feature in the Power Management Properties dialog box in Windows 98.

PRACTICE TEST QUESTIONS

1. **What type of memory module is used in a notebook computer?**
   a. SIMM
   b. DIMM
   c. SO-DIMM
   d. LDIMM

2. **Which PC Card is the thickest?**
   a. Type I
   b. Type 25
   c. Type II
   d. Type III

3. **Which type of PC Card is typically used for a modem?**
   a. Type I
   b. Type II
   c. Type III
   d. Type IV

ANSWER

4. **Hot swapping refers to:**
   a. the ability to install a component without rebooting
   b. hard drives overheating and needing to be replaced
   c. a notebook computer providing support for a PC Card that serves as a hard drive
   d. quickly rebooting a computer when components are installed

ANSWER

5. **How many pins are on a SO-DIMM?**
   a. 72
   b. 32
   c. 168
   d. 30

ANSWER

6. **A power-saving feature of a notebook computer that turns the power off after a period of inactivity is:**
   a. sleep mode
   b. hibernation
   c. Screen Saver Plus
   d. PowerSave

7. **Which bus technology is CardBus based on?**
   a. ISA
   b. AGP
   c. PCI
   d. EISA

2.1 Identify common symptoms and problems associated with each module and how to troubleshoot and isolate the problems

PROCESSOR/MEMORY SYMPTOMS • POST AUDIBLE/VISUAL ERROR CODES

UNDERSTANDING THE OBJECTIVE

Problems with a system are divided into problems that occur during booting and problems that occur after booting completes. The BIOS performs a test of the CPU, CMOS, the system board, and other vital components during booting. Errors encountered before video is active are communicated by a series of beeps and, after video is active, by error codes and messages displayed on the screen.

WHAT YOU **REALLY** NEED TO KNOW

- ◆ Errors with a system board can be discovered by interpreting beep codes, POST error codes displayed on the screen, and BIOS error messages displayed on the screen.
- ◆ Sometimes a dead computer can be fixed by disassembling and reassembling parts, reseating expansion cards, reconnecting cables, and reseating DIMMs, SIMMs, RIMMs, and the CPU.
- ◆ Bad connections and corrosion are common problems. Dust buildup can cause a system to overheat and malfunction.
- ◆ Check jumpers, DIP switches, and CMOS settings. Look for physical damage on the system board.
- ◆ If the battery is dead or low, it may cause problems. The first indication of a failing battery is the system does not keep the correct time when the power is off.
- ◆ The following are error messages that might have to do with the CMOS and their meanings:

Error	Meaning of Error Message and What to Do
Configuration/CMOS error	Setup information does not agree with the actual hardware the computer found during boot
Fixed disk configuration error	The drive type set in CMOS setup is not supported by the BIOS, or the drive setup information does not match the hard drive type
Numeric POST code displays on the screen:	Troubleshoot the subsystem identified by the POST code
• Code in the 900 range	Parallel port errors
• Code in the 1100-1200 range	System board errors: Async communications adapter errors
• Code in the 1300 range	Game controller or joystick errors
• Code in the 1700 range	Hard drive errors
• Code in the 6000 range	SCSI device or network card errors
• Code in the 7300 range	Floppy drive errors

OBJECTIVES ON THE JOB

When attempting to solve problems during booting, use beep codes and POST error messages and error codes to help in solving the problem. To interpret these beeps and codes, see the Web site of the system board manufacturer or the BIOS manufacturer.

PRACTICE TEST QUESTIONS

1. **A PC continuously reboots itself. What is the most likely cause of the problem?**
   a. corrupt operating system
   b. problems with the power source or power supply
   c. bad RAM
   d. corrupted hard drive

ANSWER

2. **POST error codes in the 1700 range indicate a problem with:**
   a. the hard drive
   b. a floppy drive
   c. a CD-ROM drive
   d. memory

ANSWER

3. **One long continuous beep or several steady long beeps most likely indicate a problem with:**
   a. the hard drive
   b. the CPU
   c. RAM
   d. the power supply

ANSWER

4. **You want to install a large hard drive on a system whose BIOS does not support large drives and you cannot upgrade the BIOS. What is the best solution?**
   a. Make the BIOS think the large drive is a SCSI drive.
   b. Use software that makes the BIOS think it is looking at a smaller drive.
   c. Replace the system board.
   d. Replace the entire PC.

ANSWER

5. **An error message, "Parity error," displays and the system hangs. The source of the problem is:**
   a. bad RAM
   b. bad CPU
   c. a corrupted hard drive
   d. a bad system board

ANSWER

6. **When a PC boots, the screen is blank and you hear a single beep. What is most likely to be the problem?**
   a. the system board or the CPU
   b. the video card
   c. the monitor
   d. ROM BIOS

ANSWER

7. **When a PC boots, the screen is blank and you hear several beeps. What is most likely to be the problem?**
   a. power to the PC
   b. a corrupted operating system
   c. the monitor
   d. RAM or the system board

ANSWER

2.1
cont.
Identify common symptoms and problems associated with each module and how to troubleshoot and isolate the problems

MOTHERBOARDS • BIOS • CMOS

UNDERSTANDING THE OBJECTIVE

PC problems are divided between those that occur during booting and those that occur after booting is successful. Problems with motherboards, BIOS, and CMOS generally cause problems during the boot process. The boot process begins when a PC is first turned on and prepares the PC to receive instructions from the user. Hardware, firmware, and the operating system are all involved in the boot process.

WHAT YOU **REALLY** NEED TO KNOW

Functions performed during the boot:

◆ Startup BIOS tests essential hardware components. This test is called the **power on self test (POST)**.

◆ The BIOS turns to information stored in CMOS to determine what hardware to expect and how that hardware is configured.

◆ Hardware devices are matched with the BIOS and device drivers that control them and with the assigned system resources that they will later use for communication.

◆ The operating system is loaded, configured, and executed.

◆ Some applications software may be loaded and executed.

◆ Steps in the boot process:
  1. When the power is first turned on, the system clock begins to generate clock pulses.
  2. The CPU turns to memory address FFFF0h, which is the memory address always assigned to the first instruction in the ROM BIOS startup program.
  3. This instruction directs the CPU to run the POST tests.
  4. POST first checks the BIOS program operating it and then tests CMOS RAM.
  5. A test is done to determine that there has not been a battery failure, and the CPU is tested and initialized.
  6. A check is done to determine if this is a **cold boot**. If so, then the first 16K of RAM is tested.
  7. Hardware devices installed on the computer are inventoried and compared to configuration information.
  8. Video, memory, keyboard, floppy disk drives, hard drives, ports, and other hardware devices are tested and configured including IRQ. I/O addresses and DMA assignments are made. The OS will later complete this process.
  9. Some devices are set up to go into sleep mode to conserve electricity.
  10. CMOS setup (a BIOS program to change CMOS setup) is run if requested.
  11. BIOS then begins its search for an operating system looking on the drives according to the order listed in CMOS setup.

OBJECTIVES ON THE JOB

Understanding the boot process is essential to troubleshooting problems that occur during booting. Problems with a PC are divided into two categories: problems during and problems after the boot. A PC technician is responsible for solving problems in both categories. One of the first steps in isolating a problem is to determine if the problem occurs during or after the boot.

PRACTICE TEST QUESTIONS

1. **During booting, the purpose of the memory test is to:**
   a. show the user how much memory is installed, but nothing else
   b. verify that the hard drive has a procedure in place to count memory
   c. verify that memory is installed and working properly
   d. hold up the boot process while a hard drive test is performed

2. **The process that determines what hardware is present and that tests critical hardware components is called:**
   a. booting
   b. the power on self test
   c. the power on startup process
   d. loading an operating system

3. **Which component could cause a blank screen during booting?**
   a. the system board
   b. the video card
   c. RAM
   d. all of the above

4. **Before video is active, errors during booting are communicated as:**
   a. messages on the screen
   b. beep codes
   c. numeric POST codes on the screen
   d. all of the above

5. **When a system repeatedly hangs during booting but finally boots successfully, the most likely cause of the problem is:**
   a. the power supply
   b. RAM
   c. the hard drive
   d. the CPU

6. **During booting, hardware devices are assigned:**
   a. system resources to be used for communication
   b. code names to be used by the OS
   c. a place in memory for their data
   d. all of the above

7. **Hardware components are checked:**
   a. by the OS after it loads
   b. during POST
   c. by a special startup program on the hard drive
   d. both a and b

2.1
cont.

Identify common symptoms and problems associated with each module and how to troubleshoot and isolate the problems

MOUSE • SOUND CARD/AUDIO • MONITOR/VIDEO • MODEMS

UNDERSTANDING THE OBJECTIVE

Problems with devices can be caused by either hardware or software failures and can occur during or after booting. To isolate the source of a problem, you can eliminate the unnecessary component, trade a suspected-bad component for a known-good component, or install a suspected-bad component into a known-good system.

WHAT YOU **REALLY** NEED TO KNOW

◆ Most problems with monitors and the video system are caused by simple things like loose cable connections and poorly adjusted brightness and contrast settings.

◆ If the LED light on the front of the monitor is lit, the monitor has power.

◆ There is sometimes a fuse on the back of a monitor; check that it is not blown.

◆ Reseat an expansion card and try to boot again before exchanging the card.

◆ Check CMOS settings, reseat socketed chips, and replace suspected bad components.

◆ Verify that Device Manager does not report any problems with the device or its port.

◆ To resolve resource conflicts, use MSD in DOS and Device Manager in Windows 9x.

◆ If a musical CD does not play, check the audio wire between the CD-ROM drive and the sound card.

◆ If the sound does not work, try adjusting the volume in Windows and the amplifier or speakers.

◆ If a mouse does not work, try cleaning the ball cavity with a clean cloth and very small amount of mild soap.

◆ You must often troubleshoot to solve problems when installing a modem. If the new modem does not work, check the following:
- Is the PC short on hard drive space or RAM? Try closing all other applications currently running.
- Is the modem set to the same COM port and IRQ to which the software is set?
- Is another device configured to the same COM port or IRQ as the modem?
- For an internal modem, check the DIP switches and jumpers. Do they agree with the modem properties in the OS?
- Try moving an internal modem to a different expansion slot.
- For an external modem, use a different serial cable.
- Did the software correctly initialize the modem? If you did not specify the correct modem type, it may be sending the wrong initialization command. Try AT&F. (In Windows 9x, click Start, Settings, Control Panel. Double-click Modem. Select the modem and click Modem Properties, Connections, Advanced Connection Settings. Enter the AT command under Extra Settings.) Retry the modem.

OBJECTIVES ON THE JOB

Follow established troubleshooting procedures when attempting to isolate and solve problems with peripheral devices.

PRACTICE TEST QUESTIONS

1. **If nothing is showing on the monitor screen, the first thing to do is:**
   a. check the monitor connections to the computer and the power
   b. reseat the video card in its expansion slot
   c. reinstall the video drivers
   d. reboot the PC

2. **If the LED light on the monitor is lit but the screen is blank, what is NOT a source of the problem?**
   a. the brightness or contrast settings
   b. video cable to the computer
   c. circuitry inside the monitor
   d. power to the monitor

3. **What IRQ does a sound card typically use?**
   a. 1
   b. 5
   c. 6
   d. 15

4. **Your modem was working fine until you installed a sound card; now neither the modem nor the sound card work. What is likely the problem?**
   a. The modem was accidentally disconnected while installing the sound card.
   b. There is a resource conflict between the two devices.
   c. The modem is the type that does not work if a sound card is installed in the system.
   d. The OS cannot support both devices at the same time.

5. **What IRQ does a monitor use?**
   a. 1
   b. 7
   c. 14
   d. A monitor does not use an IRQ.

6. **ESD is least likely to cause damage to what device?**
   a. an internal modem
   b. a keyboard
   c. a CPU
   d. RAM

7. **Which of the following is typically an input and output device?**
   a. a monitor
   b. a modem
   c. a mouse
   d. a keyboard

2.1 cont. Identify common symptoms and problems associated with each module and how to troubleshoot and isolate the problems

CD-ROM • DVD

UNDERSTANDING THE OBJECTIVE

Data and instructions (programs) are permanently stored in secondary storage devices (hard drive, floppy disk, CD-ROM, DVD, and so forth) even when the PC is turned off. A DVD disc can hold up to 17 GB of data, enough for more than 8 hours of video storage.

WHAT YOU **REALLY** NEED TO KNOW

◆ CD-ROM drives use the **ATAPI** standard to connect to the system as an IDE device using an IDE connection.

◆ If the CD-ROM drive is sharing an IDE data cable with a hard drive, set the hard drive to master and the CD-ROM drive to slave.

◆ MSCDEX.EXE is a 16-bit real mode Microsoft CD-ROM extension to DOS and is loaded in AUTOEXEC.BAT and requires a real-mode CD-ROM device driver to be loaded from CONFIG.SYS.

◆ Windows 2000 and Windows 9x provide protected mode support for CD-ROM and DVD drives.

◆ A CD-ROM drive is read only. A CD-R drive can handle CD-Recordable (both read and write) discs. A CD-RW drive manages rewriteable CDs, meaning that old data can be over-written on the disc with new data.

◆ A DVD drive can require a decoder card to uncompress video and audio data stored on the DVD disc.

◆ Several versions of DVD drives are listed in the table below:

DVD Device	Description
DVD-ROM	Read-only device; can also read CDs
DVD-R	DVD recordable; can also read DVD-ROM and CD discs
DVD-RAM	Recordable and erasable. Can read DVD and CD discs.
DVD-RW or DVD-ER	Rewritable DVD device.
DVD+RW	Rewritable DVD device. Not compatible with DVD-RAM devices.

OBJECTIVES ON THE JOB

A CD-ROM drive is considered standard equipment on computer systems today. Installing and troubleshooting problems with CD-ROM drives is an essential skill of a PC technician.

Know that Windows 95 does not automatically install the files necessary to access a CD-ROM drive on its Emergency Startup Disk (ESD). To access a CD-ROM drive in real mode from a command prompt, the ESD must include MSCDEX.EXE and the device driver file for the CD-ROM drive. Load MSCDEX.EXE from AUTOEXEC.BAT and the device driver from CONFIG.SYS. Windows 98 automatically includes these files on the ESD.

PRACTICE TEST QUESTIONS

1. How is a real-mode device driver for a CD-ROM drive loaded?
   a. from CONFIG.SYS
   b. from AUTOEXEC.BAT
   c. at the DOS prompt
   d. using the LOADHIGH command

ANSWER

2. The DOS extension that manages a CD-ROM drive is:
   a. CONFIG.SYS
   b. MSCDEX.EXE
   c. CDROM.SYS
   d. IO.SYS

ANSWER

3. What standard does a CD-ROM drive use that is installed as an IDE device in a system?
   a. ATAPI
   b. IDE CD-ROM extension
   c. MCP
   d. EISA

ANSWER

4. Which operating system(s) provides support for most CD-ROM drives?
   a. DOS
   b. Windows 2000
   c. Windows 98
   d. b and c

ANSWER

5. Which device provides the fastest data access time?
   a. an IDE hard drive
   b. a floppy disk
   c. a CD-ROM drive
   d. All of the above devices provide about the same data access time.

ANSWER

6. Which utility manages a CD-ROM drive for DOS?
   a. CONFIG.SYS
   b. COMMAND.COM
   c. MSCDEX.EXE
   d. IO.SYS

ANSWER

7. Why is MSCDEX.EXE not used with Windows 9x?
   a. It is replaced with MSCDEX.SYS.
   b. Windows 9x uses 32-bit protected mode support for CD-ROM drives.
   c. MSCDEX.EXE is required by Windows 9x.
   d. Windows 9x does not support CD-ROM drives.

ANSWER

OBJECTIVES

2.1
cont. Identify common symptoms and problems associated with each module and how to troubleshoot and isolate the problems

POWER SUPPLY • SLOT COVERS

UNDERSTANDING THE OBJECTIVE

Problems with a power supply can cause the system to hang at unexpected times, the keyboard to not work, boot failures, or other intermittent errors.

WHAT YOU **REALLY** NEED TO KNOW

◆ When a system hangs during booting, eliminate the power supply as the source of the problem by testing it with a multimeter. If there are still failures during booting, suspect the system board.

◆ Cover open slots on the rear of a PC case to keep dust and **EMI** out of the case.

◆ Line analyzers can be used to eliminate suspected problems with power surges, spikes, and sags.

◆ After you have successfully tested a power supply using a multimeter, know that the power supply might still be the source of the problem because the problem might be intermittent.

◆ A power supply contains capacitors, which retain their charge even after the power is disconnected, so don't open the case of a power supply unless you are trained to service one.

◆ Before opening the case of a power supply, discharge the power supply by placing a high-voltage prong or insulated screwdriver across the hot and ground plugs.

◆ Don't wear an anti-static ground strap when servicing a power supply; you don't want to be ground for a discharge from the power supply.

◆ Problems with a power supply might manifest themselves in the following ways:

- The PC halts or hangs during booting, but after several tries, it boots successfully.

- Error codes or beep codes occur during booting, but the errors come and go.

- The computer stops or hangs for no reason. Sometimes it might even reboot itself.

- Memory errors appear intermittently.

- Data is written incorrectly to the hard drive.

- The keyboard stops working at odd times.

- The system board fails or is damaged.

- The power supply overheats and becomes hot to the touch.

◆ Electrical problems can be caused by other devices (such as copy machines) on the same circuit as the computer and its equipment.

OBJECTIVES ON THE JOB

Problems with the power supply can sometimes appear as problems with peripheral devices or make the system unstable. Use a multimeter to test the power supply when a problem's source is not evident.

PRACTICE TEST QUESTIONS

1. **The device inside a power supply that retains a charge even after power is disconnected is a:**
   a. capacitor
   b. transistor
   c. rectifier
   d. transformer

ANSWER

2. **Covering empty slots on the back of a PC case with slot covers helps to:**
   a. prevent EMI from entering the case
   b. keep the heat inside the case so that components don't get too cold
   c. protect components from ESD
   d. prevent an electrical charge from leaving the case

ANSWER

3. **A power supply uses which IRQ?**
   a. 0
   b. 10
   c. 15
   d. A power supply does not use an IRQ.

ANSWER

4. **The IDE hard drive does not spin up when the PC is turned on. What is most likely to be the problem?**
   a. bad data cable
   b. a bad connection from the power supply
   c. a bad system board
   d. a virus

ANSWER

5. **A PC repeatedly reboots. You replace the power supply with one you know is good. What do you do next?**
   a. Use a line analyzer to eliminate the power line as the source of the problem.
   b. Replace the hard drive.
   c. Install a UPS.
   d. Install an operating system that can monitor the power input to the system.

ANSWER

6. **Which beep codes could indicate that there is a problem with the power supply?**
   a. one long beep, two short beeps
   b. three short beeps
   c. steady short beeps
   d. all of the above

ANSWER

7. **The computer system appears dead, with no lights on the front panel, nothing on the screen, and no beeps. What do you check first?**
   a. the system board
   b. the CPU
   c. the power supply
   d. the speaker

ANSWER

2.1
cont. Identify common symptoms and problems associated with each module and how to troubleshoot and isolate the problems

FLOPPY DRIVE • PARALLEL PORTS • USB

UNDERSTANDING THE OBJECTIVE

Problems with hard drives and floppy disks can be caused by physical problems with the hardware, a corrupted file system, individual files on the drive or disk, configuration information, or drivers or the BIOS used to interface with the drives. Problems with a parallel port can be physical or can be caused by errors in configuration or with how the port is used. A USB port must be enabled in CMOS, and there can be no conflicts with the resources used by the USB controller.

WHAT YOU **REALLY** NEED TO KNOW

- ◆ When trying to solve a problem with a hard drive, the best protection for data on the drive is to copy the data to another drive or storage media.
- ◆ For parallel ports, use CMOS setup to verify that the port is configured correctly in CMOS and use Device Manager to verify the OS configuration.
  - Test the port by using diagnostic software and loop-back plugs (wrap plugs).
- ◆ A floppy drive is connected to a data cable, which can connect to a controller card (on very old systems) or directly to the system board using a 34-pin data cable.
- ◆ A floppy drive cable can support two floppy drives. The twist in the cable determines which drive is A: and which drive is B:.
- ◆ Viruses sometimes hide in the boot record program on a floppy disk, which is also called the boot strap loader.
- ◆ When troubleshooting a problem with reading/writing to a floppy disk, the following can be sources of the problem:
  - The application that is running is pointing to a different drive or the OS has just encountered an unrelated error that has locked up the system.
  - System BIOS or CMOS setup is not correctly configured.
  - The disk in the drive is not formatted, is corrupted, is physically damaged, is inserted wrong, or the floppy drive is bad or out of alignment.
  - The floppy drive controller card is loose in the expansion slot or is bad, or the data cable is poorly connected or is bad.
  - The edge color on the data cable is not connected to pin 1 at both ends of the cable.
  - The power supply is bad or the power cord is loose, disconnected, or bad.
  - The command just issued has a mistake or is the wrong command.
- ◆ Floppy drive diagnostic software and floppy disks called digital diagnostic disks (data is written perfectly to these disks) can be used to check for problems with a floppy drive.
- ◆ Tests on a floppy drive include testing azimuth skew, hub centering, hysteresis, radial alignment, rotational speed, and sensitivity.

OBJECTIVES ON THE JOB

Because a floppy drive has mechanical parts, it tends to wear out earlier than other PC components. Replacing a floppy drive is a common task expected of a PC technician.

PRACTICE TEST QUESTIONS

1. **What could cause the error message, "General failure reading drive A, Abort, Retry Fail?"**
   a. The file COMMAND.COM is missing from the disk.
   b. The floppy drive is faulty.
   c. The video system has a problem.
   d. There is a parity error in RAM.

ANSWER

2. **Possible sources of problems with reading a floppy disk include:**
   a. disk in drive is not formatted
   b. application currently running has an error
   c. power supply is bad
   d. all of the above

ANSWER

3. **What could cause the error message, "Non-system disk or disk error. Replace and strike any key when ready"?**
   a. Operating system files are missing from the disk.
   b. The floppy drive data cable is faulty.
   c. Track 0 on the disk is faulty.
   d. The floppy disk is write protected.

ANSWER

4. **How many bits of data are transmitted over a parallel port at one time?**
   a. 1
   b. 8
   c. 16
   d. 32

ANSWER

5. **An external CD-ROM drive typically uses what interface with the computer?**
   a. serial
   b. keyboard
   c. parallel
   d. USB

ANSWER

6. **Which IRQ does the parallel port LPT1 typically use?**
   a. IRQ0
   b. IRQ7
   c. IRQ10
   d. IRQ14

ANSWER

7. **The user reports that a floppy drive reads the first disk inserted into the drive after a reboot but does not read subsequent disks. What might be the problem?**
   a. The IRQ for the floppy drive is in conflict with another device.
   b. The floppy drive data cable is connected backwards.
   c. Device Manager does not recognize the drive.
   d. The power to the floppy drive is fluctuating.

ANSWER

2.1
cont.
Identify common symptoms and problems associated with each module and how to troubleshoot and isolate the problems

HARD DRIVES • LARGE LBA, LBA

UNDERSTANDING THE OBJECTIVE

Problems with hard drives can be caused by physical problems with the hardware, a corrupted file system, individual files on the drive or disk, configuration information, or drivers or BIOS used to interface with the drives.

WHAT YOU REALLY NEED TO KNOW

◆ Use the Windows Defragmenter utility on a routine basis to rewrite fragmented files into contiguous clusters.

◆ A FAT can become corrupted with **cross-linked clusters** (more than one file points to a cluster as belonging to its cluster chain) and **lost clusters** (a cluster is marked as used, but no file has the cluster in its cluster chain).

◆ Use Windows Scandisk to search for and fix lost and cross-linked clusters.

◆ Keep current backups of data on a hard drive in case the drive fails.

◆ System BIOS uses LBA mode or Large mode to communicate with a hard drive that is larger than 504 MB. The hard drive mode is set in CMOS setup.

◆ Windows NT and Windows 2000 do not use system BIOS to communicate with hard drives.

◆ The following are error messages that might have to do with the hard drive and their meanings:

Error	Meaning of Error Message and What to Do
Fixed disk controller failure	The hard drive controller has failed.
No boot sector on fixed disk	The hard drive partition table is missing or corrupted.
Fixed disk error Hard drive not found No boot device available	The PC cannot locate the hard drive or the controller card is not responding.
"Bad sector" errors "Sector not found" "Track 0 not found"	Suspect a corrupted file system, corrupted boot sector, or fading track and sector markings on the drive.
Invalid drive specification	The PC is unable to find a hard drive or a floppy drive that setup tells it to expect. The hard drive may have a corrupted partition table.
"Invalid or missing COMMAND.COM" "Invalid system disk" "Command file not found"	A nonbooting disk may be in drive A: or system files on drive C: may have been erased.
Non-system disk or disk error	System files necessary to load an OS are missing from the disk or the hard drive.
"Non-DOS disk" "Unable to read from drive C" "Invalid media type" "Missing operating system" "Error loading operating system"	The OS boot record is corrupted or missing or there is a translation problem on large drives (more than 1024 cylinders).

OBJECTIVES ON THE JOB

A PC technician must be able to identify and respond to error messages during booting.

PRACTICE TEST QUESTIONS

1. **The best protection for data on a hard drive is to:**
    a. keep the data on a single logical drive
    b. routinely back up the data to another media
    c. keep a second copy of the data in a different folder on the drive
    d. routinely run diagnostic software on the hard drive

ANSWER

2. **Which of the following is considered an FRU?**
    a. the circuit board on the bottom of a hard drive
    b. the hard drive data cable
    c. the power cord from the power supply to the hard drive
    d. the jumper bank on the rear of the hard drive

ANSWER

3. **What is the first thing you should do when you get the error, "Non-system disk or disk error"?**
    a. Check for a non-bootable floppy disk in the drive during a boot.
    b. Reformat the hard drive.
    c. Use the SYS command to restore OS files to the hard drive.
    d. Replace the hard drive.

ANSWER

4. **What is the cause of the error message, "Invalid or missing COMMAND.COM" during booting?**
    a. COMMAND.COM is missing from the \Windows\System folder.
    b. COMMAND.COM is missing from the \DOS directory.
    c. COMMAND.COM is missing from the root directory of the boot device.
    d. IO.SYS is corrupted.

ANSWER

5. **When an IDE hard drive gives "Bad sector" errors, what is the first thing you should do?**
    a. Reformat the drive.
    b. Perform a low-level format of the drive using software provided by the hard drive manufacturer.
    c. Perform a thorough Scandisk of the drive.
    d. Defragment the drive.

ANSWER

6. **What is the difference between a standard and a thorough Scandisk?**
    a. Standard takes longer but does a better job than thorough.
    b. Thorough checks the disk surface for errors.
    c. Thorough is faster.
    d. There is no difference.

ANSWER

7. **A cross-linked cluster is a cluster that:**
    a. is identified in the FAT as belonging to two files
    b. is marked in the root directory as belonging to two files
    c. is not used by any file
    d. is marked as a bad cluster by the FAT

ANSWER

2.1
cont.
Identify common symptoms and problems associated with each module and how to troubleshoot and isolate the problems

TROUBLESHOOTING TOOLS, E.G., MULTIMETER

UNDERSTANDING THE OBJECTIVE

The PC technician needs tools that are used to service both hardware and software. Many are listed below. Use a **multimeter** to measure the voltage output of the power supply and to measure continuity (such as when a fuse might be blown).

WHAT YOU **REALLY** NEED TO KNOW

◆ Tools that are essential and nice to have for PC troubleshooting are listed below. Many can be purchased in one handy PC tool kit:

- Bootable rescue disk and virus detection software on disks
- Flat-head, Phillips-head, and Torx screwdrivers
- Needle-nosed pliers, tweezers, chip extractor, and spring-loaded extractor for picking up tiny bits of paper or screws
- **Multimeter** to check the power supply output
- Flashlight to see inside dark places of the PC case
- Ground bracelet and/or ground mat
- Small cups, bags, or egg cartons to help keep screws organized as you work
- Anti-static bags to store unused parts
- Pen and paper for taking notes and drawing diagrams as you disassemble a system
- Diagnostic cards and diagnostic software
- Loop-back plugs and software to use them to test ports

◆ Here are some tips on using a multimeter:

- A multimeter is sometimes called a volt-ohm meter, a digital voltage meter (DVM), or a voltage meter.
- To test a fuse, set a multimeter at continuity (if present) or to measure resistance. When set to measure resistance in the ohm range, a good fuse has a resistance of zero.
- If the multimeter does not support **autorange**, set the range slightly higher than the expected value.
- Remove a circuit board by pulling straight up on the board. If it resists, you can gently rock it back and forth end to end, but *don't* rock it side to side as you might SPREAD the expansion slot opening.

OBJECTIVES ON THE JOB

A good PC technician has the proper tools and knows how to use them.

PRACTICE TEST QUESTIONS

1. **What measurement should a DVM be set to in order to test a fuse?**

    a. ohms

    b. amps

    c. DC volts

    d. AC volts

2. **At what range do you set a multimeter to measure the voltage output as an unknown source?**

    a. 110 volts

    b. ohms

    c. the highest voltage setting

    d. the lowest voltage setting

3. **If you set a multimeter to measure resistance with a range of 20K, what will be the reading (in ohms) of a good fuse?**

    a. 0

    b. 2

    c. 20

    d. 200

4. **You suspect a problem with a serial port. The best way to test the port is to:**

    a. use diagnostic software

    b. use loop-back plugs

    c. use a port test available from CMOS setup

    d. attempt to use the port with application software

5. **When using a multimeter to measure resistance, set the meter to measure:**

    a. volts

    b. ohms

    c. farads

    d. amps

6. **When using multimeter to measure current, set the meter to measure:**

    a. volts

    b. ohms

    c. farads

    d. amps

7. **Current is measured only:**

    a. when the PC is turned off

    b. when the PC is turned on

    c. after first checking voltage

    d. when the PC is attempting to print

2.1
cont.
Identify common symptoms and problems associated with each module and how to troubleshoot and isolate the problems

NIC • CABLES • KEYBOARD • PERIPHERALS

UNDERSTANDING THE OBJECTIVE

A network card, a keyboard, and other peripherals and cables can sometimes fail. When isolating a problem, do the simple things first such as rebooting or exchanging a cable or external device before opening the case and exchanging parts inside the computer case. Work methodically when isolating a computer problem.

WHAT YOU **REALLY** NEED TO KNOW

- ◆ A network card usually has two lights on the back of the card. One light stays lit and indicates a connection with the network is established. The other light blinks to indicate network activity.

- ◆ To verify a PC using Windows 9x is working properly on a network, try to view resources in Network Neighborhood.

- ◆ Before exchanging a NIC, first try exchanging the network cable.

- ◆ Before exchanging a NIC, first try uninstalling and reinstalling the network card drivers and the network protocol (for example, TCP/IP).

- ◆ In a Microsoft network, a host is assigned a name using the Network Properties window. To access this window, right-click the Network Neighborhood icon on the desktop and select Properties from the shortcut menu.

- ◆ When a keyboard is not working properly, after making a reasonable attempt to fix the problem, replace the keyboard.

- ◆ When keys don't work, try using compressed air or a vacuum to remove crumbs and other debris from underneath the keys.

- ◆ If a keyboard fails to work intermittently, consider a faulty power supply as the source of the problem because a keyboard receives its power from the power supply.

- ◆ Always use a parallel printer cable that is rated IEEE-1284 compliant.

OBJECTIVES ON THE JOB

A good PC technician tries the simple things first. Always try replacing a cable or an external device such as a monitor before opening the computer case and replacing components inside the case.

PRACTICE TEST QUESTIONS

1. **If a light on the back of a NIC is lit solid, what can you conclude?**
   a. data is being transferred across the network
   b. the NIC is communicating with other devices on the network
   c. Network Neighborhood can access other hosts on the network
   d. the NIC has failed

2. **What is one check you can make to be certain a PC is communicating properly on a network?**
   a. Network resources can be viewed in Network Neighborhood
   b. the NIC has a solid light lit on the back of the card
   c. TCP/IP shows as an installed component in the Network window
   d. Device Manager reports the NIC has no conflicts and is working properly

3. **If a keyboard fails intermittently, what might be a source of the problem?**
   a. the mouse
   b. Windows 98 installation
   c. the power supply
   d. the NIC

4. **Video does not work. What are the things you should replace in the order you should replace them?**
   a. video cable, monitor, video card
   b. monitor, video cable, video card
   c. video card, monitor, system board
   d. video card, monitor, keyboard

5. **What standard should a parallel printer cable meet?**
   a. IEEE 1394
   b. IEEE 1284
   c. ECP
   d. Windows 98

6. **When a printer does not work, what are some things you can check?**
   a. Is the printer online?
   b. Is the printer cable connected securely at both ends?
   c. Is the printer installed correctly under Windows?
   d. all the above

7. **You have just installed a NIC, which does not work. What is the first thing you should do?**
   a. replace the NIC with a new one
   b. uninstall and reinstall the network card drivers
   c. verify the light on the NIC is lit solid
   d. exchange the network cable

2.2 **Identify basic troubleshooting procedures and how to elicit problem symptoms from customers**

TROUBLESHOOTING/ISOLATION/PROBLEM DETERMINATION PROCEDURES • DETERMINE WHETHER HARDWARE OR SOFTWARE PROBLEM

UNDERSTANDING THE OBJECTIVE

Approach each PC troubleshooting problem in a systematic way. Listed below are some common-sense approaches to this process.

WHAT YOU **REALLY** NEED TO KNOW

◆ Determine if the problem occurs during or after the boot.

◆ When isolating a problem, eliminate the unnecessary and trade good for suspected bad or install a suspected bad component into a known good system.

◆ Here are some fundamental rules for PC troubleshooting:

- **Approach the problem systematically.** Start at the beginning and walk through the situation in a thorough, careful way.

- **Divide and conquer.** Isolate the problem by eliminating components until the problem disappears.

- **Don't overlook the obvious.** Ask simple questions. Is the computer plugged in? Is it turned on? Is the monitor plugged in?

- **Check the simple things first.** It is more effective to first check the components that are easiest to replace.

- **Make no assumptions.** Check everything for yourself. Don't trust documentation or what the user tells you.

- **Become a researcher.** Take advantage of every available resource, including online help, the Internet, documentation, technical support, and books such as this one.

- **Write things down.** Keep good notes as you're working. Draw diagrams. Make lists.

- **Establish your priorities.** Decide what your first priority is. Consult the user or customer for his or her advice when practical.

- **Keep your cool.** In an emergency, protect the data and software by carefully considering your options before acting and by taking practical precautions to protect software and OS files.

- **Know your starting point.** Before trying to solve a computer problem, know for certain that the problem is what the user says it is.

OBJECTIVES ON THE JOB

Know and practice good problem solving skills, which are the essence of a PC technician's skills.

PRACTICE TEST QUESTIONS

1. **You install a second IDE hard drive in a system using the same IDE primary channel used by the first drive. When you boot up, the first drive works but the system fails to recognize the new drive. What is the most likely cause of the problem?**
   a. The second drive is bad.
   b. The data cable is bad.
   c. You failed to change the IDE setting for the first drive from single to master.
   d. The second drive is not formatted, so the system doesn't recognize the drive.

2. **A POST error code in the 6000 range indicates a problem with:**
   a. the floppy drive
   b. the system board
   c. the IDE hard drive
   d. a SCSI device

3. **POST is done when the computer is:**
   a. shut down
   b. assembled
   c. turned on
   d. configured

4. **POST is performed by:**
   a. BIOS on the system board
   b. the operating system
   c. BIOS on the hard drive
   d. software on the hard drive

5. **When you use a floppy drive cable with a twist, the order of connections on the data cable supporting two floppy drives is:**
   a. system board, drive A:, drive B:
   b. system board, drive B:, drive A:
   c. drive A:, system board, drive B:
   d. The order depends on how CMOS sees the drive assignments.

6. **A system appears dead but you notice that the small green light on the front of the monitor is on. What can you safely assume?**
   a. The computer is receiving power.
   b. The monitor is receiving power.
   c. The system board is bad.
   d. The data cable from the computer to the monitor is loose.

7. **You replace a system board because the old board is dead. You turn on the PC. It boots up correctly but hangs, dies, and refuses to reboot. What is most likely the source of the problem?**
   a. The second system board was bad.
   b. There is a problem with the power. Check the power supply next.
   c. A failed hard drive caused the system to appear dead.
   d. The RAM you installed from the old board corrupted the new system board, destroying it.

2.2
cont.
Identify basic troubleshooting procedures and how to elicit problem symptoms from customers

GATHER INFORMATION FROM USER REGARDING:
CUSTOMER ENVIRONMENT • SYMPTOMS/ERROR CODES • SITUATION WHEN THE PROBLEM OCCURRED

UNDERSTANDING THE OBJECTIVE

When approaching a PC troubleshooting situation, first, interview the user and ask questions that will help you isolate the problem and know how to reproduce it. Get background information, such as when the problem first occurred and what has happened since the system last worked properly.

WHAT YOU **REALLY** NEED TO KNOW

◆ Follow these guidelines when working with the user:
  - Don't take drastic action like formatting the hard drive before you ask the user about important data on the hard drive that may not be backed up.
  - Provide the user with alternatives (where appropriate) before you make decisions affecting him or her.
  - Protect the confidentiality of data, such as business financial information, on the PC.
  - Don't disparage the user's choice of computer hardware or software.
  - If you have made a mistake or must pass the problem on to someone with more expertise, be honest.
  - Always ask the user for information about the problem and the situation when it first occurred. Don't assume you know what happened.
  - Never leave the customer's site unless you are certain you have left the PC is good working order; don't apply a fix and just assume it worked.

◆ Here are some helpful questions to ask the user when you are first trying to discover what the problem is:
  - When did the problem start?
  - Were there any error messages or unusual displays on the screen?
  - What programs or software were you using?
  - Did you move your computer system recently?
  - Has there been a recent thunderstorm or electrical problem?
  - Have you made any hardware changes?
  - Did you recently install any new software?
  - Did you recently change any software configuration setups?
  - Has someone else been using your computer recently?
  - Can you show me what you do when you see the error?
  - If you can't show me, can you describe what happened so I can reproduce the error?

◆ Make every attempt to reproduce the error in the presence of the customer so that you and the customer are in agreement as to the starting point of the problem.

◆ When interviewing the user, the goal is to gain as much information from the user as you can before you begin investigating the hardware and the software.

OBJECTIVES ON THE JOB

People skills are often seen as unimportant skills to a successful PC technician. Nothing could be further from the truth. A satisfied customer is one who has been treated with respect and kindness. You can save a lot of time by carefully interviewing the customer before you begin troubleshooting. Discover all the information you can from the user about the problem and its source.

PRACTICE TEST QUESTIONS

1. What question might you ask a user to help you locate a problem?

    a. When was the PC purchased?

    b. Is the PC still under warranty?

    c. What software or hardware has recently been installed?

    d. Can you reproduce the problem so I can see it?

2. How can the customer help you identify the source of an intermittent problem?

    a. Call you the next time the problem occurs.

    b. Keep working until the problem recurs.

    c. Keep a log of when the problem occurs and what happened just before it occurred.

    d. Install diagnostic software to help you locate the problem.

3. Which of the following questions is not appropriate to ask the user to help you locate the source of a problem?

    a. When did the problem first begin?

    b. Has new hardware or software recently been installed?

    c. Why did you buy this brand of computer?

    d. What happened just before the problem began?

4. You are late for an appointment with a customer. What should you do when you arrive?

    a. Apologize for being late and immediately get to work.

    b. Immediately get to work without mentioning the fact you're late.

    c. Remind the customer that he or she is sometimes late, too.

    d. Spend the first 15 minutes at the customer site explaining why you're late.

5. A hard drive has failed but you think you can fix it if you reformat the drive. What should you do first?

    a. Check with the user to make sure that the data has been backed up.

    b. Immediately reformat the drive.

    c. Run diagnostic software in an attempt to save the data on the drive.

    d. Attempt to back up the data on the drive.

6. What should you always do at a customer site?

    a. Apply your fix and immediately leave the site.

    b. Apply your fix and test the system to make sure all is well.

    c. Apply your fix, reboot, and test the system to make sure all is well.

    d. Never admit to a customer that you made a mistake.

7. When you first arrive at the customer's site, what is the first thing you should do?

    a. Fill out all the paper work required by your boss.

    b. Listen carefully as the customer describes the problem.

    c. Disassemble the PC.

    d. Search the customer's desk for the PC documentation.

DOMAIN **3.0** PREVENTIVE
MAINTENANCE

3.1 Identify the purpose of various types of preventive maintenance products and procedures and when to use them

LIQUID CLEANING COMPOUNDS • TYPES OF MATERIALS TO CLEAN CONTACTS AND CONNECTIONS • NON-STATIC VACUUMS (CHASIS, POWER SUPPLIES, FANS)

UNDERSTANDING THE OBJECTIVE

Performing routine preventive maintenance is a common task for most PC technicians. Know how and when to clean a system.

WHAT YOU REALLY NEED TO KNOW

◆ Dust inside a PC case can be dangerous because it acts like a blanket, insulating components and causing them to overheat.

◆ There is disagreement in the industry about using a vacuum inside a computer case, and some believe a vacuum can cause ESD. When inside a PC case, always use a non-static vacuum to prevent ESD.

◆ Use compressed air to blow dust out of a system and vacuum the dust once it is outside the case.

◆ Corrosion on the edge connectors of circuit boards can cause poor contact, which can cause the board to fail.

◆ Clean edge connectors with contact cleaner designed for that purpose.

◆ Almost all computer equipment can be cleaned with a soft, damp cloth using a small amount of mild detergent.

OBJECTIVES ON THE JOB

Routine maintenance on the computer system is a routine task expected of PC technicians. The task is sometimes performed on a scheduled basis, but it is often expected as part of the repair process as well.

Below are a few general guidelines that a technician can follow as a regular preventive maintenance plan.

Component	Maintenance	How Often
Inside the case	Check air vents, remove dust, check that cards and chips are firmly seated.	Yearly
CMOS setup	Back up to floppy disk.	Whenever changes are made
Keyboard, monitor	Clean with damp cloth.	Monthly
Mouse	Clean mouse rollers with damp cloth.	Monthly
Printers	Remove dust, bits of paper.	Monthly
Hard drive	Perform regular backups.	Weekly or daily
	Defragment and recover lost clusters.	Monthly
	Automate a virus-scan program to run at startup.	
	Place the PC where it will not be kicked, jarred, or bumped.	

1. **Which product should be used to clean fingerprints and dirt off a keyboard?**
   a. denatured alcohol
   b. all-purpose cleaner
   c. silicone spray
   d. contact cleaner

ANSWER

2. **Which product should be used to clean a notebook computer's LCD screen?**
   a. denatured alcohol
   b. ammonia window cleaner
   c. hair spray
   d. non-abrasive cleaner

ANSWER

3. **Which of the following is most likely to do damage to data stored on a hard drive or floppy disk?**
   a. a laser printer
   b. a CRT monitor
   c. a telephone
   d. an unshielded speaker

ANSWER

4. **Why is dust inside a computer case considered dangerous?**
   a. It can cause ESD.
   b. It can get inside the CPU and corrupt it.
   c. It can insulate components and cause them to overheat.
   d. It can get down inside expansion card slots and cause them to short out.

ANSWER

5. **The best way to remove dust from inside a computer case is to:**
   a. use a regular vacuum cleaner to remove the dust
   b. use compressed air to blow the dust out
   c. use a damp, soft cloth to clean up the dust
   d. use contact cleaner on a soft cloth to clean up the dust

ANSWER

6. **Preventive maintenance on a mouse includes:**
   a. exchanging the ball inside the mouse housing
   b. cleaning the rollers and ball inside the mouse
   c. reinstalling the mouse driver
   d. all of the above

ANSWER

7. **What should you use to clean a monitor screen?**
   a. ammonia window cleaner and a paper towel
   b. denatured alcohol
   c. mild soap and water on a clean cloth
   d. clean, soft cloth

ANSWER

3.2 Identify issues, procedures and devices for protection within the computing environment, including people, hardware and the surrounding workspace

UPS (UNINTERRUPTIBLE POWER SUPPLY) AND SUPPRESSORS • DETERMINING THE SIGNS OF POWER ISSUES • PROPER METHODS OF STORAGE OF COMPONENTS FOR FUTURE USE

UNDERSTANDING THE OBJECTIVE

Use a UPS to provide uninterrupted power to the PC. Use a UPS, a line conditioner, or a surge suppressor to protect the system against power surges, lightning, and so forth. Protect a system against ESD as you work on it, and protect components against ESD when they are in storage.

WHAT YOU **REALLY** NEED TO KNOW

- ◆ Always store computer components in anti-static bags to protect against ESD.
- ◆ Wattage is calculated as volts x amps.
- ◆ If the fan on the power supply stops working, it might indicate that power is being drawn away from the fan; suspect a device drawing too much power.
- ◆ Shorts in the circuit boards, devices, or the system board will cause an overloaded power system.
- ◆ All surge protection and battery backup devices should carry the UL (Underwriters Laboratory) logo, which ensures that the device has been tested for product safety.
- ◆ Devices that filter the AC input to computers are classified as surge suppressors, power conditioners, and uninterruptible power supplies (UPSs).
- ◆ Define these terms and know what distinguishes one device from another: **surge suppressor, UPS, standby UPS, inline UPS, line-interactive UPS**, the **buck-boost** UPS feature, **intelligent UPS, line conditioner**, spikes, brownouts, and sags in current.
- ◆ A fire extinguisher is classified as Class A, Class B, or Class C, depending on the type of fire it can handle.
- ◆ Have a Class C fire extinguisher available, which can handle fires ignited by electricity.

OBJECTIVES ON THE JOB

Managing environmental hazards caused by electricity, thunderstorms, and the like is an essential task of a PC technician.

PRACTICE TEST QUESTIONS

1. **During a power outage, what should you do before the power is restored?**
    a. Unplug power cords to all equipment.
    b. Turn off all equipment.
    c. Close down all currently running software.
    d. Unplug the monitor.

ANSWER

2. **Which device helps prevent power surges to computer equipment?**
    a. a UPS
    b. a line conditioner
    c. a multimeter
    d. a power strip

ANSWER

3. **Which device prevents interruptions to power to computer equipment?**
    a. a UPS
    b. a line conditioner
    c. a multimeter
    d. a power strip

ANSWER

4. **How can computer equipment be completely protected from damage during an electrical storm?**
    a. with a surge protector
    b. with an intelligent UPS system
    c. by unplugging power cords
    d. by turning off the AC power

ANSWER

5. **What question do you ask to determine if power is getting to a computer?**
    a. Do you see lights on the front of the computer case?
    b. Do you see anything displayed on the screen?
    c. Do you hear beeps when the computer boots?
    d. Do you see a light on the front of the CRT?

ANSWER

6. **You're working at your computer and a thunderstorm begins. What do you do?**
    a. Keep on working because the power supply acts as a surge suppressor.
    b. Keep on working because you have a surge suppressor installed.
    c. Stop working and turn off the PC.
    d. Stop working, unplug the PC, and unplug the phone line from the modem.

ANSWER

7. **What is a brownout?**
    a. a slight decrease in voltage that lasts for a very short time
    b. a power outage that lasts for a few minutes
    c. a surge in current that lasts for a few seconds
    d. when AC turns to DC for just a few seconds

ANSWER

3.2
cont.

Identify issues, procedures and devices for protection within the computing environment, including people, hardware and the surrounding workspace

POTENTIAL HAZARDS AND PROPER SAFETY PROCEDURES RELATING TO:
LASERS • HIGH-VOLTAGE EQUIPMENT • POWER SUPPLY • CRT

UNDERSTANDING THE OBJECTIVE

Power supplies, CRT monitors, and other high-voltage equipment contain capacitors that retain their charge even when power is disconnected. Unless you're trained to service these devices, don't open them.

WHAT YOU **REALLY** NEED TO KNOW

- ◆ A PC technician should not open a power supply or CRT unless trained to service one because of the danger of high charges inside these components.
- ◆ When working inside a CRT or power supply, don't wear an ESD bracelet because you don't want these strong electrical charges to flow through your body to the ground.
- ◆ Unplug a laser printer before opening the cover. Protect your eyes from a laser beam.
- ◆ If a printer uses an ozone filter, replace it as recommended by the manufacturer.
- ◆ Discharge a CRT monitor before disposing of it.
- ◆ When servicing printers, don't use an ESD bracelet, as you don't want to become the ground for the device.

OBJECTIVES ON THE JOB

Know the dangers of working on high-voltage equipment and don't attempt to work on them unless trained to do so.

Spikes in electricity can damage computer equipment. To protect against spikes, be sure to properly ground equipment. When grounded, high surges of electricity are diverted through the equipment to ground. To prevent these spikes from reaching the equipment, use a surge suppressor or line conditioner. Some types of uninterruptible power supply (UPS) equipment also provide surge protection, but not all UPS devices offer this protection.

To protect modems against spikes in telephone lines, use a data line protector. Many surge protectors, line conditioners, and UPS devices include a connection for data line protection.

1. **If the fan inside a power supply stops working, what should you do?**
   a. Replace the bad fan with a new one.
   b. Replace the power supply.
   c. Replace the computer case, which comes with a power supply already installed.
   d. Do nothing; the fan is not an essential device.

   ANSWER

2. **When servicing a laser printer, why is it important to first unplug the printer?**
   a. because the current might damage the laser beam
   b. to reset the printer
   c. to prevent the printer from attempting to print while it is being serviced
   d. to prevent you from being shocked or your eyes damaged from the laser beam

   ANSWER

3. **Why do you *not* wear an ESD bracelet while servicing a monitor?**
   a. The ESD bracelet might damage the components inside the monitor.
   b. The ESD bracelet might get tangled with the cords and wires inside the monitor.
   c. You don't want your body to be a ground for stray current.
   d. You want to create as clean a work environment as possible.

   ANSWER

4. **A device that retains a high charge even after disconnected from power is:**
   a. a system board
   b. a CRT
   c. a power supply
   d. both b and c

   ANSWER

5. **The electrical component that retains a charge after the power is turned off is:**
   a. a transistor
   b. a rheostat
   c. a capacitor
   d. an electrode

   ANSWER

6. **When troubleshooting a monitor, one task a PC technician who is not trained to work inside the monitor can safely do is:**
   a. replace the cathode ray tube
   b. replace the fuse
   c. adjust the brightness and contrast settings
   d. both b and c

   ANSWER

7. **The best way to ground an ESD bracelet when servicing a power supply is to:**
   a. connect the bracelet to the ground on an AC house outlet
   b. connect the bracelet to the side of the computer case
   c. connect the bracelet to a grounding mat
   d. None of the above; don't wear an ESD bracelet when servicing a power supply.

   ANSWER

3.2
cont.
Identify issues, procedures and devices for protection within the computing environment, including people, hardware and the surrounding workspace

SPECIAL DISPOSAL PROCEDURES THAT COMPLY WITH ENVIRONMENTAL GUIDELINES: BATTERIES • CRT • TONER KITS/CARTRIDGES • CHEMICAL SOLVENTS AND CANS • MSDS (MATERIAL SAFETY DATA SHEET)

UNDERSTANDING THE OBJECTIVE

There are legal guidelines designed to protect the environment that apply to the disposal of many computer components and chemicals. Know how to properly dispose of these things.

WHAT YOU **REALLY** NEED TO KNOW

♦ A **Material Safety Data Sheet (MSDS)** is written by the material manufacturer and contains information about how to safely use the material, what to do when accidents occur, and how to properly dispose of the material.

♦ A monitor retains a dangerous charge even after it has been unplugged.

♦ Before disposing of a monitor, disconnect it from the power supply and discharge capacitors in it by placing a screwdriver or high-voltage probe across the hot and ground prongs on the back of the monitor. Also have a technician qualified to open the monitor case discharge the CRT itself.

♦ Recycle toner cartridges from a laser printer by returning them to the manufacturer.

♦ Recycle batteries and CRTs according to local environmental guidelines.

♦ A Material Safety Data Sheet (MSDS) explains how to properly handle substances such as chemical solvents. It comes in packages with the chemical or you can order it from the manufacturer or find it on the Internet.

OBJECTIVES ON THE JOB

Disposing of used equipment is often expected of a PC technician. It's important to both your company and the environment that you follow regulated guidelines when doing so.

Use the following as general guidelines for disposing computer parts.

Part	How to Dispose
Alkaline batteries including AAA, AA, A, C, D, and 9 volt	Normal trash
Button batteries used in digital cameras, Flash Path, and other small equipment Battery packs used in notebooks	These batteries can contain silver oxide, mercury, lithium, or cadmium and are considered hazardous waste. Dispose of these either by returning them to the original dealer or taking them to a recycling center. To recycle them, pack them separately from other items. If you don't have a recycling center nearby, contact your county for local regulations for disposal.
Laser printer toner cartridges	Return to the manufacturer or dealer to be recycled.
Ink jet printer ink cartridges Computers Monitors Chemical solvents and cans	Check with local county or environmental officials for laws and regulations in your area for proper disposal of these items. The county might provide a recycling center that will receive them. Before disposing of a monitor, first discharge the monitor.

PRACTICE TEST QUESTIONS

1. **Which component is easiest to environmentally recycle?**
   - a. a CMOS battery
   - b. a CRT
   - c. a toner cartridge
   - d. a battery pack from a notebook computer

   ANSWER

2. **Which component requires that you follow EPA environmental guidelines for disposal?**
   - a. a sound card
   - b. a CMOS battery
   - c. a power supply
   - d. a system board

   ANSWER

3. **How do you recycle a toner cartridge from a laser printer?**
   - a. Return it to the manufacturer.
   - b. Take it to a county recycle center.
   - c. Throw it in the trash.
   - d. Mail it to the EPA.

   ANSWER

4. **To know how to properly dispose of a can of contact cleaner, what do you do?**
   - a. Research in the local library.
   - b. Consult the product's MSDS.
   - c. Ask the EPA.
   - d. Call your county recycle center.

   ANSWER

5. **How do you dispose of a CMOS battery?**
   - a. Throw it in the trash.
   - b. Return it to the manufacturer.
   - c. Return it to the store where you purchased it.
   - d. Take it to your local recycle center.

   ANSWER

6. **Before disposing of a CRT, what must you do?**
   - a. Remove the power cord from the CRT.
   - b. Remove the CRT cover.
   - c. Discharge the CRT.
   - d. Let the CRT sit unplugged for 1 hour.

   ANSWER

7. **When disposing of an entire computer system, which components need special attention?**
   - a. the power supply, the CMOS battery, and the CRT
   - b. the CPU, the system board, and the hard drive
   - c. the floppy drive, the hard drive, and the CD-ROM drive
   - d. the CRT, the CPU, and the CMOS battery

   ANSWER

3.2
cont.
Identify issues, procedures and devices for protection within the computing environment, including people, hardware and the surrounding workspace

ESD (ELECTROSTATIC DISCHARGE) PRECAUTIONS AND PROCEDURES: WHAT ESD CAN DO, HOW IT MAY BE APPARENT, OR HIDDEN • COMMON ESD PROTECTION DEVICES • SITUATIONS THAT COULD PRESENT A DANGER OR HAZARD

UNDERSTANDING THE OBJECTIVE

When working on a PC, you must protect the equipment from ESD, which can damage the hardware and data stored on storage devices. If all devices and you are properly grounded, then ESD is not a problem. Grounding devices include ESD bracelets and grounding mats.

WHAT YOU **REALLY** NEED TO KNOW

◆ The best protection against ESD is to use an ESD bracket (also known as a static bracelet, ground bracelet, ground strap, or ESD strap) that is grounded to the house ground line.

◆ Set the equipment on a grounding mat which is connected to the house ground. Sometimes an ESD bracelet can snap to a connection on the grounding mat.

◆ ESD can be high on carpets, when bringing equipment in from the cold, and around high-voltage equipment such as monitors or powerful, unshielded speakers. Wood, plastic, vinyl, and nylon can all produce ESD.

◆ Always store or ship computer components in anti-static bags (ESD-safe bags).

◆ When you remove components from a computer system, set them on a ground mat or put them into an anti-static bag.

◆ Damage caused by ESD may not show up immediately and might cause intermittent problems that are hard to detect.

◆ Electromagnetic interference (**EMI**) is caused by the magnetic field that is produced as a side effect when electricity flows.

◆ EMI in the radio frequency range is called radio frequency interference (RFI) and can cause problems with radio and TV reception.

◆ Use a line conditioner to filter out the electrical noise that causes EMI.

◆ ESD thrives in cold, dry air.

◆ ESD does permanent damage to equipment, but the damage caused by EMI is temporary.

◆ Know how to protect disks and other hardware against ESD as well as other hazards as you work.

OBJECTIVES ON THE JOB

It's extremely important to protect computer components against ESD as you work because damage created by ESD is permanent and not easily detected.

PRACTICE TEST QUESTIONS

1. **Damage from ESD can be caused by:**
   a. placing a CPU on a ground mat
   b. touching the computer case while the power is on
   c. placing a sound card in an anti-static bag
   d. placing an IC in a plastic bag

2. **To avoid damage from ESD as you work on a computer, you should:**
   a. keep anti-static bags close by
   b. wear an ESD bracelet
   c. touch the person next to you before picking up an IC
   d. leave the power to the PC on

3. **An ESD wrist strap contains a:**
   a. diode
   b. transistor
   c. resistor
   d. capacitor

4. **What is the best ground to use when working on a computer?**
   a. an AC outlet
   b. the computer case
   c. a ground mat
   d. an ESD wrist strap

   ANSWER

5. **Which situation poses the worst possible potential danger from ESD?**
   a. hot, dry air
   b. cold, damp air
   c. cold, dry air
   d. air just after an electrical storm

6. **ESD is:**
   a. electrostatic discharge
   b. electrical storm damage
   c. electricity surge damage
   d. electrostatic device

   ANSWER

7. **A human cannot feel ESD unless it reaches a charge of _____ volts**
   a. 200
   b. 3000
   c. 20,000
   d. 50,000

4.1 Distinguish between the popular CPU chips in terms of their basic characteristics

POPULAR CPU CHIPS (INTEL, AMD CYRIX) • CHARACTERISTICS • PHYSICAL SIZE • VOLTAGE • SPEEDS • ON BOARD CACHE OR NOT • SOCKETS • SEC (SINGLE EDGE CONTACT)

UNDERSTANDING THE OBJECTIVE

Which kind of CPU can be installed in which system, the requirements of the CPU, and the performance to expect from it are important facts to know when selecting a new system or upgrading an existing one. Also, a technician is expected to be able to identify a CPU already installed in a system board.

WHAT YOU **REALLY** NEED TO KNOW

- ◆ Intel currently has five form factors used to house its processors in desktop PCs:
  - SEP (Single Edge Processor), which does not completely cover the processor
  - SECC (Single Edge Contact Cartridge), which uses Slot 1
  - SECC2 (Single Edge Contact Cartridge, version 2) used by Pentium II and Pentium III
  - PPGA (Plastic Pin Grid Array), a square box that fits into Socket 370
  - FC-PGA (Flip Chip Pin Grid Array), also a square box that fits into Socket 370 and used by the Pentium III
- ◆ A heat sink or fan fits on the top or side of most processor housing and is used to keep the processor cool.
- ◆ CPU sockets are square and use either a PGA or SPGA design; rows of pins are arranged on the socket either in even rows (PGA) or staggered (SPGA).
- ◆ CPU slots look like expansion slots. Slot 1, Slot A and Slot 2 are all designed to accommodate processors using the SEP or SECC form factors.
- ◆ The Cyrix M II competes with the Pentium II and Celeron. The Cyrix III competes with the Celeron and the Pentium III.
- ◆ AMD-K6-2 competes with the Celeron and Pentium II. AMD-K6-III competes with the Pentium II and the AMD Athlon competes with the Pentium III.
- ◆ The Cyrix MII uses Socket 7 and the Cyrix III uses Socket 370.
- ◆ The AMD-K6-2 uses Socket 7 or Super Socket and the AMD-K6-III uses Super Socket 7. The AMD Athlon uses Slot A.
- ◆ The most common speeds for the system bus (also called memory or host bus) are 66 MHz, 75 MHz, 100 MHz, 133 MHz, and 200 MHz.
- ◆ To know what CPU is installed in a system, using Windows 9x, right-click the My Computer icon on the desktop and select Properties from the shortcut menu. Select the General tab.

OBJECTIVES ON THE JOB

Recognizing a CPU type and knowing what to expect of the CPU and what is needed to install and support the CPU is an important task of a PC technician.

PRACTICE TEST QUESTIONS

1. Which processor is the most powerful?
   a. AMD Athlon
   b. AMD-K6-2
   c. AMD-K6-III
   d. Cyrix M II

2. Which processor form factor fits into Socket 370?
   a. SECC2
   b. SECC
   c. PPGA
   d. SEP

3. How wide is the data path of the Pentium CPU?
   a. 16 bits
   b. 32 bits
   c. 64 bits
   d. 128 bits

ANSWER

4. How much L1 cache is there in a Pentium II CPU?
   a. 16K
   b. 32K
   c. 128K
   d. 512K

ANSWER

5. The Pentium II typically uses what clock bus speed?
   a. 66 MHz
   b. 100 MHz
   c. 450 MHz
   d. 550 MHz

ANSWER

6. Which slot or socket is *not* used by Intel processors?
   a. Socket 370
   b. Slot 1
   c. Slot 2
   d. Slot A

7. Which processor does not have L2 cache included inside the processor housing?
   a. Pentium III
   b. Pentium III Xeon
   c. Classic Pentium
   d. Pentium II Xeon

OBJECTIVES

4.2 Identify the categories of RAM (Random Access Memory) terminology, their locations, and physical characteristics

TERMINOLOGY: EDO RAM (EXTENDED DATA OUTPUT RAM) • DRAM (DYNAMIC RANDOM ACCESS MEMORY) • SRAM (STATIC RAM) • VRAM (VIDEO RAM) • WRAM (WINDOWS ACCELERATOR CARD RAM) • SDRAM (SYNCHRONOUS DYNAMIC RAM) • RIMM (RAMBUS INLINE MEMORY MODULE 184 PIN)

UNDERSTANDING THE OBJECTIVE

RAM memory modules are considered field replaceable units. When replacing or upgrading these modules, it is important you understand what type of memory modules are available, how they are used, and when to use the different kinds of memory.

WHAT YOU **REALLY** NEED TO KNOW

- ◆ A memory cache on the system board uses static RAM (SRAM) and speeds up memory access.
- ◆ Define **primary cache, internal cache, Level 1 cache, secondary cache, external cache, Level 2 cache, backside bus**, and **frontside bus**.
- ◆ To refresh RAM means that the CPU must rewrite data to the DRAM chip because it cannot hold its data very long.
- ◆ Fast page memory (FPM) is faster than conventional memory chips.
- ◆ Extended data out (EDO) memory is faster than FPM memory and is still used on some system boards today.
- ◆ Burst EDO (BEDO) is an improved version of EDO memory.
- ◆ Synchronous DRAM (SDRAM) runs in sync with the system clock and is rated by clock speed.
- ◆ Variations of SDRAM include SDRAM II and SyncLink (SLDRAM). SDRAM II is also called Double-Data Rate (DDR SDRAM) memory and runs twice as fast as regular SDRAM.
- ◆ Direct Rambus DRAM (RDRAM or Direct RDRAM) uses a narrow 16-bit data path and transmits data in packets much like a network. RDRAM uses a proprietary memory module called a RIMM.
- ◆ Video memory:
  - Video RAM (VRAM) is a type of **dual-ported** memory used on video cards.
  - Synchronous graphics RAM (SGRAM) is designed for graphics-intensive processing and can synchronize itself with the CPU bus clock.
  - Windows RAM (WRAM) is a type of dual-ported RAM that is faster and less expensive than VRAM.
  - 3D RAM was designed to handle 3D graphics.

OBJECTIVES ON THE JOB

Upgrading memory is a typical job of a PC technician. With so many types of memory available, it's important that a technician be familiar with each type and know how to match the system board with the correct type of memory.

PRACTICE TEST QUESTIONS

1. **Which type of memory is faster?**
   - a. conventional memory
   - b. BEDO
   - c. FPM
   - d. EDO

2. **Which type of memory runs in sync with the system clock?**
   - a. FPM
   - b. SDRAM
   - c. EDO
   - d. BEDO

3. **Which type of memory is especially designed to work on a video card?**
   - a. EDO
   - b. BEDO
   - c. WRAM
   - d. SDRAM

4. **Which type of memory uses a narrow 16-bit data path?**
   - a. Rambus DRAM
   - b. WRAM
   - c. BEDO
   - d. SDRAM

5. **The connection inside a SEC between the CPU and the L2 cache is called the:**
   - a. memory bus
   - b. frontside bus
   - c. backside bus
   - d. CPU bus

6. **Why must DRAM be refreshed?**
   - a. because the power is turned off
   - b. because the CPU overwrites memory with new data
   - c. because DRAM cannot hold its data very long
   - d. because SRAM erased the data in DRAM

7. **The Pentium II backside bus is:**
   - a. visible on the system board
   - b. completely inside the Pentium II housing
   - c. completely contained on the CPU microchip
   - d. completely contained on the Level 2 cache microchip

4.2
cont.
Identify the categories of RAM (Random Access Memory) terminology, their locations, and physical characteristics

LOCATIONS AND PHYSICAL CHARACTERISTICS: MEMORY BANK • MEMORY CHIPS (8-BIT, 16-BIT, AND 32-BIT) • SIMMS (SINGLE IN-LINE MEMORY MODULE) • DIMMS (DUAL IN-LINE MEMORY MODULE) • PARITY CHIPS VERSUS NON-PARITY CHIPS

UNDERSTANDING THE OBJECTIVE

A system board is designed to hold certain types of memory modules in banks that are limited to a certain quantity of memory. This information is important when replacing or upgrading memory.

WHAT YOU **REALLY** NEED TO KNOW

- ◆ DRAM comes in three types: parity, non-parity, or ECC (error checking and correction).
- ◆ Parity is a method of checking the integrity of the memory chips.
- ◆ A parity error indicates a problem with a memory chip and brings the system to a halt.
- ◆ A SIMM can have 30 or 72 pins on the edge connector of the tiny board and can hold 8 to 64 MB of RAM on one board.
- ◆ A DIMM has 168 pins on the edge connector of the board and can hold from 8 to 256 MB of RAM on a single board.
- ◆ RAM is stored in memory banks on the system board.
- ◆ SIMMs are installed in pairs that must match in speed and size.
- ◆ DIMMs can be installed individually.
- ◆ Each 184-pin RIMM socket must be filled with either a RIMM or a placeholder module called a C-RIMM.
- ◆ The data path of a SIMM is 32 bits, the data path of a DIMM is 64 bits, and the data path of a RIMM is 16 bits.

OBJECTIVES ON THE JOB

Upgrading memory is a typical job of a PC technician. Being familiar with the types of memory, how they are physically contained, and their characteristics is an important skill for a PC technician.

PRACTICE TEST QUESTIONS

1. **How many pins does a DIMM have?**
     a. 30
     b. 72
     c. 100
     d. 168

2. **What is the data path of a SIMM?**
     a. 16 bits
     b. 32 bits
     c. 64 bits
     d. 128 bits

3. **Which type of memory has an error-checking technology that can repair the error when it is detected?**
     a. ECC memory
     b. non-parity memory
     c. parity memory
     d. self-correcting memory

4. **Which statement about SIMMs is true?**
     a. Only one SIMM module can be installed on a system board.
     b. SIMMs within a bank must match in size and speed.
     c. All SIMMs on a system board must match in size and speed.
     d. Three SIMMs are stored in a single bank on a system board.

5. **If a system contains 64 MB of RAM in two banks of 2 SIMMs each, how much memory is on one SIMM?**
     a. 16 MB
     b. 8 MB
     c. 64 MB
     d. 32 MB

6. **Which of the following can hold the most memory?**
     a. a 30-pin SIMM
     b. DIMM
     c. a 72-pin SIMM
     d. an individual microchip on the system board

7. **A SIMM is held into its socket by:**
     a. two braces, one on each end of the socket
     b. a pin in the center of each socket
     c. four pins, one on each corner of the socket
     d. a single long brace on the side of the socket

OBJECTIVES

4.3 Identify the most popular type of motherboards, their components, and their architecture (bus structures and power supplies)

TYPES OF MOTHERBOARDS: AT (FULL AND BABY) • ATX
BASIC COMPATIBILITY GUIDELINES: IDE (ATA, ATAPI, ULTRA-DMA, EIDE) • SCSI (WIDE, FAST, ULTRA, LVD (LOW VOLTAGE DIFFERENTIAL))

UNDERSTANDING THE OBJECTIVE

There are four types of system boards in use that must match in size and options the computer case and power supply. The type of system board does not affect speed or performance.

WHAT YOU **REALLY** NEED TO KNOW

◆ AT system boards have two power connections, P8 and P9, but ATX system boards have only a single power connection, P1.

◆ Most ATX system boards have a remote switch connection which must be connected to the switch on the front of the computer case in order for power to work.

◆ System boards today have several buses to accommodate slow and fast devices and different data bus widths and speeds.

◆ System boards today provide an IDE interface, which connects up to four IDE devices using two 40-pin IDE cables. For the newer IDE standard, Ultra DMA, a special 40-pin IDE cable is required that provides additional ground lines to improve signal integrity.

◆ When a system board has a SCSI interface, be aware of the different SCSI standards it supports. For example, a system might support Ultra2 SCSI and be backward compatible with single-ended SCSI devices.

◆ Low voltage differential (LVD) signaling used by Ultra2 SCSI allows for faster data transfers and longer cable lengths up to 25 meters.

Type of System Board	Description
AT	Oldest type system board still commonly used Uses P8 and P9 power connections Measures 30.5 cm × 33 cm
Baby AT	Smaller version of AT; small size is possible because the system board logic is stored on a smaller chip set Measures 22 cm × 33 cm
ATX	Developed by Intel for Pentium systems Has a more conveniently accessible layout than AT boards Uses a single P1 power connection Measures 30.5 cm × 24.4 cm
Mini ATX	An ATX board with a more compact design Measures 28.4 cm × 20.8 cm

OBJECTIVES ON THE JOB

When building a system or replacing a system board, install the type of system board that is compatible with the computer case and power supply. If a SCSI interface is required and the system board does not support SCSI, use a SCSI host adapter in an expansion slot to provide the interface.

PRACTICE TEST QUESTIONS

1. **The AT power supply connects to the system board with:**
    a. two connections, P8 and P9
    b. one connection, P1
    c. 20 connections
    d. one connection, P8

2. **The ATX power supply connects to the system board with:**
    a. two connections, P8 and P9
    b. one connection, P1
    c. 20 connections
    d. one connection, P8

3. **The SCSI standard that uses LVD is:**
    a. Fast SCSI
    b. Ultra2 SCSI
    c. Regular SCSI
    d. Wide SCSI

4. **What is one advantage that the ATX system board has over the AT system board?**
    a. Components are located on the ATX board in more convenient positions.
    b. The ATX board is much larger than the AT board.
    c. The ATX board requires less power than the AT board does.
    d. The ATX board uses more power connections than the AT board does.

5. **Which statement is true concerning the style of system board?**
    a. The Baby AT board can support more CPU types than the AT board.
    b. The ATX system board was developed by Intel for Pentium systems.
    c. The AT board measures 22 cm × 33 cm.
    d. The AT system board has a more convenient layout than the ATX system board.

6. **Which type of system board is required for a 500 MHz Pentium II that is using Slot 1?**
    a. the AT system board
    b. the Baby AT system board
    c. the ATX system board
    d. the Slot 1 system board

7. **Which type of system board measures 22 cm × 33 cm?**
    a. AT
    b. Baby AT
    c. ATX
    d. Mini ATX

4.3
cont. Identify the most popular type of motherboards, their components, and their architecture (bus structures and power supplies)

COMPONENTS: COMMUNICATION PORTS • SIMM AND DIMM • PROCESSOR SOCKETS • EXTERNAL CACHE MEMORY (LEVEL 2)

UNDERSTANDING THE OBJECTIVE

Every system board has a slot or socket for the CPU, slots for SIMMs, DIMMs or RIMMs, communication ports, and maybe some external cache memory.

WHAT YOU **REALLY** NEED TO KNOW

- Be able to identify the better known processors and the sockets or slots they use. Know the voltage requirements of these slots and sockets.
- These processors can run on system boards that run at 100 MHz and higher: Celeron, Pentium II, Pentium, Cyrix M II, Cyrix III, AMD-K6-2, AMD-K6-III, and AMD Athlon.
- Earlier sockets used a low insertion force (LIF) method, but current sockets use a zero insertion force (ZIF) mechanism to insert the CPU into the socket.
- SIMMs must be inserted in pairs in memory banks. Single DIMMs can be used on a system board, and RIMMs or a C-RIMM must fill every RIMM slot on a system board.
- Newer system boards don't have Level 2 cache memory because L2 cache is now included inside the processor housing.
- The following is a table of sockets and slots, the CPUs that use them, the voltages they support and the number of pins on the socket or slot:

Slot or Socket	Processor	Number of Pins	Voltage
Socket 4	Early Classic Pentiums	273 pins (PGA)	5 V
Socket 5	Later Classic Pentiums	320 pins (SPGA)	3.3 V
Socket 6	Not used		
Socket 7	Pentium MMX, some later Classic Pentiums, AMD K5, AMD K6, Cyrix M	321 pins (SPGA)	2.5 V to 3.3 V
Super Socket 7	AMD K6-2, AMD K6-III	321 pins (SPGA)	2.5 V to 3.3 V
Socket 8	Pentium Pro	387 pins (SPGA)	3.3 V
Socket 370 or PGA370 Socket	Pentium III FC-PGA, Celeron PPGA, Cyrix III	370 pins (SPGA)	1.5 V or 2 V
Slot 1 or SC242	Pentium II, Pentium III	242 pins in 2 rows	2.8 V and 3.3 V
Slot A	AMD Athlon	242 pins in 2 rows	1.5 V to 3.5 V
Slot 2 or SC330	Pentium II Xeon, Pentium III Xeon	330 pins in 2 rows	1.5 V to 3.5 V

OBJECTIVES ON THE JOB

Understanding the architecture of a system board and being familiar with the components on the system board, including how they work and their characteristics, is essential when a PC technician is upgrading and troubleshooting the system board and components.

PRACTICE TEST QUESTIONS

1. What slot or socket does the Intel Pentium III use?

    a. Socket 370

    b. Slot A

    c. Slot 1

    d. Either a or c

2. How many pins does Socket 7 have?

    a. 321

    b. 387

    c. 242

    d. 64

3. What socket or slot does the Pentium Pro use?

    a. Socket 7

    b. Super Socket 7

    c. Socket 8

    d. Slot 1

4. Which processor uses 5 volts of power?

    a. Pentium III Xeon

    b. The first Classic Pentiums

    c. AMD Athlon

    d. Celeron

5. How do you not install RAM on a system board?

    a. on COAST modules

    b. on individual chips on the system board

    c. on SIMMs

    d. on DIMMs

6. When is the Super Socket 7 used?

    a. to hold the Pentium II Xeon processor

    b. on system boards that run at 100 MHz

    c. to hold the Pentium III processor

    d. to hold the Pentium Pro processor

7. What is the difference between a SPGA grid and a PGA grid, as used by a CPU socket?

    a. A PGA grid has more pins than a SPGA grid.

    b. A PGA grid is shaped like a rectangle, and a SPGA grid is shaped like a square.

    c. Pins in a SPGA grid are staggered, and pins in a PGA grid are in even rows.

    d. Pins in a PGA grid are staggered, and pins in a SPGA grid are in even rows.

4.3
cont.
Identify the most popular type of motherboards, their components, and their architecture (bus structures and power supplies)

BUS ARCHITECTURE • ISA • PCI • AGP • USB (UNIVERSAL SERIAL BUS) • VESA LOCAL BUS (VL-BUS)

UNDERSTANDING THE OBJECTIVE

Know the different types of buses that can be found on a system board, their data bus width and speed, and the general purpose of each bus.

WHAT YOU **REALLY** NEED TO KNOW

◆ Know the data width of each of the common buses on a system board.
◆ The PCI bus is the fastest bus on the system board that can support peripheral devices.
◆ The USB ports connect to the USB bus that can support up to 127 devices daisy chained together. Several USB devices can connect to a USB hub.

Table of buses

Bus	Bus Speed in MHz	Address Lines	Data Width
System bus	66, 75, 100, 133, 200	32	64 bit
8-bit ISA	4.77	20	8 bit
16-bit ISA	8.33	24	16 bit
PCI	33, 66	32	32 bit
EISA	12	32	16 bit and 32 bit
AGP	66, 75, 100	NA	32 bit
USB	3	Serial	Serial
VESA	Up to 33	32	32 bit

OBJECTIVES ON THE JOB

When purchasing new devices for a system, the bus that the device will use is a critical part of the purchasing decision. Use the fastest bus possible for the device while still taking into account the expansion slots available in the system. In most cases, for peripheral devices, choose the PCI bus over the ISA bus because it is faster and easier to configure.

PRACTICE TEST QUESTIONS

1. **Which bus is primarily used on notebook computers?**
   a. 16-bit ISA
   b. PCI
   c. PC Card
   d. VESA

ANSWER

2. **Which bus only supports a video card?**
   a. AGP
   b. VESA
   c. PCI
   d. both a and b

ANSWER

3. **Which bus is fastest?**
   a. EISA
   b. PCI
   c. ISA
   d. USB

ANSWER

4. **Which bus is no longer included on new system boards?**
   a. ISA
   b. PCI
   c. VESA
   d. USB

ANSWER

5. **Which bus can support either an 8-bit or 16-bit data path?**
   a. PCI
   b. AGP
   c. ISA
   d. VESA

ANSWER

6. **Which of the following is the most common width of the data path of the PCI bus?**
   a. 8 bits
   b. 16 bits
   c. 32 bits
   d. 64 bits

ANSWER

7. **Which bus runs in synchronization with the CPU?**
   a. ISA
   b. EISA
   c. USB
   d. PCI

ANSWER

4.4 Identify the purpose of CMOS (Complementary Metal-Oxide Semiconductor), what it contains and how to change its basic parameters

EXAMPLE BASIC CMOS SETTINGS: PRINTER PARALLEL PORT: UNI-, BI-DIRECTIONAL, DISABLE/ENABLE, ECP, EPP • COM/SERIAL PORT: MEMORY ADDRESS, INTERRUPT REQUEST, DISABLE

UNDERSTANDING THE OBJECTIVE

One CMOS chip on the system board is known as CMOS and contains a small amount of RAM that is powered by a small battery when the PC is turned off. This RAM contains configuration information about the PC and user preferences.

WHAT YOU **REALLY** NEED TO KNOW

- ◆ CMOS can be changed during booting by pressing a certain key combination, depending on the system board manufacturer.
- ◆ CMOS is battery powered when the PC is off so that data stored in CMOS RAM is not lost.
- ◆ Parallel ports are enabled and disabled in CMOS and can be set to bi-directional, **ECP**, or **EPP**. ECP requires a DMA channel to work.
- ◆ Serial ports can be enabled and disabled in CMOS and configured to use certain IRQ and I/O addresses.
- ◆ If a serial port is not in use, the system resources (IRQ and I/O addresses) assigned to it should be available for other devices, however, for some systems, you must disable the port in CMOS in order to free these resources for another device.

OBJECTIVES ON THE JOB

Serial and parallel ports are enabled and disabled in CMOS, and system resources are assigned to them. When troubleshooting problems with these ports, always check CMOS for errors in configuration and to be sure that the port is enabled.

Steps to access CMOS setup for most systems are listed below.

BIOS	Keys to Press During POST to Access Setup
AMI BIOS	Del
Award BIOS	Del
Older Phoenix BIOS	Ctrl+Alt+Esc or Ctrl+Alt+S
Newer Phoenix BIOS	F2 or F1
Dell computers using Phoenix BIOS	Ctrl+Alt+Enter
Older Compaq computers like the Deskpro 286 or 386	Place the Diagnostics disk in the disk drive, reboot your system, and choose Computer Setup on the menu.
Newer Compaq computers such as the ProLinea, Deskpro, Deskpro XL, Deskpro XE, or Presario	Press F10 while the cursor is in the upper-right corner of the screen, which happens during booting just after you hear two beeps.*
All other older computers	Use a setup program on the floppy disk that came with the PC.

* For Compaq computers, the CMOS setup program is stored on the hard drive in a small, non-DOS partition of about 3 MB. If this partition becomes corrupted, you must run setup from the floppy disk. If you cannot run setup by pressing F10 at startup, suspect a damaged partition or a virus taking up space in conventional memory.

PRACTICE TEST QUESTIONS

1. **When troubleshooting a parallel port, you should verify that the port is enabled:**
   a. by setting a jumper on the system board
   b. in CMOS setup
   c. using Windows Device Manager
   d. using a parameter in the OS kernel

2. **Which setting for a parallel port gives the fastest data access time?**
   a. standard
   b. bi-directional
   c. ECP
   d. EPP

3. **When a parallel port is set to ECP, what resource is required?**
   a. a second IRQ
   b. a DMA channel
   c. an ISA bus channel
   d. a second group of upper memory addresses

ANSWER

4. **If the system is short of DMA channels, you can free one up by:**
   a. changing the parallel port CMOS setting from EPP to ECP
   b. changing the parallel port CMOS setting from Bidirectional to ECP
   c. changing the parallel port CMOS setting from ECP to EPP or Bidirectional
   d. disabling the parallel port

5. **If a serial port is not working, what should you verify?**
   a. that the port is enabled in CMOS setup
   b. that the port is set to use a 50-pin cable
   c. that the port is set to use a DMA channel
   d. that the port switch on the back of the computer case is turned on

ANSWER

6. **In CMOS setup, when a serial port is set to use IRQ4 and I/O address 03F8, the port is configured as:**
   a. COM1
   b. COM2
   c. COM3
   d. COM4

ANSWER

7. **If a parallel port in CMOS setup is configured to use IRQ5 and I/O address 0278, then the port is configured as:**
   a. LPT1:
   b. LPT2:
   c. LPT3:
   d. PRINTER 1

ANSWER

4.4
cont.
Identify the purpose of CMOS (Complementary Metal-Oxide Semiconductor), what it contains and how to change its basic parameters

FLOPPY DRIVE: ENABLE/DISABLE DRIVE OR BOOT, SPEED, DENSITY • HARD DRIVE: SIZE AND DRIVE TYPE • MEMORY: PARITY, NON-PARITY • BOOT SEQUENCE • DATE/TIME • PASSWORDS • PLUG & PLAY BIOS

UNDERSTANDING THE OBJECTIVE

CMOS settings affect floppy drives, hard drives, memory parity, the boot sequence, the date, the time, the power–on password, and how Plug & Play is used by the system.

WHAT YOU **REALLY** NEED TO KNOW

- ◆ Floppy drives are enabled and disabled in CMOS, and the floppy drive type is set in CMOS.
- ◆ Hard drive parameters are set in CMOS by auto detection or by manual entry.
- ◆ The type of memory (parity or non-parity) is set in CMOS or is automatically detected by BIOS.
- ◆ Boot sequence in CMOS determines which storage device BIOS looks to for an operating system during the boot process.
- ◆ The boot sequence can allow the system to boot from an IDE hard drive, SCSI hard drive, CD-ROM drive, Zip drive, floppy disk drive, or network device, depending on the options supported by the system BIOS.
- ◆ System date and time are set in CMOS, which are then read by the OS when it loads and then passed to applications.
- ◆ System date and time are sometimes called the real-time clock (RTC).
- ◆ Use CMOS setup to enable or disable a power-on password.
- ◆ If the password is forgotten, you can use a jumper on the system board to restore CMOS settings to default values, which will erase the forgotten password. The user settings must then be restored in CMOS.
- ◆ Use CMOS setup to reserve an IRQ or DMA channel for a legacy device so Plug & Play will not assign the IRQ or DMA channel to a Plug & Play device.
- ◆ The PCI bus IRQ steering feature allows more than one PCI device to share an IRQ. To do this, Startup BIOS and Windows can put a holder on an IRQ so that PCI can use it. This can erroneously happen when Startup BIOS does not recognize the IRQ is needed by a legacy device. Solve the problem by using CMOS setup to reserve the IRQ for the legacy device or to disable PCI bus IRQ steering.

OBJECTIVES ON THE JOB

When troubleshooting problems with floppy drives, memory, the boot sequence, and so forth, check the settings in CMOS for accuracy. When installing a floppy drive, inform CMOS of the change. A power–on password can also be set in CMOS.

PRACTICE TEST QUESTIONS

1. **When a PC boots with the incorrect date or time, what is the likely cause?**
   a. power supply is bad
   b. CMOS battery is weak
   c. hard drive is full
   d. BIOS is corrupted

2. **Which hard drive parameter is not set using CMOS setup?**
   a. the number of heads
   b. the storage capacity of the drive
   c. the number of cylinders
   d. the data access time

3. **Which of the following cannot be damaged by a virus?**
   a. data on a floppy disk
   b. CMOS
   c. the boot sector of the hard drive
   d. program files

4. **When installing a 3-1/2 inch floppy drive to replace a 5-1/4 inch floppy drive, how does the system know to expect the new type of drive?**
   a. Jumpers are set on the system board.
   b. Startup BIOS will sense the new drive.
   c. You must first change the drive type in CMOS setup.
   d. You must first change the hardware parameters stored in the root directory of the hard drive.

5. **Which of the following hard drive parameters can be set in CMOS?**
   a. the number of cylinders
   b. the number of heads
   c. the number of sectors
   d. all of the above

6. **Boot sequence as set in CMOS is the order:**
   a. that hardware is checked by BIOS during the boot process
   b. the OS files load
   c. that drives are checked when searching for an OS
   d. that BIOS and drivers are loaded into memory during the boot process

7. **System date and time can be set:**
   a. by the operating system
   b. in CMOS setup
   c. by Microsoft Word
   d. both a and b

5.1 Identify basic concepts, printer operations and printer components

PAPER FEEDER MECHANISMS • TYPES OF PRINTERS: LASER • INKJET • DOT MATRIX

UNDERSTANDING THE OBJECTIVE

Understand the basics of how the common printers work, how they are maintained, and which printer components are considered field replaceable units.

WHAT YOU **REALLY** NEED TO KNOW

◆ For laser printers:
   - The steps in laser printing are:
   1. Cleaning — The drum is cleaned of any residual toner and electrical charge.
   2. Conditioning — The drum is conditioned to contain a high electrical charge.
   3. Writing — A laser beam discharges the high charge down to a lower charge, in those places where toner is to go.
   4. Developing — Toner is placed onto the drum where the charge has been reduced.
   5. Transferring — A strong electrical charge draws the toner off the drum onto the paper.
   6. Fusing — Heat and pressure are used to fuse the toner to the paper.
◆ The primary corona used in the conditioning step creates a very high negative charge.
◆ The laser printer drum loses its high negative charge when the laser light hits it in the writing stage.
   - The lightness and darkness of printing is controlled by the transfer corona.
◆ A dot matrix printer is an impact printer; the print head containing tiny pins hits the ribbon which hits the paper, thus producing a character.
◆ For ink jet printers:
   - Ink jet printers use an ink cartridge containing three colors (magenta, cyan, and yellow) in tubes.
   - Tiny plates near the tubes heat up, causing the ink to boil and eject from the tubes.
   - More plates carrying a magnetic charge direct the path of ink onto the paper to form the desired printed image.

OBJECTIVES ON THE JOB

Supporting printers is a major part of the responsibilities of a PC technician. The first step in learning to support printers is to learn the basics of how they work.

PRACTICE TEST QUESTIONS

1. In laser printing, the step between writing and transferring is:
- a. cleaning
- b. conditioning
- c. developing
- d. fusing

ANSWER

2. What component on a dot matrix printer forms each character?
- a. the ribbon
- b. a laser beam
- c. magnetic fields around tiny pins
- d. pins on the print head

ANSWER

3. On an ink jet printer, what causes the ink to form characters and shapes on the paper?
- a. Each ink jet is directed using a highly charged fusing beam.
- b. Each ink jet is directed using magnetized plates.
- c. Each ink jet is directed using the heat from the charging plates.
- d. Each ink jet is directed using tiny mechanical levels.

ANSWER

4. In laser printing, which stage in the printing process forms the characters or shapes to be printed?
- a. writing
- b. conditioning
- c. transferring
- d. fusing

ANSWER

5. In laser printing, which stage puts the toner on the paper?
- a. writing
- b. conditioning
- c. transferring
- d. fusing

ANSWER

6. In laser printing, which is the last step?
- a. writing
- b. fusing
- c. developing
- d. transferring

ANSWER

7. In laser printing, what is the purpose of the laser beam?
- a. to cause the printer drum to loose its high negative charge
- b. to cause the toner to stick to the paper
- c. to cause the printer drum to heat up
- d. to cause the printer drum to gain a high negative charge

ANSWER

OBJECTIVES

5.1 Identify basic concepts, printer operations and printer components
cont.

PARALLEL • NETWORK • USBO INFRARED • SERIAL

UNDERSTANDING THE OBJECTIVE

A printer can be connected directly to a PC (local printer) or a PC can access a printer that is shared on a network. A printer can also be connected directly to the network (network printer). When installing a printer using the OS, you tell the OS which connection is used as well as the printer configuration and type.

WHAT YOU **REALLY** NEED TO KNOW

- ◆ A local printer can be connected to a computer using a parallel, serial, infrared or USB port.
- ◆ A local printer can be shared with others over a network. First, the PC must configure the printer to be shared across the network (print sharing).
- ◆ A printer is made available to many on a network by one of the following three methods:
  - The printer can be connected to a PC on the network, and the PC can then share the printer on the network.
  - A network printer with embedded logic can manage network communication and be connected directly to the network and be assigned its own network address (IP address).
  - A computer called a print server can control several printers connected to a network. (For example, HP Jet Direct is software that supports HP printers on a network.)

OBJECTIVES ON THE JOB

One important use of a LAN is printer sharing. When servicing PCs on a network, be aware that the PC might support a printer that is shared on the network. Before the service is completed, verify that other users on the network still have access to the printer.

If there are problems printing when using a parallel port to connect to a printer, verify that the parallel port is enabled and configured correctly. In CMOS setup, choices for the parallel port mode might be Output Only, Bidirectional, ECP, and EPP. Because ECP mode uses a DMA channel, when the mode is set to ECP, an option for DMA channel might appear. When the mode is set to Output Only, the printer cannot communicate with the PC.

For fastest communication with the printer, select ECP. If problems arise, first try EPP, then Bidirectional. Only use Output Only if other options don't work. When using this option, disable bi-directional support for the printer using the Printer Properties dialog box in Windows 9x. If this method works when others don't, suspect the parallel printer cable. Verify that the cable is a bi-directional cable that complies with IEEE 1284 standards. Also use loop back plugs to test the port.

PRACTICE TEST QUESTIONS

1. **In what ways can a printer connect to a computer system?**
   a. by a parallel, serial, or infrared port
   b. by a parallel, serial, or USB port
   c. by a parallel, serial, infrared, or USB port
   d. by a parallel, serial, infrared, USB or mouse port

ANSWER

2. **If a printer is connected to a computer by way of a parallel cable and the computer is connected to a network, what must be done before others on the network can use this printer?**
   a. The computer must share the printer use file and print sharing.
   b. The printer must be connected to a network server.
   c. The printer must be converted to use a serial cable.
   d. The printer must be moved to a Windows NT computer.

ANSWER

3. **To access file and print sharing in Windows 9x, you should do which of the following?**
   a. Click Start, Programs, Control Panel, Network.
   b. Click Start, Settings, Control Panel, Network.
   c. Click Start, Settings, Printers, Sharing.
   d. Click Start, Settings, Network, Sharing.

ANSWER

4. **To share a printer over a network, you must:**
   a. click Start, Settings, Printers, and select Sharing on the drop-down menu
   b. click Start, Settings, Printers, and select File and Print Sharing on the drop-down menu
   c. click Start, Settings, Control Panel, and select Sharing from the icons displayed
   d. double-click the Shared icon on the desktop

ANSWER

5. **When sharing a printer over a network, you must:**
   a. disconnect the printer from the PC when you set up printer sharing
   b. give the shared printer a name
   c. use a modem to allow others on the network to use the printer
   d. keep the printer off line

ANSWER

6. **To use a shared printer on another PC, you must:**
   a. add the new printer to your list of installed printers
   b. be connected to the network when you install the printer
   c. know the name of the shared printer
   d. all of the above

ANSWER

7. **When troubleshooting problems with shared printers on a network, what is a good question to ask?**
   a. Is the printer online?
   b. Is the network printer on the remote PC configured correctly?
   c. Is there enough hard drive space available on the remote PC?
   d. all of the above

ANSWER

5.2 Identify care and service techniques and common problems with primary printer types

FEED AND OUTPUT • ERRORS (PRINTED OR DISPLAYED) • PAPER JAM • PRINT QUALITY • SAFETY PRECAUTIONS • PREVENTIVE MAINTENANCE

UNDERSTANDING THE OBJECTIVE

Troubleshooting, maintaining, and servicing printers are skills needed by a PC technician. Know what errors and problems can occur and what to do about them.

WHAT YOU **REALLY** NEED TO KNOW

◆ Define **enhanced metafile format (EMF)** and **spooling** as used by Windows 9x and Windows 2000. Most Windows printing is done using EMF spooling.

◆ When troubleshooting print problems, try disabling EMF conversion and disabling spooling of print jobs.

◆ When troubleshooting print problems, the source of the problem might be with bi-directional communication with the printer. From the Printer Properties dialog box, choose "Disable bidirectional support for this printer."

◆ When performing preventive maintenance on a dot matrix printer, never lubricate the print head pins; the ink on the ribbon serves as a lubricant for the pins.

◆ When performing preventive maintenance on a laser printer, replace the ozone filter, if there is one.

◆ Dark spots on the paper indicate loose toner particles on a laser printer. The solution is to run extra paper through the printer.

◆ When servicing a laser printer, beware that the fuser assemblage can be hot to the touch. Also, remember to protect the toner cartridge from light as you work.

◆ A dot matrix print head can overheat, which can lessen the life of the printer.

◆ When troubleshooting problems with jammed paper in a printer, note the location of the leading edge of jammed paper. It indicates where the jam begins and what component is causing the problem.

◆ If you can print a test page from the operating system (for Windows, double-click the Printer icon in the Control Panel to use the Printer Properties dialog box), then all is working correctly between the OS, the device drivers, the connectivity to the printer, and the printer itself.

◆ For a dot matrix printer, do the following:
- If the head moves back and forth but nothing prints, suspect a problem with the ribbon.
- Smudges on the paper can be caused by the ribbon being too tight.
- Incomplete characters can be caused by broken print head pins.
- If the printing is inconsistent, look for a problem with the ribbon advancing.

◆ For an ink jet printer, poor print quality can sometimes be solved by cleaning the ink jet nozzles by following the directions of the printer manufacturer.

OBJECTIVES ON THE JOB

Troubleshooting problems with printers is a common task for a PC technician.

PRACTICE TEST QUESTIONS

1. **Into what format does Windows 9x convert a print job file before printing?**
   a. a text document
   b. a Word document
   c. enhanced metafile
   d. spool job

2. **Spooling print jobs:**
   a. relieves an application from the delay of printing
   b. allows several print jobs to be placed into a queue
   c. is used by Windows 9x
   d. all of the above

3. **When troubleshooting a print problem, you can:**
   a. disable EMF conversion
   b. disable spooling of print jobs
   c. test the printer using a printer self test
   d. all of the above

ANSWER

4. **If there is a problem with the printer communicating with the computer, the problem can be solved by:**
   a. disconnecting the printer cable
   b. taking the printer off line
   c. disabling bi-directional support for this printer
   d. lubricating the print head pins

ANSWER

5. **When servicing a dot matrix printer, what device might be hot to the touch?**
   a. the print ribbon
   b. the print head
   c. the roller mechanism
   d. the paper carriage assembly

ANSWER

6. **When servicing a laser printer, which component might be hot to the touch?**
   a. the print head
   b. the paper drum
   c. the fuser assemblage
   d. the toner cartridge

ANSWER

7. **When troubleshooting a dot matrix printer, if the head moves back and forth but nothing prints, then suspect a problem with the:**
   a. pins on the print head
   b. paper feeder
   c. ribbon
   d. printer cable

6.1 Identify basic networking concepts, including how a network works and the ramifications of repairs on the network

WAYS TO NETWORK A PC • PHYSICAL NETWORK TOPOGRAPHIES • HARDWARE PROTOCOLS • FULL-DUPLEX, HALF-DUPLEX

UNDERSTANDING THE OBJECTIVE

Most PCs in the home or business environment are connected to a network. A PC technician needs a fundamental understanding of the different network topographies and protocols and also must know about the several ways a PC can connect to a network.

WHAT YOU **REALLY** NEED TO KNOW

- A **local area network (LAN)** is a group of computers and other equipment contained in a relatively small area.
- A wide area network (WAN) is a network that connects geographically separated areas.
- A metropolitan area network (MAN) can contain several LANs and telecommunications equipment and is smaller and usually faster than a WAN.
- The most popular hardware protocols are Ethernet, **Token Ring**, and Fiber Distributed Data Interface **(FDDI)**. A relatively new protocol is Asynchronous Transfer Mode (ATM). Each network technology is designed to meet a particular network need and has its own advantages and disadvantages.
- The most popular network for LANs is **Ethernet**, which can be configured in either a bus or star topology and can use coaxial and twisted pair wiring. It supports speeds of 10 to 100 Mbps.
- **Full-duplex** is communication in both directions simultaneously; **half-duplex** allows communication in only one direction at a time.
- In its simplest form a network can be two PCs connected to each other by a single network cable.
- A **hub** connects computers and other devices on a network and is used when several PCs are networked together in an Ethernet LAN using a star topology.
- A **bridge** or **router** connects network segments.
- A **backbone** is a network used to link several networks together.
- An Ethernet NIC, called a **combo card**, can support more than one cabling media by containing more than one transceiver on the card.
- A **media access control (MAC) address** or **adapter address** is a unique number that is hard-coded into a NIC and that is used to uniquely identify the NIC on the network.
- A network is often used to share printers (print services) and to share space on a hard drive (network drives) across the network.

OBJECTIVES ON THE JOB

Servicing PCs on a network requires that you have a basic understanding of how networks work and be able to recognize network hardware.

PRACTICE TEST QUESTIONS

1. **Which of the following is not a type of network?**
   a. LAN
   b. FAN
   c. WAN
   d. MAN

 ANSWER

2. **Which of the following is not a type of hardware protocol?**
   a. Internet
   b. Ethernet
   c. Token Ring
   d. FDDI

 ANSWER

3. **What does FDDI stand for?**
   a. fitting dirty data interface
   b. fiber distributed data interface
   c. fine dirty data for the Internet
   d. fiber deep down Internet

ANSWER

4. **Which of the following is the most popular network architecture?**
   a. FDDI
   b. Token ring
   c. Ethernet
   d. Metropolitan network

ANSWER

5. **What device connects two computers or other components within a network?**
   a. a hub
   b. a bridge
   c. a router
   d. a node

ANSWER

6. **Full-duplex communication is communication in:**
   a. two directions, but not at the same time
   b. two directions simultaneously
   c. only a single direction
   d. one direction at a time

ANSWER

7. **A number permanently assigned to a NIC that uniquely identifies the computer to the network is:**
   a. an IP address
   b. a MAC address
   c. a combo card address
   d. a NIC Handle

 ANSWER

6.1
cont.
Identify basic networking concepts, including how a network works and the ramifications of repairs on the network

INSTALLING AND CONFIGURING NETWORK CARDS • NETWORK ACCESS • CABLING: TWISTED PAIR, COAXIAL, FIBER OPTIC, RS-232 • INFRARED

UNDERSTANDING THE OBJECTIVE

A PC technician is often expected to service a PC connected to a network. You should be able to recognize when the PC is network ready, disconnect it from the network, reconnect it, and verify that connectivity is working properly. Be able to recognize the different network cabling systems and how they can be used to network a PC.

WHAT YOU **REALLY** NEED TO KNOW

◆ Coaxial, twisted pair, and **fiber optic** cables are all used in networks.

◆ RS-232 is a standard that controls serial cables.

◆ An infrared device (for example, an infrared printer) can access a network by way of a PC that has an infrared port. The device is installed on the PC and then shared with others on the network.

◆ The most common LAN setup today is Ethernet 10BaseT star formation using UTP cabling with RJ-45 connectors.

◆ Listed below are the several cabling systems used by Ethernet

Cable System	Cable and Connectors	Notes
10Base5 (Thicknet) Speed = 10 Mbps	Thick coaxial cable uses an AUI 15-pin D-shaped connector.	Maximum segment length of Thicknet is 500 meters
10Base2 (Thinnet) Speed = 10 Mbps	Thin coaxial cable uses a BNC connector (T-connector).	Maximum segment length of Thinnet is 185 meters
10BaseT (Twisted pair) Speed = 10 Mbps	Unshielded twisted-pair (UTP) cable uses an RJ-45 connector. (The most common cabling system.)	There are several grades of UTP. A lower grade of UTP not suitable for 10BaseT is often used for telephone wire.
100 BaseT (Fast Ethernet) Speed = 100 Mbps	Unshielded twisted-pair (UTP) of shielded twisted pair (STP) cable with RJ-45 connector. Category 5 (Cat-5) UTP cable is most common.	STP is rigid and thick and costs more than UTP.
10BaseFL and 100BaseFX (Fiber Optic) Speeds = 10 Mbps or 100 Mbps	Optical fiber (fiber-optic cable) uses an ST or SC fiber-optic connector.	These cables use light rather than electricity to transmit signals.

OBJECTIVES ON THE JOB

A PC technician is often called on to service PCs on a network. You should be able to recognize the different network topologies, cables, and network card ports so as to know what type of network you are dealing with. Always depend on the network administrator to answer specific questions about the network configuration and its hardware.

PRACTICE TEST QUESTIONS

1. **What is the shape of a BNC connector?**
   a. square
   b. round
   c. looks like a large phone jack
   d. rectangular

2. **The term 10BaseT refers to what network speed?**
   a. megabits per second
   b. megabytes per second
   c. bits per second
   d. bytes per second

3. **What is the most common Ethernet technology today?**
   a. 10Base5
   b. 100BaseT
   c. 10BaseFL
   d. 10BaseT

4. **Which connector is typically used in an Ethernet bus topology?**
   a. BNC
   b. STP
   c. RJ-45
   d. CAT 5

5. **Which is the more reliable network cable?**
   a. UTP
   b. STP
   c. RJ-45
   d. BNC

6. **Which Ethernet technology uses fiber optic cable?**
   a. 10Base5
   b. 100BaseT
   c. 10BaseFL
   d. 10BaseT

7. **Which Ethernet topology uses a hub?**
   a. a star topology
   b. a bus topology
   c. a fixed length fiber optic topology
   d. a token ring topology

6.1
cont.
Identify basic networking concepts, including how a network works and the ramifications of repairs on the network

INCREASING BANDWIDTH • LOSS OF DATA • NETWORK SLOWDOWN

UNDERSTANDING THE OBJECTIVE

You should have a procedure in place to remove a PC from a network, service it, and restore connectivity to the network. When a PC demonstrates a slowdown when accessing the network, a variety of problems can be the source.

WHAT YOU **REALLY** NEED TO KNOW

◆ When a PC demonstrates a slowdown when accessing the network, all the following can be a source of the problem:
- A virus or worm on the PC or on the network
- A failing network card
- A failing hub or other network device
- Hard drive space too full
- Not enough memory or hard drive space on the PC
- Too many applications open at the same time and thus reducing PC resources
- Problems with a corrupted operating system

◆ When troubleshooting a problem with a PC on a network, first isolate the problem to the PC or the network. Do other PCs on the network have the same problem? Does the PC work well when disconnected from the network? Does the problem only occur when the PC is accessing data or resources across the network? Try disconnecting the PC from the network and reproducing the problem.

◆ When replacing a NIC on a PC, use a NIC that is identical to the one you are replacing. If you cannot match the NIC, then consult with the network administrator as to how to install and configure the new NIC.

◆ The following are the steps to disconnect a PC from a network, repair the PC, and reconnect it to the network with the least possible disturbance of network configuration:
1. If possible, verify that the PC is network-ready.
2. Log off the network.
3. Save the network files and parameters to disk if you think you might destroy them on the hard drive as you work.
4. Disconnect the network cable and repair the PC.
5. Restore the network configurations.
6. Reconnect the PC to the network.
7. Verify that network resources are available to the PC.

Objectives On the Job

When servicing a PC on a network, you must be able to perform the service with as little disturbance to the network as possible. The PC should be fully restored to the network before your work is considered finished.

PRACTICE TEST QUESTIONS

1. **When servicing a PC on a network, before you turn off the PC, you should:**
   a. disconnect the network cable from the NIC
   b. log off the network
   c. write down the MAC address of the computer
   d. turn off the monitor

2. **When replacing a NIC in a computer system, it is important to use an identical NIC because:**
   a. only one kind of NIC works on a particular network
   b. it is easier to fit the replacement NIC in the expansion slot
   c. the drivers for the NIC will not need replacing
   d. you cannot tell what kind of NIC will work on this network

ANSWER

3. **Before connecting a computer back to the network, you should:**
   a. verify that the network parameters are still configured correctly
   b. ask the user to verify that the computer has access to the network drives
   c. back up the entire hard drive
   d. reboot from a floppy disk

ANSWER

4. **If you must install a different type of NIC than the one currently installed, what must you do?**
   a. Verify that the new NIC uses the same type network cable.
   b. Ask the network administration for the proper drivers for the new NIC.
   c. Verify that network parameters are entered correctly.
   d. all of the above

ANSWER

5. **When the light on the back of the NIC is not lit solid, what can be the problem?**
   a. the NIC, the network cable or the hub
   b. the NIC, the OS, or the hub
   c. the NIC, the OS, or the application using the network
   d. the OS, the user, or the application using the network

ANSWER

6. **Which type of network port uses a T-connector?**
   a. the FDDI port
   b. RJ-45
   c. BNC
   d. RJ-11

ANSWER

7. **What type of NIC works on an Ethernet network and supports more than one cabling media?**
   a. a dual NIC
   b. a combo card
   c. a NIC NIC
   d. a double-NIC

Objectives

The following descriptions of the A+ DOS/Windows Objective domains are taken from the CompTIA Web site at *www.comptia.org/index.asp?ContentPage=/certification/aplus/aplus.asp*

% OF EXAM

DOMAIN 1.0 OPERATING SYSTEM FUNDAMENTALS   30%

This domain requires knowledge of underlying DOS (command prompt functions) in Windows 9x, Windows 2000 operating systems in terms of its functions and structure, for managing files and directories, and running programs. It also includes navigating through the operating system from command line prompts and Windows procedures for accessing and retrieving information.

DOMAIN 2.0 INSTALLATION, CONFIGURATION, AND UPGRADING   15%

This domain requires knowledge of installing, configuring, and upgrading Windows 9x and Windows 2000. This includes knowledge of system boot sequences and minimum hardware requirements.

DOMAIN 3.0 DIAGNOSING AND TROUBLESHOOTING   40%

This domain requires the ability to apply knowledge to diagnose and troubleshoot common problems relating to Windows 9x and Windows 2000. This includes understanding normal operation and symptoms relating to common problems.

DOMAIN 4.0 NETWORKS   15%

This domain requires knowledge of network capabilities of Windows, and how to connect to networks on the client side, including what the Internet is about, its capabilities, basic concepts relating to Internet access, and generic procedures for system setup. The scope of this topic is only what is needed on the desktop side to connect to a network.

1.1 Identify the operating system's functions, structure, and major system files to navigate the operating system and how to get to needed technical information

MAJOR OPERATING SYSTEM FUNCTIONS

UNDERSTANDING THE OBJECTIVE

Know how to navigate through menus to get to important system information and perform routine and troubleshooting tasks. Sometimes the mouse is not working during a troubleshooting session, so you should know the key combinations for performing critical tasks. Know more than one way to locate and execute an OS utility such as Windows Explorer or Device Manager. Also know the program file names of Windows utilities such as Disk Cleanup (Cleanmgr.exe) and where these programs are located (Cleanmgr.exe is in the \Windows folder).

WHAT YOU **REALLY** NEED TO KNOW

◆ Know how to step through the menus to find the Device Manager, System Monitor, and other commonly used Windows utilities.
◆ The Control Panels in Windows 9x and Windows 2000 are used mainly to configure system settings.
◆ Know the following key combinations, which must be used if the mouse is not working:

General Action	Key Combinations and Mouse Actions	Description
Managing program windows	Alt+Tab	While holding down the Alt key, press Tab to switch from one loaded application to another.
	Ctrl+Esc	While holding down the Ctrl key, press Esc to display the Start menu.
	Alt+Esc	While holding down the Alt key, press Esc to move from one window to another.
	Alt+F4	While holding down the Alt key, press F4 to close a program window.
	Double-click	Double-click an icon or program name to execute the program.
Selecting	Shift+click	To select multiple entries in a list (such as filenames items in Explorer), click the first item, and then hold down the Shift key and click the last item you want to select in the list. All items between the first and last are selected.
	Ctrl+click	To select several items in a list that are not listed sequentially, click the first item to select it. Hold down the Ctrl key as you click other items anywhere in the list. All items you have clicked on are selected.
Using menus	Alt	Press the Alt key to activate the menu bar.
	Alt, letter	Press Alt to activate the menu bar, and then press a letter to select a menu option. The letter must be underlined on the menu.
	Alt, arrow keys	Press Alt to activate the menu bar; then use arrow keys to highlight menu options.
	Alt, arrow keys, Enter	Press Alt to activate the menu bar, press the arrow keys to highlight an option, and then press Enter to select the option.
	Esc	Press Esc to exit a menu without making a selection.

OBJECTIVES ON THE JOB

Navigating through Windows 2000 and Windows 9x is an essential skill of a PC technician. Being able to function without the use of a mouse is also important and should not be overlooked when preparing to support PCs.

PRACTICE TEST QUESTIONS

1. **What key combination closes a program window?**
   a. Ctrl+Esc
   b. Alt+Tab
   c. Alt+F4
   d. Alt+F5

   ANSWER

2. **From a program window, how do you bring focus to or activate the menu bar?**
   a. Press the Ctrl key.
   b. Press the Alt key.
   c. Press the Esc key.
   d. Press Ctrl+Alt.

   ANSWER

3. **In Windows 9x, an application is open on the screen, the mouse does not work, and you want to do an orderly shutdown. What do you do?**
   a. Turn off the PC.
   b. Press Ctrl+Esc and use the arrow key to select Shutdown.
   c. Press Alt+Tab to go to the Task List and select Shutdown.
   d. Press Ctrl+F4.

   ANSWER

4. **In Windows 9x, what do you press to move from one loaded application to another?**
   a. Alt+Tab
   b. Ctrl+Esc
   c. F4
   d. Shift+F2

   ANSWER

5. **In Windows 2000 Explorer, how do you select several files that are listed consecutively?**
   a. Click the first filename, hold down the Ctrl key, and click the last filename in the list.
   b. Click the first filename, hold down the Shift key, and click the last filename in the list.
   c. Drag your mouse over the entire list, clicking as you go.
   d. all of the above

   ANSWER

6. **If you delete a file in Explorer, how can you recover it?**
   a. Run UNERASE from a DOS box.
   b. Restore it from the Recycle Bin.
   c. Run DEFRAG.
   d. Go to Control Panel and double-click the Recover icon.

   ANSWER

7. **What is one way to access Device Manager in Windows 98?**
   a. Right click My Computer, select Properties, Device Manager
   b. Right click Start, Settings, select Device Manager
   c. Click Start, Settings, Control Panel, select System, Device Manager
   d. Either a or c

   ANSWER

1.1
cont. Identify the operating system's functions, structure, and major system files to navigate the operating system and how to get to needed technical information

MAJOR OPERATING SYSTEM FUNCTIONS • CREATE FOLDERS • CHECKING OS VERSION

UNDERSTANDING THE OBJECTIVE

There are many skills required by a user when performing the daily routines of working with a PC including creating folders, creating shortcuts, managing files and storage media and making backups. A PC technician is expected to be proficient at all these skills and more.

WHAT YOU **REALLY** NEED TO KNOW

- ◆ Software works in layers. From the top down, the layers are applications software, the operating system, device drivers and BIOS, and hardware.
- ◆ Applications relate to the user and pass on some commands to the operating system. The operating system depends on the device drivers and BIOS to relate to the hardware.
- ◆ The OS is responsible for managing memory, diagnosing problems with software and hardware, managing the file system on secondary storage devices, and performing routine housekeeping chores such as formatting diskettes, deleting files, and changing the system date and time.
- ◆ Know how to perform routine tasks of the OS including copying files, running utilities, and creating folders and shortcuts. Know more than one way of doing things and memorize the menu paths to utilities and functions.
- ◆ To know which OS version is installed, right-click the My Computer icon and select Properties from the shortcut menu. Select the General tab.
- ◆ Create a folder using Windows Explorer. Select the folder under which the new folder should be created and click File, New from the menu.
- ◆ You can create shortcuts on the desktop in several ways, and you should know more than one way. One way to create a shortcut is to right-click the taskbar, select Properties, Start Menu Programs, Add. When given the option, choose to create the shortcut on the desktop.
- ◆ You can also use Windows Explorer to create a shortcut. Right-click a program file name and select Create Shortcut from the shortcut menu. Then drag and drop the shortcut created onto the desktop or move it to the Desktop folder.
- ◆ A shortcut on the desktop can give an error if the program file it points to has been moved, deleted or renamed. To verify the target to the shortcut, right-click the shortcut and select Properties.

OBJECTIVES ON THE JOB

Understanding the functions of Windows 9x and Windows 2000 is essential to making decisions about which OS to purchase, when to upgrade the OS, and supporting the OS and applications that use it. Also, customizing the user's desktop and troubleshooting problems with the desktop is a common chore of a PC technician.

PRACTICE TEST QUESTIONS

1. **What are the steps to hide the Windows 98 taskbar?**
   a. Right-click the taskbar, select Properties, Taskbar Options
   b. Right-click the taskbar, select Properties, Hide Taskbar
   c. Click Start, Settings, Control Panel, Desktop, Taskbar Options
   d. Click Start, Settings, Desktop, Taskbar Options

    ANSWER

2. **What steps can you use to create a shortcut on the Windows 98 desktop?**
   a. Using Windows Explorer, add a shortcut file to the \Windows\Desktop folder.
   b. Right-click the taskbar, select Properties, Start Menu, Programs, Add.
   c. Using Windows Explorer, create a shortcut file and drag and drop it on the desktop.
   d. all of the above

   ANSWER

3. **In Windows 2000, how do you add an item to the Start menu?**
   a. Right-click the taskbar and select Properties, Advanced, Add
   b. Right-click the taskbar and select Properties, Start Menu, Add
   c. Click Start, Settings, Control Panel, Start Menu
   d. Right-click the taskbar and select Options, Add

   ANSWER

4. **Which is not a function of an operating system?**
   a. Format a floppy disk.
   b. Partition a hard drive.
   c. Load application software.
   d. Check spelling.

   ANSWER

5. **How do you access Windows Explorer in Windows 2000?**
   a. Click Start, Programs, Accessories, Windows Explorer
   b. Right-click Start and select Windows Explorer
   c. Click Start, Programs, Windows Explorer
   d. Either a or b

   ANSWER

6. **Which of the following is a function of an operating system?**
   a. change the system date and time
   b. change the real time clock date and time
   c. determine which hard drive in a dual drive system is the boot device
   d. format a paragraph using left justified alignment

    ANSWER

7. **How do you discover the version number of the operating system?**
   a. Using Windows Explorer, right-click My Computer and select Properties
   b. On the desktop, right-click the My Computer icon and select Properties
   c. Click Start, Settings, Control Panel. Double-click System icon, select General tab.
   d. all of the above

    ANSWER

1.1
cont.

Identify the operating system's functions, structure, and major system files to navigate the operating system and how to get to needed technical information

MAJOR OPERATING SYSTEM COMPONENTS: EXPLORER • MY COMPUTER • CONTROL PANEL

UNDERSTANDING THE OBJECTIVE

Every operating system has tools to manage files and folders, view and use system resources, add and remove hardware and software, and perform other tasks. Windows 9x and Windows 2000 provide three tools for most of these functions: Explorer, My Computer, and Control Panel.

WHAT YOU **REALLY** NEED TO KNOW

◆ Use Control Panel to add and remove hardware and software and configure system resources. Be familiar with each icon or entry in Control Panel and know its primary purpose.

◆ My Computer is accessible from the desktop and from Windows Explorer. Use My Computer to view and access storage devices, Control Panel, Dial-Up Networking, and Network Neighborhood and other resources.

◆ The System Properties window can be accessed from Control Panel or My Computer.

◆ Use either My Computer or Explorer to determine how much space is available on a hard drive.

◆ The following is a list of tasks and where to find them in Windows 2000, 98 and NT.

Task	Windows 98	Windows NT	Windows 2000
Add and delete users	Control Panel, Users	Start, Programs, Administrative Tools	Control Panel, Users and Passwords
System and administrative tools	Start, Programs, Accessories, System Tools	Start, Programs	Control Panel, Administrative Tools
MS-DOS command prompt	Start, Programs, MS-DOS prompt	Control Panel, Console	Start, Programs, Accessories, Command Prompt
Configure a hardware device	Control Panel, System, Device Manager	Control Panel, Devices	Control Panel, System, Hardware, Device Manager
Dial-up connections and networking	Control Panel, Modems	Control Panel, Modems	Control Panel, Network and Dial-up Connections
Display options	Control Panel, Display	Control Panel, Display	Control Panel, Display
Install new hardware	Control Panel, Add New Hardware	Property window of a new device	Control Panel, Add/Remove Hardware
Network configuration	Control Panel, Network	Control Panel, Network	Control Panel, Network and Dial-up Connections
Set password	Control Panel, Passwords	Start, Programs, Administrative Tools	Control Panel/ Users and Passwords
Configure scanners and cameras	Not available	Not available	Control Panel, Scanners and Cameras
Configure UPS device	Control Panel, Power Management	Control Panel, UPS	Control Panel, Power Options

OBJECTIVES ON THE JOB

A PC technician is expected to know how to use the major operating system components to service, maintain, and troubleshoot a computer system.

PRACTICE TEST QUESTIONS

1. **In Device Manager, a diamond icon with a short line through one side of it stands for?**
   a. ISA bus
   b. USB device
   c. SCSI
   d. Video card

2. **A yellow exclamation point through a device in Device Manager indicates:**
   a. the device is disabled
   b. resources have been manually assigned
   c. there is a problem with the device
   d. the device is Plug and Play

3. **Which icon in Windows 2000 Control Panel do you use to configure a modem for a dial-up connection to a network?**
   a. Network and Dial-up Connections
   b. Network
   c. Dial-Up Networking
   d. Add/Remove Hardware

4. **Which icon in Windows 98 Control Panel do you use to change the user's password?**
   a. Passwords and Users
   b. Passwords
   c. Network
   d. Add New Programs

5. **How do you change a password in Windows 2000?**
   a. Control Panel, Users and Passwords
   b. Control Panel, Network
   c. Start, Programs, Accessories, Administrative Tools
   d. Start, Programs, Administrative Tools

6. **How can you determine how much space is available on a hard drive?**
   a. My Computer, Properties, System
   b. From Explorer, right click the drive and select Properties
   c. From My Computer, right click the drive and select Properties
   d. Either b or c

7. **How do you access a command line prompt using Windows 98?**
   a. Start, Programs, Accessories, Command Prompt
   b. Control Panel, MS-DOS Prompt
   c. Start, Programs, MS-DOS Prompt
   d. Either b or c

OBJECTIVES

1.1
cont.

Identify the operating system's functions, structure, and major system files to navigate the operating system and how to get to needed technical information

CONTRASTS BETWEEN WINDOWS 9X AND WINDOWS 2000

UNDERSTANDING THE OBJECTIVE

Windows 2000 was built on Windows NT and is basically the next evolution of Windows NT with the added user-friendly features of Windows 9x. Windows 2000 is more reliable than Windows 9x. Windows 9x is a combination of 16-bit and 32-bit OS components and supports legacy hardware and software that Windows 2000 does not support.

WHAT YOU **REALLY** NEED TO KNOW

- ◆ Because of improved power management features, Windows 2000 is better than Windows 9x for newer notebooks.
- ◆ Because of advanced security features, Windows 2000 is better for the corporate and business environments, and Windows 9x is better for the home market because it best supports games and legacy hardware and software.
- ◆ Windows 9x is similar to DOS in that it includes a DOS-based core with many 16-bit programs and manages base, upper, and extended memory in fundamentally the same way as DOS.
- ◆ Windows 9x assigns virtual memory addresses to a page table. The VMM manages the page table by moving data in and out of the page table to RAM and virtual memory (a swap file).
- ◆ Windows NT and Windows 2000 manage networks by assigning them to domains. The OS is the domain controller for the network.
- ◆ Windows 9x is a combination of 16-bit and 32-bit coding, but Windows 2000 uses all 32-bit code.
- ◆ Windows 9x installs applications, the DLLs for all applications are stored in a common folder, but Windows 2000 keeps an application's DLL files separate from other applications.
- ◆ Windows 9x does not ask permission before it overwrites or deletes a critical system file, but Windows 2000 protects that from happening and thereby improves system reliability.
- ◆ Windows 2000 is a suite of operating systems. Windows 2000 Professional is the choice for desktop and notebook computers.
- ◆ Windows 9x and Windows 2000 both use power management features for notebook computers, although Windows 2000 offers more features than Windows 9x.
- ◆ Windows 2000 and Windows 9x both use Plug and Play, but Windows NT does not.
- ◆ The suite of Windows 2000 operating systems will ultimately replace Windows NT and Windows 9x in the corporate, business, and home markets.

OBJECTIVES ON THE JOB

Understanding differences and similarities between Windows 9x and Windows 2000 is essential to knowing when to upgrade to Windows 2000 and how to support applications and the OS.

PRACTICE TEST QUESTIONS

1. **Which operating system uses dynamically loaded device drivers?**
   a. Windows 95
   b. Windows NT
   c. Windows 2000
   d. all of the above

   ANSWER

2. **Which operating system does not support Plug and Play?**
   a. Windows 95
   b. Windows 98
   c. Windows NT
   d. Windows 2000 Professional

   ANSWER

3. **Which operating system provides a feature to allow a user at home to connect a notebook computer to a network at his workplace using a virtual private network?**
   a. Windows 2000
   b. Windows 95
   c. Windows 98
   d. all of the above

   ANSWER

4. **Which operating system does not offer the NTFS file system?**
   a. Windows NT
   b. Windows 2000 Professional
   c. Windows 9x
   d. Windows 2000 Server

   ANSWER

5. **How does the Windows 95 Virtual Memory Manager assign memory addresses for applications to use?**
   a. Addresses are assigned to a page table that points to RAM and virtual memory.
   b. Addresses are assigned to areas in RAM.
   c. Addresses are assigned to virtual memory, which can represent either a swap file or RAM.
   d. Addresses are assigned by the CPU and VMM is not involved in the process.

   ANSWER

6. **Why would a user choose to use the NTFS file system on a notebook computer?**
   a. The hard drive is very large
   b. For added security over the FAT file system
   c. To allow the notebook to connect to the private network at his workplace
   d. To be able to use the Windows 2000 Active Directory on his network file server

   ANSWER

7. **Which operating system is best designed for small, inexpensive PCs where the user needs to run 16-bit application programs that require a graphical interface?**
   a. Windows 98
   b. Windows 2000
   c. Windows NT
   d. UNIX

   ANSWER

OBJECTIVES

1.1
cont.
Identify the operating system's functions, structure, and major system files to navigate the operating system and how to get to needed technical information

MAJOR SYSTEM FILES: WHAT THEY ARE, WHERE THEY ARE LOCATED, HOW THEY ARE USED AND WHAT THEY CONTAIN

UNDERSTANDING THE OBJECTIVE

Every operating system has a kernel or group of core components that performs the basic OS functions such as managing memory, managing the file system, and loading and executing programs. In addition, in this kernel, the OS must manage peripheral resources that interact with the user and with applications. Windows 9x accomplishes all this with three core components (Kernel, User, and GDI), and Windows NT and Windows 2000 use two modes (User mode and Kernel mode).

WHAT YOU **REALLY** NEED TO KNOW

◆ The three core components of Windows 9x are listed in the table below and are all located in the \Windows\System folder:

Component Name	Main Files Holding the Component	Functions
Kernel	KERNEL32.DLL, KRNL386.EXE	Handles the basic OS functions such as managing memory, file I/O, loading and executing programs
User	USER32.DLL, USER.EXE	Controls the mouse, keyboard, ports, and the desktop, including position of windows, icons, and dialog boxes
GDI	GDI32.DLL, GDI.EXE	Draws screens, graphics, lines, and prints

◆ All of these three core components use some 16-bit code and some 32-bit code. The 16-bit code primarily provides backward compatibility with 16-bit applications.

◆ The Windows 9x core components use the following components to relate to hardware:
- The Virtual Memory Manager (VMM) manages memory
- The Installable File System (IFS) Manager controls disk access
- The Configuration Manager is responsible for Plug and Play and other hard configuration tasks
- The Win32 Driver Model (WDM) is new with Windows 98 and manages device drivers

◆ Windows 9x uses the virtual machine (VM) concept to manage 16-bit and 32-bit applications.

◆ DOS requires IO.SYS, MSDOS.SYS, and COMMAND.COM to load. IO.SYS is the DOS kernel.

◆ DOS is a 16-bit OS; Windows 2000 and Windows NT is a 32-bit OS, and Windows 9x uses a combination of 16-bit and 32-bit code.

◆ Windows 2000 runs 32-bit applications and will also run 16-bit applications only when they don't attempt to access system resources independently of the OS.

OBJECTIVES ON THE JOB

Identifying the core components of an OS and understanding how they work with other components is essential to supporting the OS.

PRACTICE TEST QUESTIONS

1. **Which operating system does not allow an application to directly access system resources?**

   a. DOS

   b. Windows 95

   c. Windows 98

   d. Windows 2000

   ANSWER

2. **Where does Windows 9x store most configuration information?**

   a. SYSTEM.INI and WIN.INI

   b. the registry

   c. AUTOEXEC.BAT and CONFIG.SYS

   d. none of the above

   ANSWER

3. **Which core component of Windows 9x manages printing?**

   a. the kernel

   b. the user

   c. the GDI

   d. the Print services

   ANSWER

4. **Which core component of Windows 95 controls the mouse?**

   a. the kernel

   b. MOUSE.BAT

   c. the user

   d. GDI

   ANSWER

5. **Which Windows 95 component is responsible for managing Plug and Play tasks?**

   a. Virtual Memory Manager

   b. Installable File System

   c. Plug and Play Manager

   d. Configuration Manager

   ANSWER

6. **The Windows 2000 Hardware Abstraction Layer (HAL) operates in what mode?**

   a. the user mode

   b. the kernel mode

   c. the hardware mode

   d. the WIN32 subsystem mode

   ANSWER

7. **Which service or system operates in the kernel mode under Windows 2000?**

   a. WIN32 subsystem

   b. Executive Services

   c. Windows Explorer

   d. NTVDM

   ANSWER

OBJECTIVES

1.1
cont.
Identify the operating system's functions, structure, and major system files to navigate the operating system and how to get to needed technical information

MAJOR SYSTEM FILES: WHAT THEY ARE, WHERE THEY ARE LOCATED, HOW THEY ARE USED AND WHAT THEY CONTAIN: SYSTEM, CONFIGURATION, AND USER INTERFACE FILES: IO.SYS, MSDOS.SYS, AUTOEXEC.BAT, CONFIG.SYS

UNDERSTANDING THE OBJECTIVE

Each operating system has a group of core system files that are essential to loading and running the OS. You can manually edit some of these files to accommodate custom settings, software requirements, and hardware configurations. The system automatically changes other files when hardware or software is installed or uninstalled. Other system files never change for the current operating system installation. Since you are sometimes required to operate in a DOS environment, understand how DOS uses these system, configuration, and user interface files.

WHAT YOU **REALLY** NEED TO KNOW

- ◆ With DOS, when the BIOS turns to secondary storage to load an OS, the files are loaded or executed in this order: IO.SYS, MSDOS.SYS, CONFIG.SYS, COMMAND.COM, and AUTOEXEC.BAT.
- ◆ Of the above five files, CONFIG.SYS and AUTOEXEC.BAT are optional and both can be edited by the user.
- ◆ IO.SYS contains basic device drivers for standard system devices. MSDOS.SYS contains the DOS kernel and it possesses a majority of the low-level operating system routines such as file handling. MSDOS.SYS executes CONFIG.SYS during the boot process. IO.SYS and MSDOS.SYS are hidden, system files.
- ◆ CONFIG.SYS loads device drivers into memory and controls some of the system configuration.
- ◆ The FILES= line in CONFIG.SYS tells DOS how many files it can have open at one time.
- ◆ The BUFFERS= line in CONFIG.SYS tells DOS how many file buffers to create. (Buffers are memory locations set aside by the operating system to temporarily hold data.) The number is determined by the DOS applications using the buffers.
- ◆ BUFFERS= and SMARTDRV are both used to cache hard drive access in DOS.
- ◆ The DEVICE= line in CONFIG.SYS loads a device driver into base memory and DEVICEHIGH= loads a device driver into upper or reserved memory.
- ◆ The Microsoft files IO.SYS and MSDOS.SYS are named IBMBIO.COM and IBMDOS.COM under IBM DOS.
- ◆ A program can be executed from AUTOEXEC.BAT each time the PC boots by including the filename and path to the file in AUTOEXEC.BAT.

OBJECTIVES ON THE JOB

When supporting an OS, the PC technician must know how system files are used, where they are located, and the symptoms of a corrupted file. A technician must also know how to change these files as the hardware, software, and user needs change.

PRACTICE TEST QUESTIONS

1. **What file contains the BUFFERS= command line?**
   a. AUTOEXEC.BAT
   b. SYSTEM.INI
   c. CONFIG.SYS
   d. WIN.INI

ANSWER

2. **In which file is the command PROMPT PG located?**
   a. CONFIG.SYS
   b. AUTOEXEC.BAT
   c. SYSTEM.INI
   d. CONTROL.INI

ANSWER

3. **Which command is executed first during the boot process?**
   a. DEVICE=C:\DOS\EMM386.EXE
   b. PATH C:;C:\DOS
   c. DEVICE=C:\DOS\HIMEM.SYS
   d. PROMPT PG

ANSWER

4. **What is the purpose of the FILES= command?**
   a. to set how many files can be open at any one time
   b. to tell DOS how many files to create during the boot process
   c. to set how many files DOS can create as temporary files
   d. to set the location of the temporary directory used for temp files

ANSWER

5. **What software can be used to edit CONFIG.SYS?**
   a. Notepad
   b. EDIT.COM
   c. SYSEDIT
   d. all of the above

ANSWER

6. **Which files are hidden system files?**
   a. WIN.COM, AUTOEXEC.BAT, and IO.SYS
   b. IO.SYS and MSDOS.SYS
   c. WIN.COM and IO.SYS
   d. all of the above

ANSWER

7. **Which file is the DOS kernel?**
   a. KERNEL.EXE
   b. SYS.COM
   c. MSDOS.SYS
   d. COMMAND.COM

ANSWER

1.1
cont. Identify the operating system's functions, structure, and major system files to navigate the operating system and how to get to needed technical information

MAJOR SYSTEM FILES: WHAT THEY ARE, WHERE THEY ARE LOCATED, HOW THEY ARE USED AND WHAT THEY CONTAIN: SYSTEM, CONFIGURATION, AND USER INTERFACE FILES: IO.SYS, BOOT.INI, WIN.COM, MSDOS.SYS, AUTOEXEC.BAT, CONFIG.SYS, COMMAND LINE PROMPT

UNDERSTANDING THE OBJECTIVE

Each operating system has a group of core system files that are essential to loading and running the OS. Windows 9x uses some of the same system, configuration, and user interface files used by DOS, but the file can be used in a different way.

WHAT YOU **REALLY** NEED TO KNOW

◆ Windows 9x does not require that Config.sys or Autoexec.bat be present, but, if they are present, they are executed during the boot process in the same way they are used by DOS.

◆ After BIOS completes Plug and Play configuration, it turns the boot process over to Windows 9x. The first Windows file to execute is IO.SYS, which checks the contents of two text files, Msdos.sys and Config.sys.

◆ Msdos.sys contains these and other boot parameters:
- BootMulti – Allows for a dual boot
- BootWin – Allows the system to boot to a previous version of DOS
- BootMenu – Displays the Startup menu during booting
- BootKeys – Controls whether the function keys work during booting
- BootDelay – Controls number of seconds the boot process pauses for user intervention
- Logo – Displays logo screen
- BootFailSafe – Controls Safe mode as one option in the Startup Menu
- LoadTop – Controls loading Command.com at the top of conventional memory

◆ Control the logo screen that displays when loading Windows by storing your own BMP file in Logo.sys in the root directory.

◆ Win.com is loaded after IO.SYS loads and is responsible for loading the real mode core components of Windows 9x.

◆ Vmm32.vxd creates virtual machines, loads static VXDs named in the registry and System.ini, and then shifts the operating system to protected mode.

◆ The Configuration Manager loads Plug-and-Play dynamic device drivers (VxDs). Next in the boot process, the Kernel, GDI, and User core components are loaded, and the shell and desktop are built.

◆ In Windows 9x, DOS-like commands can be entered at a command line prompt similar to the DOS prompt. The program Command.com is executed that provides the prompt in a "DOS box."

◆ Windows NT and Windows 2000 use Boot.ini, which is stored in the root directory of the startup disk, to provide boot parameters that include the ability to customize a dual boot.

OBJECTIVES ON THE JOB

When supporting an OS, the PC technician must know how system files are used, where they are located, and the symptoms of a corrupted file. A technician must also know how to change these files as the hardware, software, and user needs change.

PRACTICE TEST QUESTIONS

1. **Which entry in the Msdos.sys file in Windows 98 controls the function keys during startup?**
    a. BootFunction
    b. BootKeys
    c. FunctionKeys
    d. BootDelay

    ANSWER

2. **Which program file executes to provide a command line prompt in Windows 95?**
    a. Command.sys
    b. Command.com
    c. Prompt.sys
    d. Config.sys

    ANSWER

3. **Which operating system uses the text file Boot.ini to control the boot process?**
    a. Windows 95
    b. DOS
    c. Windows NT
    d. Windows 98

    ANSWER

4. **Where is the file located that contains the logo screen that displays when loading Windows 9x?**
    a. \Windows
    b. \Windows\Logo
    c. Root directory
    d. \Windows\System

    ANSWER

5. **What software can be used to edit the Windows file Msdos.sys?**
    a. Notepad
    b. EDIT.COM
    c. SYSEDIT
    d. all of the above

    ANSWER

6. **Which Windows 9x system file is responsible for loading the real mode core components of Windows 9x?**
    a. Win.com
    b. Msdos.sys
    c. IO.SYS
    d. Command.com

    ANSWER

7. **Where is Boot.ini stored?**
    a. \Windows\System
    b. Root directory
    c. \Windows
    d. \DOS

    ANSWER

1.1
cont. Identify the operating system's functions, structure, and major system files to navigate the operating system and how to get to needed technical information

MAJOR SYSTEM FILES: WHAT THEY ARE, WHERE THEY ARE LOCATED, HOW THEY ARE USED AND WHAT THEY CONTAIN: MEMORY MANAGEMENT: CONVENTIONAL • EXTENDED/UPPER MEMORY • HIGH MEMORY

UNDERSTANDING THE OBJECTIVE

Memory addresses are divided into conventional, upper, and extended memory. For DOS, the memory device driver HIMEM.SYS must be used to gain access to upper and extended memory. Windows 9x automatically uses HIMEM.SYS for this purpose. Memory addresses are considered to be a system resource needed by the operating system, device drivers, and applications software. Physical memory is RAM stored on SIMMs, DIMMs or RIMMs installed on the system board, and memory addresses are the numbers assigned to memory so that the CPU can access it.

WHAT YOU **REALLY** NEED TO KNOW

◆ Know the details of the following map of memory addresses:

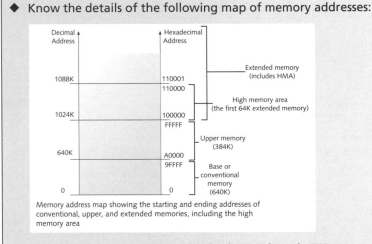

Memory address map showing the starting and ending addresses of conventional, upper, and extended memories, including the high memory area

◆ For real-mode device drivers and other real-mode TSRs to use upper memory, HIMEM.SYS and EMM386.EXE must have been loaded from CONFIG.SYS during the boot process.

◆ Part of system BIOS is stored in the F range of upper memory.

◆ The high memory area (HMA) is the first 64K of extended memory that is used to hold a portion of DOS or Windows. Putting DOS in this high memory area is called loading DOS high.

OBJECTIVES ON THE JOB

Managing memory requires understanding the different areas of the memory map, how each is used, and how to access each area for use by device drivers, the operating system, and applications. Occasionally, a PC technician is expected to create a DOS environment for a legacy DOS application. You must be able to load device drivers in upper memory to conserve conventional memory for these applications. Generally, it is better to run a DOS application in a DOS box under Windows rather than boot into a real-mode DOS environment because you can use 32-bit disk access, protected mode drivers, and VCACHE which can improve performance. Some legacy applications, however, will not run in a DOS box and require MS-DOS mode.

PRACTICE TEST QUESTIONS

1. **What command do you use to load DOS into the high memory area?**
   a. DEVICE=DOS
   b. DEVICEHIGH=DOS
   c. DOS=HIGH
   d. DOS=UMB

   ANSWER

2. **What command do you use to load a device driver into an upper memory block?**
   a. LOADHIGH
   b. DEVICEHIGH=
   c. DEVICE=
   d. DOS=UMB

   ANSWER

3. **What area of memory is known as extended memory?**
   a. memory above 640K
   b. memory above 1024K
   c. memory that is contained on a SIMM module
   d. memory between 640K and 1024K

   ANSWER

4. **When running a legacy DOS application, what is an advantage to running the application in MS-DOS mode rather than in a DOS box under Windows?**
   a. the application uses fewer system resources when run in MS-DOS mode
   b. the application generally runs faster
   c. the application might not function properly under a DOS box in Windows
   d. you have the added advantage of using 32-bit disk access when running in MS-DOS mode

   ANSWER

5. **What is true when running a DOS application in a DOS box under Windows 9x?**
   a. protected mode device drivers can be used
   b. all drivers must be run in real mode
   c. 32-bit disk access must be disabled
   d. conventional memory is not available to the application

   ANSWER

6. **What command can you use to determine if DOS loaded high?**
   a. MEMMAKER
   b. MEM
   c. DIR
   d. CHKDSK

   ANSWER

7. **What programs can use upper memory addresses without any special memory management software?**
   a. BIOS program
   b. device drivers
   c. TSRs
   d. DOS command files

   ANSWER

Identify the operating system's functions, structure, and major system files to navigate the operating system and how to get to needed technical information

MAJOR SYSTEM FILES: WHAT THEY ARE, WHERE THEY ARE LOCATED, HOW THEY ARE USED AND WHAT THEY CONTAIN: MEMORY MANAGEMENT: VIRTUAL MEMORY

UNDERSTANDING THE OBJECTIVE

Virtual memory is created by a file on the hard drive called a swap file, and this file acts like memory. Virtual memory results in a net increase in memory addresses available for the OS and applications, but is slower than regular memory.

WHAT YOU **REALLY** NEED TO KNOW

- ◆ Swap files are generally stored in the root directory of the hard drive where Windows is installed and are hidden, read-only system files.
- ◆ The Windows 9x swap file is dynamic, meaning that it can increase and decrease in size as needed. It can also be fragmented over the hard drive without a significant performance loss, and can reside on a compressed drive.
- ◆ Provide plenty of hard drive space so that the swap file has room to grow.
- ◆ Windows 9x manages the swap file for you; you shouldn't need to change virtual memory settings.
- ◆ In Windows 9x, to view virtual memory settings, choose Start, Settings, Control Panel, System, Performance, and then Virtual Memory. In this dialog box, you should usually select the "Let Windows manage my virtual memory settings" option.
- ◆ In the Virtual Memory dialog box for Windows 9x, you can specify the location of the swap file.
- ◆ Disk thrashing results when the Virtual Memory Manager (VMM) moves data in and out of virtual memory at an excessive rate and can result in slow system performance and can even cause premature hard drive failure.
- ◆ The opposite of virtual memory is a RAM drive in which part of extended memory is set up to act like a hard drive and is assigned a drive letter.
- ◆ The Windows NT and Windows 2000 swap file is named Pagefile.sys, and the Windows 9x swap file is named Win386.swp.

OBJECTIVES ON THE JOB

Virtual memory is an essential method of memory management. Windows 9x and Windows 2000 can manage their own swap files without a technician's intervention. Allow plenty of extra room on a hard drive so the swap file can increase in size as needed.

PRACTICE TEST QUESTIONS

1. **The name of the temporary swap file in Windows 98 is:**
   a. SWAP.FLE
   b. WIN386.SWP
   c. 386SPART.PAR
   d. WIN.COM

2. **Which statement about the Windows 95 methods of managing virtual memory is true?**
   a. The swap file is always a temporary version.
   b. The swap file is always stored in the root directory of the hard drive where Windows is installed.
   c. The name of the swap file is SWAP.SWP.
   d. The location of the swap file can be changed by the user.

3. **What is the purpose of a swap file?**
   a. to provide virtual memory which increases the overall memory addresses available for use
   b. to increase the amount of usable space on a hard drive
   c. to improve system performance by storing the operating system in RAM rather than on the hard drive
   d. to create a virtual hard drive in RAM which an application can use to store data

4. **Which operating system does not use virtual memory?**
   a. Windows 2000
   b. DOS
   c. Windows 95
   d. Windows NT

5. **Conceptually, the opposite of virtual memory is:**
   a. a RAM drive
   b. a swap file
   c. a compressed drive
   d. a hard disk cache

6. **What is the name of the Windows 2000 swap file?**
   a. 386SPART.PAR
   b. WIN386.SWP
   c. SWAP.FLE
   d. Pagefile.sys

7. **In Windows 95, how can you change the location of the swap file?**
   a. On the Control Panel, select System, Performance, and then Virtual Memory.
   b. On the Control Panel, select 386 Enhanced Mode.
   c. Select Start, Programs, Accessories, System Tools, and then Memory.
   d. You cannot change the location of the swap file in Windows 95.

OBJECTIVES

1.1
cont.
Identify the operating system's functions, structure, and major system files to navigate the operating system and how to get to needed technical information

MAJOR SYSTEM FILES: WHAT THEY ARE, WHERE THEY ARE LOCATED, HOW THEY ARE USED AND WHAT THEY CONTAIN: MEMORY MANAGEMENT: HIMEM.SYS, EMM386.EXE • WINDOWS 9X: COMMAND.COM, RUN COMMAND, SETVER.EXE, DOSSTART.BAT

UNDERSTANDING THE OBJECTIVE

Some system files are essential and some are optional. EMM386.EXE and HIMEM.SYS are used to manage the hardware resource, memory. Himem.sys is required by Windows 9x, but Emm386.exe is optional. Legacy DOS applications can run under a virtual DOS machine in Windows 9x, and DOS commands can be executed from a command prompt provided by Command.com.

WHAT YOU **REALLY** NEED TO KNOW

◆ DOS does not let device drivers and applications access memory above 640K unless DOS extensions (HIMEM.SYS and EMM386.EXE) are executed to manage this memory.

◆ HIMEM.SYS is a device driver that accesses and manages memory above 640K. Windows automatically loads Himem.sys, but for DOS, it must be loaded from CONFIG.SYS.

◆ EMM386.EXE makes upper memory blocks (UMBs) available to legacy device drivers and other TSRs and can emulate expanded memory by causing some extended memory to act like expanded memory.

◆ The command in CONFIG.SYS for EMM386.EXE to make UMBs available without creating emulated expanded memory is DEVICE=C:\DOS\EMM386.EXE NOEMS.

◆ Emm386.exe is not automatically loaded by Windows 9x, therefore, if Emm386.exe is needed, it must be manually loaded from Config.sys.

◆ COMMAND.COM is the command interpreter for DOS and Windows 9x. Under Windows, it provides a command prompt in a DOS box or virtual DOS machine.

◆ In DOS, internal DOS commands (DIR, for example) are included in COMMAND.COM and are loaded into memory when COMMAND.COM loads during booting.

◆ In DOS, external DOS commands are stored in individual program files found in the DOS directory of the hard drive (FORMAT.COM, for example) and are loaded into memory when the program is first required by the user.

◆ In Windows 9x, click Start, Run to access the Run dialog box. From it, you can execute a command to evoke either a 32-bit or 16-bit program.

◆ Batch files have a .BAT file extension and contain DOS commands executed as a group. Put the batch file name in AUTOEXEC.BAT to run the batch file at startup.

◆ When running Windows 95 from a command prompt, to run existing CD-ROM drivers, execute the Windows utility DOSStart.bat.

◆ Setver.exe is available under Windows for backward compatibility with legacy applications that require a specific version of DOS to run.

OBJECTIVES ON THE JOB

A PC technician is often called on to configure an OS to accommodate the needs of application software and to troubleshoot problems with the OS. Many situations still require legacy 16-bit applications to run under Windows. A technician must know how to configure a virtual DOS machine environment to accommodate these applications.

1. **Which Windows file holds settings for several DOS applications to be run under Windows?**
    - a. DOSStart.bat
    - b. Apps.inf
    - c. Autoexec.bat
    - d. Legacy.inf

2. **The purpose of HIMEM.SYS is:**
    - a. to allow access to extended memory
    - b. to emulate expanded memory
    - c. to load DOS high
    - d. to create virtual memory

3. **The purpose of EMM386.EXE is:**
    - a. to allow access to extended memory
    - b. to emulate expanded memory
    - c. to allow programs to use upper memory blocks
    - d. both b and c

4. **Where in memory are upper memory blocks located?**
    - a. between 640K and 1024K
    - b. above 1024K in extended memory
    - c. below 640K
    - d. in conventional memory

ANSWER

5. **The executable program that accommodates legacy DOS applications that require a specific version of DOS is:**
    - a. Autoexec.bat
    - b. Setver.exe
    - c. Config.sys
    - d. Version.exe

ANSWER

6. **What are the steps to access the Run command?**
    - a. Click Start, Accessories, Command
    - b. Click Start, Programs, MS-DOS
    - c. Click Start, Run
    - d. Right-click the taskbar and select Run

7. **The location of the Windows file Apps.inf is:**
    - a. the root directory
    - b. \Windows
    - c. \Windows\Inf
    - d. \Windows\System

OBJECTIVES

1.1
cont.
Identify the operating system's functions, structure, and major system files to navigate the operating system and how to get to needed technical information.

MAJOR SYSTEM FILES: WHAT THEY ARE, WHERE THEY ARE LOCATED, HOW THEY ARE USED AND WHAT THEY CONTAIN: WINDOWS 9X: IO.SYS • WIN.INI • SYSEDIT • SYSTEM.INI • MSCONFIG (98) • SMARTDRV.EXE • DRIVESPACE

UNDERSTANDING THE OBJECTIVE

Windows 9x requires a core group of system files to load beginning with IO.SYS. Most Windows configuration information is stored in the registry, but some can be stored in Win.ini and System.ini. The Windows System Configuration Utility (Msconfig.exe) can edit these files and other startup parameters to make it easier to change the startup environment when diagnosing a Windows problem. Also, utilities to manage a hard drive include Smartdrv.exe and Drivespace.

WHAT YOU **REALLY** NEED TO KNOW

- ◆ When the BIOS loads Windows 9x, the boot record program first searches for and loads IO.SYS, a hidden file stored in the root directory of the boot device.
- ◆ Use the System Configuration Utility (Msconfig.exe in the \Windows\System folder) to change the Windows 98 startup environment. It provides a GUI to edit Config.sys, System.ini, the registry and Win.ini. It can also enable or disable the loading of certain device drivers and software.
- ◆ To access the System Configuration Manager, click Start, Programs, Accessories, System Tools, System Information. From the Tools menu, click System Configuration Utility.
- ◆ The six tabs on the System Configuration Utility window are General, Config.sys, Autoexec.bat, System.ini, Win.ini, and Startup.
- ◆ Use the Sysedit.exe text editor in the \Windows\System folder to edit these and other text files: Autoexec.bat, Config.sys, Win.ini, System.ini, and Protocol.ini.
- ◆ DOS and Windows 3.x used a legacy 16-bit disk drive cache called SmartDrive (Smartdrv.exe). You might still need to use SmartDrive when troubleshooting a system and you have booted from a floppy disk. In that case, run SmartDrive to speed up 16-bit disk access.
- ◆ Windows 9x uses the 32-bit disk drive cache called VCACHE which automatically loads when Windows starts up. VCACHE replaces SmartDrive.
- ◆ Use Windows 9x DriveSpace to compress a hard drive. Click Start, Programs, Accessories, System Tools, DriveSpace. DriveSpace does not support FAT32.

OBJECTIVES ON THE JOB

Supporting Windows 9x requires an understanding of how the OS is loaded, how device drivers are referenced and loaded, and the differences between real-mode and protected-mode components of the OS. You must also know how to alter the Windows startup process when troubleshooting a problem. By eliminating elements of the startup, you can isolate the source of the problem.

PRACTICE TEST QUESTIONS

1. Which of the following Windows 9x system files is a text file?

    a. IO.SYS

    b. VMM32.VXD

    c. MSDOS.SYS

    d. COMMAND.COM

2. To function properly under Windows 9x, a Plug and Play device requires:

    a. that system BIOS be Plug and Play

    b. a 32-bit VxD driver

    c. that CMOS setup reserve the IRQ needed by the device

    d. that the device already be installed at the time Windows 9x is installed

3. If CONFIG.SYS is present when Windows 9x loads:

    a. it will be ignored because Windows 9x does not support CONFIG.SYS

    b. all device drivers listed in it are loaded except HIMEM.SYS

    c. it will be executed even though CONFIG.SYS is not a required Windows 9x file

    d. none of the above

4. How are device drivers loaded under Windows 9x?

    a. from CONFIG.SYS

    b. from SYSTEM.INI

    c. from the registry

    d. all of the above

5. What is one thing that Msconfig.exe can do?

    a. restore a corrupted registry

    b. disable a device driver at startup

    c. disable or enable a startup parameter for an application

    d. all of the above

6. When is it appropriate to use SmartDrive on a Windows system?

    a. at all times in order to speed up disk access

    b. when VCACHE is not loaded during Windows startup

    c. when there is more than one hard drive on a system

    d. when you are booting to a DOS prompt from a floppy disk

7. What is one limitation of DriveSpace under Windows 9x?

    a. it does not support FAT32

    b. it cannot be used if VCACHE is enabled

    c. it is a legacy Windows 3.x utility and is slow to execute

    d. it must be executed from Autoexec.bat

Identify the operating system's functions, structure, and major system files to navigate the operating system and how to get to needed technical information

MAJOR SYSTEM FILES: WHAT THEY ARE, WHERE THEY ARE LOCATED, HOW THEY ARE USED AND WHAT THEY CONTAIN: WINDOWS 9X: REGEDIT.EXE • SYSTEM.DAT • USER.DAT

UNDERSTANDING THE OBJECTIVE

Windows 9x stores most configuration information in the registry, a hierarchical database with a tree structure. The registry is most often changed when you use the Control Panel to modify settings or when you install hardware or software, but you can also manually edit the registry using the editor REGEDIT.EXE. The registry is stored in two files in the \Windows folder.

WHAT YOU **REALLY** NEED TO KNOW

◆ The Windows 9x registry is stored in two files, System.dat and User.dat. The OS keeps a backup copy of each file under System.da0 and User.da0.

◆ During booting, if the OS cannot find the registry files, or if they are corrupt, it reverts to SYSTEM.DA0 and USER.DA0.

◆ During booting, if the OS detects a corrupted registry, it boots into Safe Mode and asks if you want to restore from backup. If you respond with Yes, it reverts to SYSTEM.DA0 and USER.DA0.

◆ To manually edit the registry, first back up the two files, SYSTEM.DAT and USER.DAT, and then type Regedit in the Run dialog box.

◆ Windows 98 includes Registry Checker that backs up, verifies, and recovers the registry. (From the Start menu, choose Programs, Accessories, System Tools, System Information, Tools, and then Registry Checker.)

◆ The registry is divided into six major keys or branches. Keys contain subkeys, which contain values. The six major keys are listed below.

Key	Description
HKEY_CLASSES_ROOT	Contains information about file associations and OLE data. (This branch of the tree is a mirror of HKEY_LOCAL_MACHINE\ Software\Classes.)
HKEY_USERS	Includes user preferences, including desktop configuration and network connections.
HKEY_CURRENT_USER	If there is only one user of the system, this is a duplicate of HKEY_USERS, but for a multi-user system, this key contains information about the current user preferences.
HKEY_LOCAL_MACHINE	Contains information about hardware and installed software.
HKEY_CURRENT_CONFIG	Contains the same information in HKEY_LOCAL_MACHINE\ Config and has information about printers and display fonts.
HKEY_DYN_DATA	Keeps information about Windows performance and Plug-and-Play information.

OBJECTIVES ON THE JOB

A PC technician is expected to know how to recover from a corrupted or deleted registry and how to manually edit the registry.

PRACTICE TEST QUESTIONS

1. **What are the two Windows 9x registry back-up files?**
   a. SYSTEM.DAT and USER.DAT
   b. REGEDIT.EXE and REGISTRY.SYS
   c. AUTOEXEC.BAT and CONFIG.SYS
   d. SYSTEM.DA0 and USER.DA0

   ANSWER

2. **What program do you execute when you want to edit the Windows 95 registry?**
   a. SYSTEM.DAT
   b. SYSEDIT.EXE
   c. REGEDIT.EXE
   d. WIN.COM

   ANSWER

3. **Which registry key stores current information about hardware and installed software?**
   a. HKEY_USERS
   b. HKEY_CURRENT_USER
   c. HKEY_LOCAL_MACHINE
   d. HKEY_DYN_DATA

   ANSWER

4. **How many major branches or keys are there in the Windows 9x registry?**
   a. 10
   b. 5
   c. 4
   d. 6

   ANSWER

5. **What are the names of the Windows 9x registry files?**
   a. SYSTEM.INI and WIN.INI
   b. WIN.COM and COMMAND.COM
   c. SYSTEM.DAT and USER.DAT
   d. SYSTEM.DA0 and USER.DA0

   ANSWER

6. **What is one reason that Windows 9x supports using SYSTEM.INI and WIN.INI during the boot process?**
   a. These files can support 16-bit programs that can't use the Windows registry.
   b. The only way Windows 95 can load HIMEM.SYS is through SYSTEM.INI.
   c. Windows 9x depends on real-mode device drivers to operate Plug and Play devices.
   d. none of the above; Windows 9x does not support SYSTEM.INI and WIN.INI.

   ANSWER

7. **Most configuration information for Windows 9x is stored in:**
   a. SYSTEM.INI and WIN.INI
   b. the registry
   c. VMM32.VXD
   d. none of the above

   ANSWER

1.1
cont.

Identify the operating system's functions, structure, and major system files to navigate the operating system and how to get to needed technical information

MAJOR SYSTEM FILES: WHAT THEY ARE, WHERE THEY ARE LOCATED, HOW THEY ARE USED AND WHAT THEY CONTAIN: WINDOWS 2000: COMPUTER MANAGEMENT • REGEDIT32 • REGEDIT

UNDERSTANDING THE OBJECTIVE

Windows 2000 and Windows NT store most configuration information in a registry which is built differently from the Windows 9x registry. Computer Management is a Windows 2000 console that contains several problem solving utilities in a single, easily accessed location. Also, the Windows 2000 boot process can be controlled by entries in the text file, Boot.ini.

WHAT YOU **REALLY** NEED TO KNOW

◆ The Windows NT and Windows 2000 registry is a hierarchical database containing all the hardware, software, device drivers, network protocols, and user configuration information needed by the OS and applications.

◆ The registry is logically organized into five keys or subtrees:
  - HKEY_CURRENT_USER – contains information about the currently logged-on user HKEY_CLASSES_ROOT – contains information about software and software configuration
  - HKEY_CURRENT_CONFIG – contains information about the active hardware configuration
  - HKEY_USERS – contains information used to build the logon screen and the ID of the current user
  - HKEY_LOCAL_MACHINE – contains all information about the computer including device drivers

◆ The keys that change depending on the user currently logged on are the HKEY_CURRENT_USER and HKEY_CURRENT_CONFIG.

◆ Windows 2000 uses two registry editors: Regedt32.exe which shows each key in a separate window, and Regedit.exe, which shows all keys in the same window. Microsoft recommends you use Regedt32.exe.

◆ To backup the Windows NT registry, use Rdisk.exe, which creates an emergency repair disk and also copies the registry files (called hives) to *winnt_root*\repair folder.

◆ To back up the Windows 2000 registry and other critical system files, use the Backup utility. Click Start, Programs, Accessories, System Tools, Backup.

◆ To access the Windows 2000 Computer Management console, click Start, Programs, Administrative Tools, Computer Management. From it you can monitor problems with hardware, software, and security. You can share folders, view device configurations, add new device drivers, start and stop services, and manage server applications.

◆ A Windows 2000 console is a window that contains applets or applications called snap-ins in an easy-to-access, single location.

OBJECTIVES ON THE JOB

Supporting Windows NT and Windows 2000 requires that a PC technician understand how the registry is organized, how to edit and back it up, and how to affect the boot process when troubleshooting. Computer Management is only one tool that can help when managing a Windows 2000 system and troubleshooting problems with the system.

PRACTICE TEST QUESTIONS

1. **What are the files that hold the Windows NT registry called?**
   - a. registry files
   - b. hives
   - c. system files
   - d. tree files

   ANSWER

2. **Which program is the best one to use to edit the Windows NT registry?**
   - a. Regedt32.exe
   - b. Sysedit.exe
   - c. Regedit.exe
   - d. Word for Windows

   ANSWER

3. **Which Windows 2000 registry key stores information about hardware and installed software and does not change when a new user logs on?**
   - a. HKEY_USERS
   - b. HKEY_CURRENT_USER
   - c. HKEY_LOCAL_MACHINE
   - d. HKEY_CLASSES_ROOT

   ANSWER

4. **How many major branches or keys are there in the Windows NT registry?**
   - a. 10
   - b. 5
   - c. 4
   - d. 6

   ANSWER

5. **Where is the Windows 2000 registry located?**
   - a. \Winnt\System32\config
   - b. \Winnt\System
   - c. \Winnt\System32
   - d. \Winnt\Profiles

   ANSWER

6. **What utility do you use to back up the Windows NT registry?**
   - a. Rdisk.exe
   - b. Regedit.exe
   - c. Device Manager
   - d. Windows Explorer

   ANSWER

7. **How do you back up the Windows 2000 registry?**
   - a. Click Start, Programs, Accessories, System Tools, Backup
   - b. Click Start, Programs, Administrative Tools, Backup
   - c. Click Start, Settings, Control Panel, Backup
   - d. Click Start, Programs, Accessories, Backup

   ANSWER

1.1
cont.
Identify the operating system's functions, structure, and major system files to navigate the operating system and how to get to needed technical information

MAJOR SYSTEM FILES: WHAT THEY ARE, WHERE THEY ARE LOCATED, HOW THEY ARE USED AND WHAT THEY CONTAIN: WINDOWS 2000: BOOT.INI • RUN CMD • NTLDR • NTDETECT.COM • NTBOOTDD.SYS

UNDERSTANDING THE OBJECTIVE

Windows 2000 and Windows NT use the same boot process. Know the files needed to success-fully boot Windows and the purpose of each file. Also, the Windows 2000 and Windows NT boot process can be controlled by entries in the text file, Boot.ini.

WHAT YOU **REALLY** NEED TO KNOW

- ◆ The files needed to successfully boot Windows NT and Windows 2000 include Ntldr, Boot.ini, Bootsect.dos, Ntdetect.com, Ntbootdd.sys (used only with a SCSI boot device), Ntoskrnl.exe, Hal.dll, System, and device drivers.
- ◆ The Bootsect.dos file contains information from the partition table of the hard drive. This file is custom built for this system and cannot be copied to another system.
- ◆ The Boot.ini file is a text file that can be used to control a dual boot and multiple proces-sors on the same system.
- ◆ The main steps in the Windows NT and Windows 2000 boot process are:
  - System BIOS performs POST and then turns to the MBR on the hard drive for an OS.
  - The MBR looks to the bootstrap loader program in the boot sector of the active partition. The bootstrap loader program executes Ntldr, the Windows 2000/NT boot loader program.
  - Ntldr reads Boot.ini and provides a boot loader menu for a dual booting system, if so indicated by the entries in the Boot.ini text file.
  - Ntldr executes NTdetect.com to detect and configure the hardware present, reads information from the registry about device drivers, and loads them.
  - Ntldr loads the Windows 2000 kernel, including the Hal.dll and Ntoskrnl.exe files, and passes control to Ntoskrnl.exe, the kernel-controlling module.
- ◆ To access a Windows 2000 command line window, click Start, Run, and enter CMD in the Run dialog box. CMD.exe is a 32-bit command-line interpreter.

OBJECTIVES ON THE JOB

A PC technician needs to understand the boot process to troubleshoot problems when they arise. The Boot.ini file is a text file that can be edited to control part of the boot process. Use it to create a dual boot with Windows NT or Windows 2000 and another operating system such as Windows 98 or DOS.

PRACTICE TEST QUESTIONS

1. Where is the Ntldr file located?
- a. Root directory of the system partition
- b. \Winnt\System32 folder
- c. \Winnt folder
- d. \Winnt\Boot folder

2. Which file is only used in the Windows 2000 boot process when a SCSI boot device is used?
- a. Ntldr
- b. Scsi.sys
- c. Ntbootdd.sys
- d. Hal.dll

3. Which of the following is a hidden text file?
- a. Ntldr
- b. Boot.ini
- c. Ntdetect.com
- d. System.sys

ANSWER

4. Which Windows 2000 file is responsible for most of the booting process?
- a. Ntdetect.com
- b. Ntldr
- c. Boot.ini
- d. IO.SYS

ANSWER

5. Which two files are used to create most of the Windows NT kernel?
- a. IO.SYS and MSDOS.SYS
- b. Ntldr and NtDetect.com
- c. SYSTEM.DAT and USER.DAT
- d. Hal.dll and Ntoskrnl.exe

6. How can you attain a Windows 2000 command line prompt?
- a. Click Start, Run and enter CMD in the Run dialog box
- b. Click Start, Programs, Accessories, Command Prompt
- c. Click Start, Command Prompt
- d. Either a or b

7. Which Windows 2000 component is responsible for loading device drivers at startup?
- a. NTDetect.com
- b. Hal.dll
- c. Ntoskrnl.exe
- d. Ntldr

ANSWER

1.1
cont.
Identify the operating system's functions, structure, and major system files to navigate the operating system and how to get to needed technical information

MAJOR SYSTEM FILES: WHAT THEY ARE, WHERE THEY ARE LOCATED, HOW THEY ARE USED AND WHAT THEY CONTAIN: COMMAND PROMPT PROCEDURES (COMMAND SYNTAX): DIR, ATTRIB, VER, MEM, SCANDISK, DEFRAG, EDIT, XCOPY, COPY, FORMAT, FDISK, MSCDEX, SETVER, SCANREG

UNDERSTANDING THE OBJECTIVE

Even though DOS is a real mode operating system that does not support today's GUI, protected-mode applications, a PC technician needs DOS commands to recover a failed system or bring up a new hard drive. Because DOS is command driven, navigating requires knowledge of using commands and the parameters or switches each command supports.

WHAT YOU **REALLY** NEED TO KNOW

◆ The following is a list of the commands and common switches or parameters:

Command	Some Common Parameters or Switches
DIR	Displays a list of files and folders DIR/P – Displays one page at a time DIR l MORE – Displays one page or item at a time
ATTRIB	Displays or changes the read-only, archive, system, and hidden attributes of a file ATTRIB +H +R +S filename.ext – Sets the hidden, read-only, and system attribute to a file
VER	Displays the version of the operating system loaded
MEM	Displays a report of memory MEM /C l MORE – A complete MEM report paged to screen
SCANDISK	Examines a hard drive for errors and repairs them if possible SCANDISK /A – Scans and repairs all drives in the system SCANDISK C: /P – Displays problems found but does not repair them
DEFRAG	Examines a hard drive for fragmented files and rewrites them in contiguous clusters DEFRAG C: /S:N – Arranges files in alphabetical order by filename
EDIT	Opens a full-screen text editor EDIT filename.ext
XCOPY	Copies directories, their subdirectories, and files (not including hidden files) XCOPY A:*.* C:\DOS /S – Copies all files to DOS folder on hard drive including subdirectories
COPY	Same as XCOPY but does not include subdirectories
FORMAT	Formats a floppy disk or hard drive FORMAT C: /S – Formats a hard drive and writes system files on the drive, making it bootable
MSCDEX	Supports a CD-ROM drive when booting from a floppy disk. MSCDEX is a real mode extender that requires a driver be loaded from Config.sys. In the command below, MYTAG points to that driver. MSCDEX.EXE /D:MYTAG/L:E /M:10 – Use drive letter E and 10 memory buffers
SETVER	Fixes a problem with legacy DOS applications that require a certain version of DOS
SCANREG	Restores or repairs the registry using backups that Registry Checker creates each day. ScanReg /Restore – Restores the registry from backup ScanReg /Fix – Repairs a corrupted registry ScanReg /Opt – Optimizes the registry by deleting unused entries

OBJECTIVES ON THE JOB

Using DOS commands to solve problems is an essential skill of a PC technician, who should be comfortable with all the commands mentioned above.

PRACTICE TEST QUESTIONS

1. **Which command can make a file a hidden system file?**
   - a. SYS
   - b. ATTRIB
   - c. MEM
   - d. VER

2. **What is the purpose of the /C switch in the MEM command (MEM /C)?**
   - a. Saves a memory report to drive C
   - b. Displays a complete report
   - c. Pages the report one screen at a time
   - d. Displays the current memory status

3. **What command scans and repairs errors on a hard drive?**
   - a. SCANREG
   - b. SCANDISK
   - c. DEFRAG
   - d. FORMAT C: /S

   ANSWER

4. **What is a text editor that can be used to edit a text file?**
   - a. EDIT
   - b. WordPad
   - c. NotePad
   - d. all the above

   ANSWER

5. **Which command copies files including files in the subdirectories of the current folder?**
   - a. COPY
   - b. TREE
   - c. EDIT
   - d. XCOPY

   ANSWER

6. **What is the purpose of the SETVER command?**
   - a. Tells a DOS application that the correct version of DOS is running
   - b. Sets the Windows 98 version that will run the application correctly
   - c. Sets the parameters that allows the application to access the hard drive
   - d. none of the above

   ANSWER

7. **Which command lets you access a CD-ROM drive during a DOS session?**
   - a. MSCDEX
   - b. SETVER
   - c. SCANREG
   - d. CDROM.EXE

Identify basic concepts and procedures for creating, viewing and managing files, directories and disks. This includes procedures for changing file attributes and the ramifications of those changes (for example, security issues)

FILE ATTRIBUTES • READ ONLY, HIDDEN, SYSTEM, AND ARCHIVE ATTRIBUTES

UNDERSTANDING THE OBJECTIVE

This objective involves the details of managing files and directories. You should understand the concepts of file attributes as well as the commands that manage them and when and how to use these commands.

WHAT YOU **REALLY** NEED TO KNOW

◆ The attributes assigned to a file are stored in the directory entry for the file. Using the FAT file system, the attributes are stored in an 8-bit byte called the attribute byte.

◆ The attribute byte contains an on/off setting for each of the file attributes. Each file attribute can be set by changing the specific file attribute to on (logical '1') or off (logical '0'). The specific file attributes are hidden, system, archive, and read-only.

◆ A hidden file is not seen or accessed with many DOS commands, such as DIR.

◆ The archive bit is used by the DOS BACKUP command or other third-party backup software to know to back up the file because it has changed since the last backup. If the archive bit is set to on, the backup software knows that the file has been created or modified since the last backup and includes the file during a backup procedure. Some types of backups reset the archive bit at the end of the backup process.

◆ In DOS the file attributes are changed using the ATTRIB command, as in the following examples.
  - ATTRIB +R –H MYFILE.TXT Makes the file a read-only file and removes the hidden status on the file.
  - ATTRIB -A MYFILE.TXT Turns the archive bit off.

◆ For Windows 9x, Windows NT and Windows 2000, change file attributes using the file Properties dialog box.

◆ To help protect a file from damage by the user, set the file attributes of the file to hidden, read-only.

◆ In order to see hidden files such as IO.SYS or MSDOS.SYS, use the /AH switch on the DIR command. For example, to see hidden files in the root directory of drive C, use this command: DIR C:*.* /AH.

◆ In Windows 9x, before you can edit MSDOS.SYS, you must make the file available for editing. Use this command: ATTRIB -R -H -S MSDOS.SYS.

OBJECTIVES ON THE JOB

A PC technician is expected to understand the meaning and purpose of each of the file attributes and use commands in DOS and Windows to change these attributes as appropriate to service or troubleshoot a PC.

PRACTICE TEST QUESTIONS

1. What command can make a file read-only?
   a. READONLY
   b. ATTRIB
   c. COPY
   d. DIR

2. Which of the following is a hidden file?
   a. WIN.COM
   b. AUTOEXEC.BAT
   c. SYSTEM.DAT
   d. REGEDIT.EXE

3. What is the result of the ATTRIB -R MYFILE.TXT command?
   a. The file MYFILE.TXT cannot be edited.
   b. The file MYFILE.TXT can be edited.
   c. The file MYFILE.TXT is erased.
   d. The file MYFILE.TXT is not affected.

4. What is the command to hide AUTOEXEC.BAT?
   a. ATTRIB +H AUTOEXEC.BAT
   b. HIDE AUTOEXEC.BAT
   c. UNERASE AUTOEXEC.BAT
   d. ATTRIB -H AUTOEXEC.BAT

ANSWER

5. Before you edit the registry files, what must you do?
   a. Use ATTRIB to show the hidden files and then use COPY to back them up.
   b. Use XCOPY to back them up because it can copy hidden system files directly.
   c. First rename SYSTEM.DAT to SYSTEM.DA0 and rename USER.DAT to USER.DA0.
   d. Move the files to a new directory.

ANSWER

6. What in Windows 95 performs a function similar to the ATTRIB command in DOS?
   a. Regedit
   b. Scandisk
   c. a file's Properties dialog box
   d. a PIF file

ANSWER

7. What file attribute does the DOS BACKUP command use to determine if the file is to be backed up?
   a. the hidden status of the file
   b. the read-only status of the file
   c. the archive bit of the file
   d. none of the above; BACKUP backs up all files it finds.

1.2
cont.

Identify basic concepts and procedures for creating, viewing and managing files, directories and disks. This includes procedures for changing file attributes and the ramifications of those changes (for example, security issues)

FILE NAMING CONVENTIONS (MOST COMMAND EXTENSIONS) • WINDOWS 2000 COMPRESS, ENCRYPT • IDE/SCSI • INTERNAL/EXTERNAL • BACKUP/RESTORE

UNDERSTANDING THE OBJECTIVE

Windows 95 introduced long filenames. To maintain backward compatibility, each file having a long filename is also assigned a DOS filename. When using DOS commands or DOS-like commands in Windows 9x, the syntax of the command line is crucial. Know the rules and how to read documentation that gives you the specific information for each command. In addition, Windows 2000 offers several tools to compress and encrypt files.

WHAT YOU **REALLY** NEED TO KNOW

- ◆ DOS files consist of two parts: a filename, which is required, and a file extension, which is optional but strongly recommended.
- ◆ DOS filenames must have one to eight characters with no spaces or punctuation in the filename. The file extension can have up to three characters.
- ◆ Windows 9x uses long filenames that can contain up to 255 characters. Know how these names are converted to DOS 8-character and 3-character filename formats for backward compatibility.
- ◆ When adding parameters or optional switches to the end of a command line, the parameter is usually preceded by a slash, as in FORMAT C: /S.
- ◆ Wildcard characters ? and * are allowed in DOS command lines to represent parts of filenames.
- ◆ In documentation, optional command line parameters or switches are included in brackets [ ].
- ◆ Use Windows Explorer to manage files, renaming, copying, deleting, and moving them.
- ◆ Using Windows 2000, run the Compress command in the Run dialog box to compress a file. Later, you can use the Expand.exe program to uncompress it.
- ◆ Windows 2000 has an Encrypting File System (EFS) that allows users to encrypt files on an NTFS file system volume.
- ◆ Use the utility program Ifsinfo.exe to display information about encrypted files.
- ◆ Some DOS commands are internal (included in the Command.com file) and others are external (stored in individual program files).
- ◆ Use the Scheduled Tasks icon in My Computer to schedule a routine backup under Windows 9x.
- ◆ To access the Windows 98 backup utility, click Start, Programs, Accessories, System Tools, Backup. If the utility is not showing in the menu list, install it from the Windows 98 CD using the Add/Remove Programs icon in Control Panel.

OBJECTIVES ON THE JOB

Servicing and troubleshooting a PC is impossible without a thorough working knowledge of command syntax and file naming conventions. As many users are concerned about security, supporting file compression and encryption is a common task expected of a technician. Also, making routine backups is something a technician must know how to set up and support those who are responsible for exchanging tape cartridges, Zip drives, or other backup storage media.

PRACTICE TEST QUESTIONS

1. **In DOS, what is the combined maximum number of characters a filename and file extension can have?**
    a. 8
    b. 3
    c. 11
    d. 255

ANSWER

2. **A file named My Long File Document in Windows 95 will be displayed in DOS as:**
    a. MYLONG~1
    b. MYLONG.FLE
    c. Mylongfiledocument.txt
    d. MY LONG1

ANSWER

3. **What is a valid file extension for DOS?**
    a. TXT
    b. T?T
    c. T*
    d. *

ANSWER

4. **What is the maximum number of characters allowed in a Windows 95 filename?**
    a. 8
    b. 255
    c. 1024
    d. 256

ANSWER

5. **Which file will be listed using this DIR command: DIR TA*.?**
    a. TAXES.TXT
    b. TAXES.T
    c. TA.TXT
    d. TAXES.TX

ANSWER

6. **In Windows 95, how do you format a floppy disk?**
    a. Go to Control Panel and double-click the System icon.
    b. In Explorer, right-click the floppy disk drive and select Format.
    c. In Explorer, select Tools on the menu bar, and then select Format.
    d. none of the above

ANSWER

7. **In Windows 2000, what is the utility that displays information about encrypted files?**
    a. NTFS
    b. Encrypt.exe
    c. Ifsinfo.exe
    d. Compress.exe

ANSWER

1.2
cont.

Identify basic concepts and procedures for creating, viewing and managing files, directories and disks. This includes procedures for changing file attributes and the ramifications of those changes (for example, security issues)

PARTITIONING/FORMATTING/FILE SYSTEM (FAT, FAT16, FAT32, NTFS4, NTFS5, HPFS)

UNDERSTANDING THE OBJECTIVE

Part of installing a hard drive involves installing an operating system, which includes installing a file system on the drive. DOS supports FAT16, and Windows 9x supports FAT16 and FAT32. Windows NT Version 4 supports NTFS4 and FAT16. Windows 2000 supports FAT16, FAT32, and NTFS. Either file system requires first partitioning and then formatting the drive.

WHAT YOU **REALLY** NEED TO KNOW

- ◆ The partition table at the very beginning of a hard drive (cylinder 0, track 0, sector 0) contains information about each partition on the drive, including what type of file system is used for the partition. The partition table also contains the master boot program called the boot strap loader.
- ◆ The High Performance File System (HPFS) used by OS/2 is not supported by Windows 9x, Windows NT, or Windows 2000.
- ◆ If a system uses the HPFS file system, you can convert it to an NTFS partition using Convert.exe utility.
- ◆ Windows 2000 can access an NTFS volume (NTFS4) created with Windows NT 4.0 or 3.51. Windows NT 4.0 with Service Pack 5 can access a Windows 2000 NTFS volume (NTFS5).
- ◆ With FAT file systems, the file allocation table (FAT) contains an entry for each cluster of the logical drive.
- ◆ Floppy drives use a 12-bit FAT (12 bits for each FAT entry, which equates to three hex numerals).
- ◆ For hard drives, DOS supports a 16-bit FAT and Windows 9x supports either FAT16 (16-bit FAT) or FAT32 (32-bit FAT).
- ◆ The OS considers a hard drive a group of logical drives. Each logical drive has a root directory and FAT.
- ◆ CHKDSK and DIR report the size of a hard drive as well as other information.
- ◆ FAT32 was introduced with Windows 95, Service Release 2 (Windows 95b or Windows 95 OSR2).
- ◆ Wasted space on a hard drive caused by unused entries at the end of a cluster is called **slack**. With FAT32, slack is reduced because the cluster size is smaller, which optimizes usable hard drive space.
- ◆ Formatting a logical drive writes the boot record to the first sector of the volume and creates a root directory and two copies of the FAT (1 copy of the FAT for floppy disks). Use the /S option to format and then write system files to the drive to make it bootable (example: FORMAT C: /S).

OBJECTIVES ON THE JOB

A PC technician must be able to install a hard drive. After the physical installation, the drive must be prepared for data and software. Partitioning, formatting, and installing software are essential steps in the process. A technician is also expected to make decisions about which file system to use and understand the consequences of these decisions.

PRACTICE TEST QUESTIONS

1. **For very large hard drives, which file system provides the smallest cluster size?**
    a. FAT12
    b. FAT16
    c. FAT32
    d. Choices a, b, and c all yield the same cluster size.

2. **Where is the boot strap loader located?**
    a. near the FAT on drive C:
    b. in the partition table sector
    c. at the very end of the hard drive, after all data
    d. in drive D:

3. **The master boot program is located at:**
    a. cylinder 1, track 1, sector 1
    b. cylinder 1, track 0, sector 0
    c. cylinder 0, track 0, sector 1
    d. cylinder 0, track 0, sector 0

4. **What are the functions of FDISK?**
    a. It creates the partition table.
    b. It displays partition table information.
    c. It creates partitions and logical drives.
    d. all of the above

5. **What file system is used by floppy disks?**
    a. FAT16
    b. FAT12
    c. FAT32
    d. FAT8

6. **Which file system is not supported by Windows NT?**
    a. FAT16
    b. FAT32
    c. NTFS
    d. none of the above; they are all supported by Windows NT

7. **What is the first Microsoft OS to support FAT32?**
    a. Windows 95, Release 1 (Windows 95a)
    b. Windows NT
    c. DOS version 6.0
    d. Windows 95, Release 2 (Windows 95b)

1.2
cont. Identify basic concepts and procedures for creating, viewing and managing files, directories and disks. This includes procedures for changing file attributes and the ramifications of those changes (for example, security issues)

WINDOWS-BASED UTILITIES: SCANDISK • DEFRAG.EXE • FDISK.EXE • SCANREG • ATTRIB.EXE • EXTRACT.EXE • EDIT.COM

UNDERSTANDING THE OBJECTIVE

The Windows utilities listed above are used to troubleshoot problems with the file system and Windows registry on a hard drive. These problems can appear in application software and the operating system, and may include errors during the boot process.

WHAT YOU **REALLY** NEED TO KNOW

- ◆ Use ATTRIB.EXE to display and change file attributes.
- ◆ Use EXTRACT.EXE to manage cabinet files. Windows 9x stores Windows files in cabinet files on installation disks to save space.
- ◆ EDIT.COM is a 16-bit real-mode text editor that can be used in DOS mode.
- ◆ Use SYSEDIT.EXE to edit Windows configuration files. When launched, the editor automatically opens AUTOEXEC.BAT, CONFIG.SYS, SYSTEM.INI, WIN.INI, and PROTOCOL.
- ◆ The utilities that can be useful when stored on an emergency boot disk for DOS are ATTRIB.EXE, CHKDSK.EXE, EDIT.COM, FDISK.EXE, SCANDISK.EXE, DEFRAG.EXE, HIMEM.SYS, EMM386.EXE, FORMAT.COM, MSCDEX.EXE, SYS.COM, and UNDELETE.EXE.
- ◆ Run FDISK to verify that the partition table and partition information on a hard drive are reported with the correct information. FDISK/MBR repair a damaged master boot record program stored at the beginning of the partition table.
- ◆ Run ScanDisk and then Defrag when you get the "Insufficient disk space," "Bad or missing file," "Bad sector or sector not found," or other errors that indicate a problem with the hard drive or file system on the drive.
- ◆ The system locking up can be caused by excessive fragmentation on the drive.
- ◆ Without a good partition table, all information on the hard drive is not accessible.
- ◆ If you are unable to boot to Windows 9x, initiate a DOS prompt and run ScanDisk.
- ◆ If you run DOS DEFRAG, long filenames under Windows 9x are lost.
- ◆ Run SCANREG to restore or repair a corrupted Windows 9x registry. The utility can use a backup copy of the registry created earlier by Registry Checker.
- ◆ Be familiar with options listed under the Control Panel, System Properties, Performance, File System, and File System Properties windows.

OBJECTIVES ON THE JOB

When solving problems with the operating system or application software, sometimes the problem is caused by the hard drive. Corrupted files, directories, and FAT, as well as bad sectors on the disk surface and excessive fragmentation can be corrected using ScanDisk and Defragmenter.

PRACTICE TEST QUESTIONS

1. **Which programs are used to test a hard drive for errors?**
   a. CHKDSK
   b. ATTRIB
   c. SCANDISK
   d. both a and c

2. **Which program rewrites files in contiguous cluster chains?**
   a. DEFRAG
   b. SCANDISK
   c. CHKDSK
   d. FDISK

3. **What is a fragmented drive?**
   a. a drive that contains files that are not stored in consecutive clusters
   b. a drive that contains partitions that are not located next to each other
   c. a drive that contains logical drives that are not yet formatted
   d. a drive that contains sectors and tracks that are not being used

4. **You have Windows 95 installed on your PC, but you boot from a DOS version 6.22 bootable diskette. From the DOS prompt, you run DEFRAG to defragment your hard drive. What happens to the Windows 95 long filenames?**
   a. They are retained; DOS 6.22 supports long filenames.
   b. DEFRAG recognizes a problem and stops the process so that the long filenames are not lost.
   c. Because DOS DEFRAG does not support long filenames, the long filenames are lost.
   d. The long filenames are saved, but are temporarily unavailable until you boot into Windows 95.

ANSWER

5. **The system repeatedly hangs when applications are running. What is a possible cause of this problem?**
   a. The hard drive is fragmented.
   b. There is a problem with the power supply.
   c. Disk caching is not working properly.
   d. Any one of the above can cause this problem.

ANSWER

6. **When is it appropriate to run the Thorough version of ScanDisk?**
   a. when you suspect problems with bad sectors on the hard drive
   b. when software needs to be installed
   c. when you are ready to install a new printer
   d. when you are connecting to the Internet

ANSWER

7. **When troubleshooting problems with accessing data on the hard drive, which command sequence do you follow to find the "Disable write-behind caching for all drives" option?**
   a. System Properties, Device Manager, Hard drive, Properties
   b. System Properties, Performance, File System, Troubleshooting
   c. System Properties, Device Manager, Computer, Properties
   d. Control Panel, Add/Remove Programs, Windows Setup

ANSWER

1.2
cont.

Identify basic concepts and procedures for creating, viewing and managing files, directories and disks. This includes procedures for changing file attributes and the ramifications of those changes (for example, security issues)

WINDOWS-BASED UTILITIES: DEVICE MANAGER • SYSTEM MANAGER • COMPUTER MANAGER • MSCONFIG.EXE • REGEDIT.EXE (VIEW INFORMATION/BACKUP REGISTRY) • REGEDT32.EXE • WSCRIPT.EXE • HWINFO.EXE • ASD.EXE (AUTOMATIC SKIP DRIVER) • CVT1.EXE (DRIVE CONVERTER FAT16 TO FAT32)

UNDERSTANDING THE OBJECTIVE

The operating system utilities listed above are all tools that can help troubleshoot problems with both hardware and software. Use Device Manager, System Manager and Computer Manager to help resolve problems, resolve system resource conflicts, and monitor system performance.

WHAT YOU **REALLY** NEED TO KNOW

◆ Device Manager is a Windows utility that lets you view, enable, display, and set parameters for hardware devices.

◆ In Windows 9x, if you suspect a resource conflict, use Device Manager to report the I/O addresses, DMA channels, IRQs, and upper memory addresses currently in use and to report conflicts with these resources.

◆ In Device Manager, recognize these symbols: Open diamond with a bar, red X, yellow exclamation point, and blue "I" on a white field.

◆ Computer Management is a Windows 2000 window that consolidates several tools to manage the local PC or other computers on the network. To access the Manager, click Start, Programs, Administrative Tools, Computer Management. Some Manager tools include Event Viewer, System information, Disk Defragmenter, and Device Manager.

◆ MSCONFIG.EXE is a Windows 9x utility that allows you to temporarily modify the system configuration to troubleshoot problems.

◆ Regedit.exe and Regedt32.exe are two registry editors. For Windows NT or Windows 2000, use Regedt32.exe to edit the registry.

◆ The same information displayed by the Windows 9x System Information tool can be displayed in text format by the Hardware Diagnostic tool (Hwinfo.exe).

◆ Wscript.exe is a utility that can execute a file that contains commands written in a scripting language such as VBScript or Jscript. These scripting files are sometimes used like batch files to perform routine tasks such as backups.

◆ Automatic Skip Driver Agent (Asd.exe) automatically skips drivers that prevent Windows from loading and records problems encountered in a log file, Asd.log.

◆ CVT.exe is the drive converter utility that converts a FAT16 drive to FAT32. Click Start, Programs, Accessories, System Tools, Drive Converter.

OBJECTIVES ON THE JOB

Device Manager, Computer Manager, System Configuration Utility, Automatic Skip Driver Agent and other utilities help you solve problems with an operating system.

PRACTICE TEST QUESTIONS

1. **In Device Manager, a red X through a device icon indicates:**
   a. The device is working using 16-bit drivers.
   b. The device is not Plug and Play.
   c. Device Manager changed the manual settings to its own default settings.
   d. The device is not working.

2. **What is the purpose of the file Asd.exe?**
   a. Displays system information when new hardware is installed
   b. Automatically skips loading certain drivers that are causing a problem
   c. Restores a corrupted registry
   d. Scans a hard drive for errors

3. **Using Windows 98, how do you see a list of the I/O addresses currently used by the system?**
   a. Control Panel, System, Hardware Profiles
   b. Control Panel, System, Device Manager, Computer, Properties
   c. Control Panel, System, Device Manager, View devices by connection
   d. Control Panel, System, Performance, Virtual Memory

4. **Which Windows program file can execute a file containing a script?**
   a. Wscript.exe
   b. Script.exe
   c. Asd.exe
   d. Msconfig.exe

ANSWER

5. **Which icon represents SCSI in Device Manager?**
   a. a red X
   b. a yellow S
   c. an open diamond with a bar through it
   d. an S with a circle around it

ANSWER

6. **What are the steps to access the Windows 98 utility to convert a hard drive from FAT16 to FAT32?**
   a. Click Start, Programs, Accessories, System Tools, Drive Converter
   b. Click Start, Programs, Accessories, Drive Converter
   c. Run Driveconvert in the Run dialog box
   d. From the Control Panel, double-click the File System icon

ANSWER

7. **When a new hardware device is added to a system, Windows 9x usually detects the device at startup and automatically begins the process of installing the device. What might be a reason that Windows 9x never detects a new hardware device?**
   a. When Windows 9x was installed, Plug and Play was not selected as an installed component.
   b. Plug and Play has not been enabled under Control Panel, Add/Remove Programs, Windows Setup.
   c. The system BIOS is not Plug and Play.
   d. Device Manager has been set so as to not detect new devices.

2.1 Identify the procedures for installing Windows 9x, and Windows 2000 for bringing the software to a basic operational level

START UP • PARTITION • FORMAT DRIVE • LOADING DRIVERS • RUN APPROPRIATE SET UP UTILITY

UNDERSTANDING THE OBJECTIVE

Windows 9x and Windows 2000 are often installed from a CD-ROM drive, although Windows 2000 can easily be installed over a network. Part of installation is partitioning and formatting the hard drive, installing device drivers for all hardware, and configuring the system to meet user needs.

WHAT YOU **REALLY** NEED TO KNOW

◆ The four setup options for Windows 9x are:
- Typical – Use this option to install all components most users require
- Portable – Use this option when installing Windows 9x on a notebook
- Compact – Use this option when you are short on hard drive space
- Custom – Use this option if you want to install more components than those installed with the Typical setup

◆ Switches that can be added to the Windows 9x Setup command are:
- Setup /D – Don't use the existing version of Windows
- Setup /IC – Perform a clean boot. Use this option if you suspect corrupted drivers are stalling the installation
- Setup /IN – Do not set up the network

◆ Before installing Windows 9x or Windows 2000 decide on the file system you will use.

◆ The Windows 9x FDISK command can create up to two partitions on the drive: one primary and one extended. The partition table is written at the very beginning of the hard drive and is 512 bytes (1 sector) long.

◆ A logical drive or volume is assigned a drive letter by FDISK. The drive must then be formatted before the logical drive or volume can be used.

◆ The primary partition contains only one logical drive (drive C:) and is called the active partition because it is bootable, and should be at least 150 MB for it to hold Windows 9x.

◆ The extended partition can contain several logical drives.

◆ The beginning of the partition table contains the master boot record (MBR) that BIOS executes when booting from the drive.

◆ Use FAT32 instead of FAT16 on the hard drive to eliminate as much slack as possible.

◆ When installing Windows 2000, know the following before beginning the installation: The computer name and workgroup name for a peer-to-peer network, the user name, user password, and host name for a domain network, and, for TCP/IP networks, how the IP address is assigned.

OBJECTIVES ON THE JOB

Partitioning and formatting a hard drive is a skill expected of a PC technician.

PRACTICE TEST QUESTIONS

1. **What command do you use to eliminate the partition table as the source of a problem with a hard drive?**
    a. FORMAT
    b. DISPLAY
    c. FDISK
    d. PARTITION

2. **Which Windows setup option should you use when installing Windows 98 on a notebook?**
    a. Typical
    b. Portable
    c. Notebook
    d. Custom

3. **What is the command to begin installing Windows 9x?**
    a. Install
    b. Setup
    c. Start
    d. Makeboot

4. **After partitioning the hard drive using FDISK, the next step is to:**
    a. low-level format the drive
    b. use the SYS C: command to make the hard drive bootable
    c. use FORMAT to format each logical drive
    d. enter the drive parameters in CMOS setup

5. **When the FORMAT program is formatting the drive, how are bad sectors handled?**
    a. FORMAT tests each sector and marks the sector as bad.
    b. FORMAT does not distinguish bad sectors from good sectors, but uses all just the same way.
    c. FORMAT reads bad sector information left on the sector by the low-level format program and records the sector as bad in the FAT.
    d. FORMAT reads bad sector information from the partition table and records that information in the FAT.

6. **How many partitions can a hard drive have using Windows 9x?**
    a. one primary and one extended partition
    b. one primary and up to three extended partitions
    c. one primary and up to two extended partitions
    d. two primary and one extended partition

7. **How many logical drives can the primary partition contain?**
    a. 1 to 8
    b. only 1
    c. 1 or 2
    d. none

UPGRADING WINDOWS 95 TO WINDOWS 98 • UPGRADING FROM WINDOWS NT WORKSTATION 4.0 TO WINDOWS 2000 • REPLACING WINDOWS 9X WITH WINDOWS 2000 • DUAL BOOT WINDOWS 9X/WINDOWS NT 4.0/2000

UNDERSTANDING THE OBJECTIVE

When upgrading from one Windows operating system to another, an important decision is whether you will overwrite the existing OS (clean install) or if you will upgrade the existing OS (upgrade). If you choose to upgrade, the system configuration, device drivers, and applications will carry forward to the new installation. If you do a clean install, you must start fresh and install all device drivers and applications from the ground up. Perform a clean install if the existing OS is corrupted.

WHAT YOU **REALLY** NEED TO KNOW

◆ Before upgrading from Windows 9x to Windows NT or Windows 2000, check that all hardware and applications on the system are compatible, as Windows NT and Windows 2000 do not support all legacy hardware and software.

◆ To upgrade from Windows 9x to Windows 2000, insert the Windows 2000 CD in the drive. If your PC does not automatically recognize the CD, click Start, Run, and enter this command: D:\i386\winnt32.exe. Select the option to upgrade on the opening menu.

◆ To perform a clean install of Windows 2000 when Windows 9x is the current OS, on the opening Windows 2000 setup menu, select the option, "Install a new copy of Windows 2000 (Clean Install)."

◆ When upgrading from Windows NT to Windows 2000, be aware that the NTFS file system on Windows 2000 (NTFS5) is not compatible with the NTFS file system used by Windows NT (NTFS4). For that reason, using a dual boot between Windows NT and Windows 2000 is not recommended.

◆ For a dual boot system, use a file system that is compatible with both operating systems. Windows 2000 requires that a second OS be installed in a different partition than the one holding Windows 2000.

◆ When installing Windows 9x from a CD, CD-ROM drivers must be available. The Windows 9x upgrade expects the CD-ROM drivers to already be loaded. You can load these from the DOS bootable disk in real mode.

◆ During a Windows 9x installation, Setup records information in the following log files:
  - SETUPLOG.TXT Records how far Setup got in the installation
  - DETLOG.TXT Records hardware detected
  - DETCRASH.LOG A binary file that helps Setup recover from a failed installation due to a hardware problem
  - NETLOG.TXT Records problems with network setup
  - BOOTLOG.TXT Records problems during the boot

◆ Executable files that perform the Windows 9x installation are SETUP.EXE, WINIT.EXE, and GRPCONV.EXE.

◆ Windows 98 and Windows 2000 have an upgrade CD and a new install CD. The cost for each is different. An upgrade CD requires that a previous OS be installed.

OBJECTIVES ON THE JOB

Installing an operating system is a typical task expected of a PC technician. Know how to do this in a variety of situations.

PRACTICE TEST QUESTIONS

1. **During a Windows 98 upgrade, VMM32.VXD is built specifically for this PC. Why is that so?**
   a. because each PC has a different serial number that is recorded in this file
   b. because VMM32.VXD contains the serial number for this specific Windows 98 license
   c. because VMM32.VXD contains drivers for devices specific to this hardware system
   d. because VMM32.VXD contains user preferences specific for this installation

2. **What is the purpose of the Windows 95 Setup option "Portable"?**
   a. The installation can be ported from one computer platform to another.
   b. The installation is for notebook computers and includes utilities for remote computing.
   c. The installation requires minimum user interaction.
   d. This minimum installation requires little hard drive space.

3. **To create a dual boot between Windows 2000 and Windows 98, which file system should be used?**
   a. NTFS
   b. FAT16
   c. FAT32
   d. FAT12

4. **The name of the setup program to install Windows NT is:**
   a. SETUP.COM
   b. SETUP.EXE
   c. WINNT.EXE
   d. INSTALL.EXE

5. **Which operating system requires it be the only OS installed on a partition?**
   a. Windows 95
   b. Windows 98
   c. Windows NT
   d. Windows 2000

6. **What is the purpose of the program MSCDEX.EXE?**
   a. It is used as an installation support program when installing Windows 95.
   b. It is a DOS extension that supports CD-ROM drives.
   c. It is a universal CD-ROM driver that works with any CD-ROM.
   d. It is part of the Windows 95 kernel.

7. **What are the four options for a Windows NT installation?**
   a. Typical, Portable, Express, Custom
   b. Typical, Portable, Compact, Custom
   c. Typical, Compact, Express, Custom
   d. Typical, Express, Custom, Extensive

2.3 Identify the basic system boot sequences and boot methods, including the steps to create an emergency boot disk with utilities installed for Windows 9x, Windows NT, and Windows 2000

STARTUP DISK • CREATING EMERGENCY REPAIR DISK (ERD)

UNDERSTANDING THE OBJECTIVE

An emergency boot disk is essential in a troubleshooting situation. The boot disk must be created before the problem occurs and is specific to the operating system installed. An emergency boot disk can also contain information specific to the computer and the hardware configuration.

WHAT YOU **REALLY** NEED TO KNOW

◆ When installing a new OS, make emergency startup disks when prompted to do so. These disks can later be used to recover from a failed installation.

◆ A startup disk contains the software necessary to boot the OS. For Windows 9x, when formatting a floppy disk, select the Copy System Files option in the Format dialog box.

◆ For Windows 95, include on an emergency boot disk the necessary driver files to access a CD-ROM drive, so that you can access the Windows 95 CD during a troubleshooting session.

◆ To create an emergency boot disk under Windows 9x, access the Control Panel and choose Add/Remove Programs. Choose Startup Disk and then Create Disk.

◆ Files on a Windows 9x emergency startup disk differ depending on the version of Windows installed. A typical group of files on the disk include ATTRIB.EXE, CHKDSK.EXE, EDIT.COM, FC.EXE, FDISK.EXE, FORMAT.COM, MEM.EXE, MORE.COM, MSCDEX.EXE, MSD.EXE, SCANDISK.EXE, SETVER.EXE, SYS.COM, and XCOPY.EXE. Know the purpose of each file.

◆ The Windows 98 emergency startup disk contains a cabinet file, EXTRACT.EXE (a utility program needed to manage the cabinet file), and drivers necessary to access a CD-ROM drive.

◆ Windows NT has three disks that together can boot a system. Create these disks using this command entered in the Run dialog box: D:\i386\winnt32.exe /ox, where D: is the CD-ROM drive with the Windows NT CD.

◆ Create an emergency repair disk (ERD) for Windows NT using this command: C:\Winnt\System32\rdisk.exe /s. The ERD contains information specific to the system configuration. Update the disk after you have installed new hardware. The disk contains a backup of the registry.

◆ Windows 2000 has an ERD that does not contain the registry, but does contain information specific to this installation. To create the disk, click Start, Programs, Accessories, System Tools, Backup, Emergency Repair Disk.

◆ Windows 2000 uses four disks to boot from floppies. Create the four disks using this command: D:\bootdisk\makeboot.exe A:, where D: is the CD-ROM drive containing the Windows 2000 CD.

OBJECTIVES ON THE JOB

A PC technician should never be without an emergency startup disk. Be sure to run a current version of antivirus software against the disk before using it on a customer's PC to be certain you don't spread a virus while troubleshooting.

PRACTICE TEST QUESTIONS

1. **To create an emergency startup disk in Windows 95:**
   a. use the System icon in Control Panel
   b. use the Add/Remove Programs icon in Control Panel
   c. use the Utilities icon in Control Panel
   d. use Explorer

   ANSWER

2. **The purpose of the MORE.COM program on the Windows 95 rescue disk is:**
   a. to control file display
   b. to configure memory when it is added to a system
   c. to add a new partition to a hard drive
   d. to diagnose problems with the hard drive

   ANSWER

3. **The purpose of the FC.EXE program on the Windows 95 rescue disk is:**
   a. to fix problems with CD-ROM drives
   b. to compare two files
   c. to format drive C:
   d. to fix clusters on a hard drive that have been marked as bad in the FAT

   ANSWER

4. **What command is used to manage cabinet files?**
   a. FC.EXE
   b. EDIT.COM
   c. SETUP.EXE
   d. EXTRACT.EXE

   ANSWER

5. **What is the program used by Windows 2000 to create a set of startup disks?**
   a. Startup.exe
   b. Makeboot.exe
   c. Winnt32.exe
   d. Rdisk.exe

   ANSWER

6. **What is the purpose of a cabinet file?**
   a. to hold several compressed files
   b. to create a file after the Windows 95 installation is complete
   c. to create the Windows 95 Registry
   d. to replace a directory or folder

   ANSWER

7. **In Windows 95, what is the difference between a system disk and an emergency startup disk?**
   a. An emergency startup disk is bootable, but a system disk is not.
   b. An emergency startup disk is created using Explorer, but a system disk is created at a DOS prompt.
   c. An emergency startup disk contains utility programs used for troubleshooting.
   d. An emergency startup disk does not contain as many files as a system disk does.

   ANSWER

2.3
cont.
Identify the basic system boot sequences and boot methods, including the steps to create an emergency boot disk with utilities installed for Windows 9x, Windows NT, and Windows 2000

FILES REQUIRED TO BOOT • NTLDR (NT LOADER), BOOT.INI

UNDERSTANDING THE OBJECTIVE

Knowing what files are required to boot the OS is the first step in being able to manage the boot process and troubleshoot problems with it. Know the files required to boot DOS, Windows 9x, Windows NT, and Windows 2000.

WHAT YOU **REALLY** NEED TO KNOW

◆ These files are needed in the boot sequence for DOS: IO.SYS, MSDOS.SYS, CONFIG.SYS (optional), COMMAND.COM, and AUTOEXEC.BAT (optional).

◆ For IBM DOS, IO.SYS is named IBMBIO.COM and MSDOS.SYS is named IBMDOS.COM.

◆ These are the files required in the Windows 9x boot sequence up to the point that Windows 9x switches to protected mode: IO.SYS, which checks the contents of CONFIG.SYS (optional), MSDOS.SYS, COMMAND.COM, AUTOEXEC.BAT (optional), WIN.COM, and VMM32.VXD.

◆ VMM32.VXD loads static device drivers listed in the registry and in SYSTEM.INI; these drivers have a .vxd file extension.

◆ The Windows 9x kernel consists of the Kernel (KERNEL32.DLL and KRNL386.EXE), the GDI component (GDI.EXE and GDI32.DLL), and the User component (USER.EXE and USER32.DLL).

◆ Files needed to boot Windows NT and Windows 2000:
  - Ntldr – NT loader
  - Boot.ini - text file with boot switches
  - Bootsect.dos – manages a dual boot and contains information about the hard drive partition
  - Ntdetect.com - detects hardware and loads drivers
  - Ntbootdd.sys - needed when booting from a SCSI device
  - Ntoskrnl.exe and Hal.dll – kernel components
  - System - registry hive containing hardware information
  - Device drivers

OBJECTIVES ON THE JOB

A PC technician is expected to understand and be able to troubleshoot the process of loading an OS.

PRACTICE TEST QUESTIONS

1. **Which Windows 2000 system file is required to boot only when booting from a SCSI device?**
   a. Ntldr
   b. Ntdetect.com
   c. Ntbootdd.sys
   d. Ntoskrnl.exe

2. **What is the correct boot sequence using DOS?**
   a. IO.SYS, CONFIG.SYS, MSDOS.SYS
   b. IO.SYS, MSDOS.SYS, CONFIG.SYS
   c. IO.SYS, AUTOEXEC.BAT, CONFIG.SYS
   d. AUTOEXEC.BAT, CONFIG.SYS, COMMAND.COM

3. **Which Windows 9x component is responsible for loading static device drivers?**
   a. Kernel32.dll
   b. Vmm32.vxd
   c. Io.sys
   d. Gdi.exe

4. **Which Windows 2000 component is part of the kernel?**
   a. Ntldr
   b. Boot.ini
   c. Hal.dll
   d. System

5. **Where can installed device drivers be listed so they are loaded when Windows 98 loads?**
   a. the registry
   b. System.ini
   c. Config.sys
   d. all the above

6. **What are the three core components of Windows 9x?**
   a. Kernel, GDI, Windows Explorer
   b. Kernel, GDI, User
   c. COMMAND.COM, IO.SYS, and MSDOS.SYS
   d. WIN.COM, the registry, and Windows Explorer

7. **How does Windows 98 use COMMAND.COM?**
   a. Just as DOS uses it; it is the command interpreter.
   b. Windows 98 does not use COMMAND.COM since it is a GUI operating system.
   c. As a bridge to DOS; it passes older DOS application instructions to DOS to execute.
   d. Only to load Windows 98. Once Windows 98 is loaded, COMMAND.COM is
      not used.

2.3
cont. Identify the basic system boot sequences and boot methods, including the steps to create an emergency boot disk with utilities installed for Windows 9x, Windows NT, and Windows 2000

SAFE MODE

UNDERSTANDING THE OBJECTIVE

An operating system offers a variety of tools you can use to troubleshoot a problem with booting the OS. For Windows 9x, tools include Safe Mode, the Windows 9x Startup menu, and the emergency boot disk. Windows 2000 Safe Mode works similar to that of Windows 9x. In addition, Windows 2000 offers the Windows 2000 Advanced Options Menu, Recovery Console, and the Emergency Repair Process.

WHAT YOU **REALLY** NEED TO KNOW

◆ Important function keys that can be used during the Windows 9x boot process:

Function Key	Purpose
F4	Load previous version of MS-DOS
F5	Start in Safe Mode
F8	Display Startup menu
Shift+F8	Step-by-step confirmation during bootup

◆ You can force Windows 9x to boot in Safe Mode by pressing F5 while Windows loads. Windows also selects Safe Mode if it detects a problem with the OS.

◆ Safe Mode starts Windows 9x with a minimum default configuration to give you an opportunity to correct an error in the configuration.

◆ Safe Mode loads Windows 9x, but does not execute entries in the Registry, CONFIG.SYS, AUTOEXEC.BAT, or the [Boot] and [386Enh] sections of SYSTEM.INI. Only the mouse, keyboard, and standard VGA drivers are loaded.

◆ Once in Safe Mode, try to fix the setting or hardware or software installation that caused the problem, and then reboot.

◆ Option 4 only displays if Windows recognizes the PC to be network ready. Option 8 displays only if Windows recognizes that a previous version of MS-DOS is installed. These options may differ depending on your version of Windows.

◆ In Windows 2000, press F8 during startup to display the Advanced Options Menu. Safe Mode and Last Known Good Configuration are options on this menu.

◆ If booting from the hard drive using Windows 2000 fails, the next tool is Recovery Console. Access it by booting from the four startup disks and having the Windows 2000 CD available.

OBJECTIVES ON THE JOB

A PC technician is often called upon to solve problems with booting the operating system. Understanding and knowing how to use OS tools to help in the troubleshooting process are essential skills.

PRACTICE TEST QUESTIONS

1. Which function key allows you to choose between Normal, Safe Mode, Step-by-Step Confirmation, Command Prompt Only, and Previous Version of MS-DOS when booting Windows 9x?

    a. F4

    b. F5

    c. F8

    d. Shift+F8

2. Which function key allows you to boot directly into Safe Mode when using Windows 9x?

    a. F4

    b. F5

    c. F8

    d. Shift+F8

3. Which function key allows you to boot Windows 2000 into Safe Mode?

    a. F4

    b. F5

    c. F7

    d. F8

4. What is the name of the command line interface offered by Windows 2000 to recover from a failed installation?

    a. MS-DOS prompt

    b. DOS box

    c. Recovery Console

    d. Safe Mode

5. Which statement is not true about Safe Mode in Windows 9x?

    a. CONFIG.SYS and AUTOEXEC.BAT are not executed.

    b. Standard VGA drivers are loaded.

    c. The mouse driver is not loaded, so you do not have use of the mouse in Safe Mode.

    d. Entries in the Registry are not executed.

6. How many startup disks are required to boot Windows NT from floppy disks?

    a. 1

    b. 2

    c. 3

    d. 4

7. When using Windows 95, if you boot from the Startup menu to Option 6, Command Prompt Only, what command do you use to load Windows?

    a. SCANDISK

    b. DEFRAG

    c. WIN

    d. EXIT

OBJECTIVES

2.3
cont.
Identify the basic system boot sequences and boot methods, including the steps to create an emergency boot disk with utilities installed for Windows 9x, Windows NT, and Windows 2000

MS-DOS MODE

UNDERSTANDING THE OBJECTIVE

Windows 9x runs with the microprocessor in protected mode, but offers a way to use real mode for troubleshooting as well as to run DOS applications that require it. MS-DOS mode can be accessed by using the Shut Down menu or during the boot process.

WHAT YOU **REALLY** NEED TO KNOW

- ◆ Select the Restart in MS-DOS mode option in the Shut Down dialog box to restart the PC in DOS mode. Windows 9x unloads itself and does not run when DOS mode is running.
- ◆ Another way to run in MS-DOS mode is to select the Command Prompt Only option from the Windows 9x Startup menu.
- ◆ When the PC boots in MS-DOS mode, CONFIG.SYS and AUTOEXEC.BAT are executed.
- ◆ In MS-DOS mode, to load Windows 9x, type WIN at the DOS prompt.
- ◆ MS-DOS mode can be used to troubleshoot problems with loading Windows 9x. From the command prompt, run ScanDisk and Defrag to help eliminate problems with corrupted files and the file system.
- ◆ From the command prompt, examine the BOOTLOG.TXT file for errors.
- ◆ A DOS box on a Windows 9x screen is not the same as it is in DOS mode. From a DOS box, you can execute DOS commands using COMMAND.COM as the command interpreter.
- ◆ Windows 2000 uses the Recovery Console to provide a command prompt. Commands available include ATTRIB, CD, CHKDSK, COPY, DEL, DIR, DISABLE, DISKPART, ENABLE, EXPAND, FIXBOOT, FORMAT, MD, RD, RENAME, SYSTEMROOT.
- ◆ Using the Recovery Console, you can restore the registry from backups by copying the five hives from the backup folder to the system root folder.

OBJECTIVES ON THE JOB

The DOS mode is one tool that can be used by the PC technician to troubleshoot problems with loading Windows 9x.

PRACTICE TEST QUESTIONS

1. **When Windows 9x executes MS-DOS mode, what happens to Windows 9x?**
   a. It runs in the background.
   b. It is minimized at the bottom of the DOS mode screen.
   c. It unloads itself.
   d. It doesn't show on the screen, but is still loaded in the background.

   ANSWER

2. **What is the purpose of the SYSTEMROOT command issued from the Windows 2000 Recovery Console?**
   a. Makes the root directory the current directory
   b. Makes the Windows directory the current directory
   c. Restores the system files necessary to boot Windows 2000
   d. Erases all files in the root directory

   ANSWER

3. **If you are running MS-DOS mode, how do you load Windows 9x?**
   a. Reboot the PC.
   b. Select Load Windows 9x on the menu.
   c. Type WIN at the DOS prompt.
   d. Run ScanDisk, which loads Windows 9x as the last step of the process.

   ANSWER

4. **From Windows 9x, how do you enter MS-DOS mode?**
   a. Double-click COMMAND.COM in Explorer.
   b. Select Start, Shutdown, and then Restart in MS-DOS mode.
   c. Double-click the MS-DOS shortcut on the Windows 9x desktop.
   d. all of the above

   ANSWER

5. **Which of the following is an internal DOS command?**
   a. COPY
   b. XCOPY
   c. FDISK
   d. FORMAT

   ANSWER

6. **You suspect a problem when Windows 9x loads. Where is one place to look for information about the problem?**
   a. the BOOTLOG.TXT file
   b. the HKEY_ERRORS log in the Windows 9x Registry
   c. the [Errors] section of SYSTEM.INI
   d. the DETLOG.TXT file

   ANSWER

7. **What happens when you double-click COMMAND.COM in Windows Explorer?**
   a. Windows 9x enters DOS mode.
   b. A DOS box displays on the screen from which you can enter DOS commands.
   c. Windows 9x unloads.
   d. all of the above

   ANSWER

2.4 Identify procedures for loading/adding and configuring application device drivers, and the necessary software for certain devices

WINDOWS 9X PLUG AND PLAY AND WINDOWS 2000

UNDERSTANDING THE OBJECTIVE

Plug and Play is a technology that helps automate the process of installing new hardware devices. For a system to be truly Plug and Play compliant, the OS, the system BIOS, and the device must all support Plug and Play.

WHAT YOU **REALLY** NEED TO KNOW

- ◆ Windows 9x and Windows 2000 support Plug and Play, but Windows NT does not.
- ◆ Most system BIOS produced after 1994 support Plug and Play.
- ◆ A device that is Plug and Play compliant includes text such as "Windows 98 Ready" on the box or in the documentation.
- ◆ Install a device driver when a new hardware device is installed. Choose Start, Settings, Control Panel, and Add New Hardware.
- ◆ To change a device driver for a device, open the Properties dialog box for the device and select Settings, and then Update Driver. The Update Device Driver Wizard steps you through the process.
- ◆ During the Windows 9x load process, VMM32.VXD creates virtual machines, loads static Virtual Device Drivers (VxD drivers) named in the Windows registry and System.ini and shifts the OS to protected mode.
- ◆ Static VxDs are device drivers that remain in memory while Windows 9x is running.
- ◆ Dynamic VxDs are 32-bit protected mode device drivers that Plug and Play devices require.
- ◆ The following is a summary of the two kinds of device drivers in Windows 9x and when and how to use them:

	16-bit Device Drivers	32-bit Device Drivers
Operating Mode	Real mode	Protected mode
Use of memory	May use upper memory addresses	Stored in extended memory
How loaded	Loaded by a DEVICE= line in CONFIG.SYS at startup	Automatically loaded by Windows 9x
How changed	Edit the CONFIG.SYS file	From Device Manager, select the device and use Properties, Device tab
How to identify the type	In Device Manager, look for an exclamation point beside the device name	Look for no exclamation point beside the device name in Device Manager. Also, "32" is typically included in the driver filename.
When to use this type	Use a 16-bit driver under Windows only when a 32-bit driver is not available.	When you can, always use 32-bit drivers. They are faster.

OBJECTIVES ON THE JOB

When upgrading to Windows 9x from DOS, make every effort to convert all 16-bit drivers to 32-bit versions. If Windows 9x does not support a device, check the device manufacturer Web site for a 32-bit version of the driver.

PRACTICE TEST QUESTIONS

1. **Which operating system supports Plug and Play?**
   a. DOS
   b. Windows NT
   c. Windows 98
   d. UNIX

2. **In order for a system to be fully Plug and Play compliant, what must be true?**
   a. The BIOS, operating system, and devices must be Plug-and-Play.
   b. The operating system and devices must be Plug-and-Play.
   c. The operating system, device drivers, and devices must be Plug-and-Play.
   d. The operating system and application software must be Plug-and-Play.

3. **A 16-bit device driver is loaded from:**
   a. CONFIG.SYS
   b. the registry
   c. Plug and Play configuration information in Device Manager
   d. AUTOEXEC.BAT

4. **One advantage a 32-bit driver has over a 16-bit driver is that the 32-bit driver:**
   a. can easily be disabled by commenting out the line in CONFIG.SYS
   b. can be stored in upper memory
   c. can be stored in extended memory
   d. does not require as much memory

5. **Using Windows 9x, where do you look to find the name of a 32-bit device driver used by a device?**
   a. the Properties dialog box for the device under Device Manager
   b. the device driver name in SYSTEM.INI
   c. the device driver name in the Windows 95 registry
   d. in CONFIG.SYS for the driver name

6. **Plug and Play requires:**
   a. all 16-bit drivers
   b. all 32-bit drivers
   c. that virtual device drivers be loaded from SYSTEM.INI
   d. that the system BIOS be Plug and Play

7. **The message "Windows 98 Ready" on the packaging of a new hardware device probably means that:**
   a. the device package includes a disk or CD that contains 32-bit drivers
   b. the device is Plug and Play
   c. the device was manufactured after 1994
   d. all of the above

Identify procedures for loading/adding and configuring application device drivers, and the necessary software for certain devices

IDENTIFY THE PROCEDURES FOR INSTALLING AND LAUNCHING TYPICAL WINDOWS AND NON-WINDOWS APPLICATIONS (NOTE: THERE IS NO CONTENT RELATED TO WINDOWS 3.1)

UNDERSTANDING THE OBJECTIVE

Software is installed using a setup program that comes with the application. Insert the floppy disk or CD in the drive and, at the command prompt or Run dialog box, type SETUP or INSTALL, preceded by the drive letter of the drive. Each OS has more than one way to launch an application, either automatically at startup or by the user after startup.

WHAT YOU **REALLY** NEED TO KNOW

◆ For DOS, applications can be automatically loaded at startup by entering the name of the program file in AUTOEXEC.BAT.

◆ Parameters can be added to the command line that execute an application and are then passed to the application.

◆ For Windows 9x, to automatically load an application at startup, place a shortcut to the application in the Startup folder.

◆ A .dll file is a dynamic-link library file that holds program segments that applications will call. The .dll files are stored in the \Windows\System folder.

◆ A GPF error can result if a .dll file is corrupted or has been overwritten by a newer version than an application can use.

◆ A program information file (PIF) contains settings that are used by Windows to know how to execute a DOS application.

◆ Windows 9x uses the application's Property box instead of a PIF file to track settings.

◆ Settings about several applications are stored in the Windows 9x file Apps.inf. Settings about DOS applications are stored under the section [PIF95].

◆ Windows 9x applications can be launched from the Start, Programs menu, from Explorer, or from shortcuts on the desktop.

◆ Install new software in Windows using the Add/Remove Programs icon of Control Panel.

◆ To configure the virtual DOS machine environment for a legacy application, right-click the application filename and select Properties. Save any changes in the Apps.inf file, which holds settings for several applications, or a PIF file stored in the same folder as the program executable file.

OBJECTIVES ON THE JOB

Installing software, setting up short cuts, and configuring applications to load at startup are typical jobs expected of a PC technician.

PRACTICE TEST QUESTIONS

1. **What is the result when the same memory is allocated to more than one application?**
   a. General Protection Fault
   b. two applications can share the same data
   c. only one application can run at a time
   d. IRQ conflict

2. **What is one thing you can do so that more applications can be loaded at the same time?**
   a. Add more RAM.
   b. Upgrade the CPU.
   c. Add a second hard drive.
   d. Uninstall some Windows components.

3. **What type of multitasking does Windows 9x support?**
   a. preemptive multitasking
   b. cooperative multitasking
   c. true multitasking
   d. single multitasking

4. **Where are most DLL files stored under Windows 9x?**
   a. the Windows folder
   b. the application folder
   c. the Windows\System folder
   d. the Program Files folder

5. **How do you change the environmental settings for a DOS application running under Windows 2000?**
   a. Make the changes directly in the registry.
   b. Right-click the application file name and select Properties from the shortcut menu.
   c. Click Start, Programs, Command Prompt. Enter the changes at the command prompt.
   d. Make the changes in the Autoexec.bat file.

6. **What is an example of OLE?**
   a. An object in a word processing document points to the application that created it, such as Paint.
   b. An object in a word processing document was created by Paint and then inserted into this document.
   c. An object from one application is embedded into the document created by another application.
   d. all of the above

7. **What is one way to cause an application under Windows 9x to load at startup?**
   a. place a shortcut to the application in the Program Files folder
   b. create a shortcut to the application on the desktop
   c. place a shortcut to the application in the Startup folder
   d. either a or b

Identify procedures for loading/adding and configuring application device drivers, and the necessary software for certain devices

PROCEDURES FOR SET UP AND CONFIGURING WINDOWS PRINTING SUBSYSTEM: SETTING DEFAULT PRINTER • INSTALLING/SPOOL SETTING • NETWORK PRINTING (WITH HELP OF LAN ADMIN)

UNDERSTANDING THE OBJECTIVE

Windows provides support for many printers and automates the printing process for applications. Windows keeps track of installed printers and relieves applications of providing printer dialog boxes, preparing and formatting print jobs, and managing the print queue.

WHAT YOU **REALLY** NEED TO KNOW

- ◆ Windows 9x manages a print job in one of three ways:
  - For non-PostScript printers, print job data is converted to enhanced metafile format (EMF), which embeds print commands in the data to speed up printing.
  - For PostScript printers, Windows 9x converts the print job data to the PostScript language.
  - For DOS applications, data is not converted, but sent to the printer as is (called raw data).
- ◆ Windows 9x places print jobs into a queue so that applications need not wait for the printing to complete before releasing the job. This process is called **spooling**. Clean out the print spool to remove all pending print jobs.
- ◆ Most Windows 9x printing is done using EMF spooling.
- ◆ To install a new printer, click the Start button on the taskbar, point to Settings, click Printers, and then double-click the Add New Printer icon.
- ◆ Change the Windows default printer using the Printer window. Select the printer and choose Set as Default on the File menu.
- ◆ Know the steps to install a new printer and share it to others on the network. Know how to install a network printer on a remote PC.

OBJECTIVES ON THE JOB

Installing and maintaining printers and resolving printer problems are typical tasks for a PC technician. Understanding how Windows 9x manages printers is essential to this skill.

If you can print a self-test page, but cannot print a test page from the OS, try these things:

- ◆ Verify that the printer is online and the proper printer cable is connected.
- ◆ In the printer's Properties dialog box, verify the correct parallel (LPT) port. In the Services tab, verify that the printer can communicate with the OS by clicking Test printer communications. If communication is not bi-directional, the printer will print, but without making all of its features available to the OS. In the Details tab, click Port Settings to try disabling "Check Port State Before Printing."
- ◆ Enter CMOS setup of the PC and verify that the parallel port is enabled.
- ◆ Check the parallel port mode. If ECP mode is selected, verify that a DMA channel is available and not conflicting with another device. Try setting the port to bi-directional.
- ◆ Try printing from DOS. If you can print from DOS, try disabling EMF spooling.

PRACTICE TEST QUESTIONS

1. **What does EMF stand for?**
   a. extra measure format
   b. enhanced metafile format
   c. enhanced manufacturing factory
   d. enhanced method of formatting

2. **What is EMF printing?**
   a. a Windows 9x method of embedding print commands in a print job
   b. printing that is designed to use a bi-directional parallel cable under Windows
   c. printing designed to use laser printers
   d. storing print jobs in a queue

3. **What is print spooling?**
   a. storing print jobs in a queue for later printing
   b. installing a new printer under Windows 95
   c. a print setting that controls the parallel port
   d. when an application, rather than the OS, controls the printing process

ANSWER

4. **When troubleshooting a problem with printing, what can you check in CMOS setup?**
   a. what printer is installed and if the PC can communicate with it
   b. if the parallel port is communicating properly
   c. if the parallel port is enabled and configured correctly
   d. if the printer I/O address and IRQ have been assigned correctly

ANSWER

5. **What is PostScript?**
   a. a method of printing a document in landscape orientation
   b. a page-description language developed by Adobe Systems
   c. a method of compressing a print job in order to save disk space
   d. a protocol used to send word processing documents over a network

6. **What is raw data?**
   a. data that has not been processed by the CPU
   b. data that has not been cooked
   c. data that does not contain any embedded commands
   d. data that has not yet been saved to a file

ANSWER

7. **What is one advantage of using print spooling?**
   a. to make it easier to troubleshoot problems with printing
   b. to allow a PC to use a laser or ink jet printer
   c. to allow the use of graphics in print documents
   d. to release the application from the printing process so the user can continue working

3.1 Recognize and interpret the meaning of common error codes and startup messages from the boot sequence, and identify steps to correct the problems

SAFE MODE

UNDERSTANDING THE OBJECTIVE

Problems with loading an operating system are communicated to the user as error messages on screen or the system may simply lock up. Safe Mode is only one of several options Windows 9x and Windows 2000 offer to help resolve problems when loading the OS.

WHAT YOU **REALLY** NEED TO KNOW

- ◆ When Windows encounters problems with loading the OS, it might enter Safe Mode or it might offer the Startup menu from which you can select Safe Mode.
- ◆ Here's what to expect when you select each option on the Windows 9x Startup menu:
  - **Normal** In MSDOS.SYS, if BootGUI=1, then this option starts Windows 9x. If BootGUI=0, then this option will boot to the DOS 7.0 or DOS 7.1 prompt. Either way, the commands in AUTOEXEC.BAT and CONFIG.SYS are executed.
  - **Logged (\BOOTLOG.TXT)** Same as Normal, except Windows 9x tracks the load and startup activities and logs them to this file.
  - **Safe Mode** Windows loads with a minimum configuration.
  - **Safe mode with Network Support** Network drivers are loaded when booting into Safe Mode.
  - **Step-by-Step Confirmation** The option asks for confirmation before executing each command in IO.SYS, CONFIG.SYS, and AUTOEXEC.BAT.
  - **Command Prompt Only** Also called DOS mode. Executes CONFIG.SYS and AUTOEXEC.BAT.
  - **Safe mode Command Prompt Only** Does not execute the commands in AUTOEXEC.BAT or CONFIG.SYS. You will be given a DOS prompt. Type WIN to load Windows 9x.
  - **Previous Version of MS-DOS** Loads a previous version of DOS if one is present. This is the same as pressing F4 when the message "Starting Windows 95/98" displays.
- ◆ Once in Safe Mode in Windows 9x or Windows 2000, the following may help resolve a problem:
  - Reboot the system; sometimes this is all that's needed.
  - Run antivirus software to check for a virus.
  - If the Safe Recovery dialog box appears, select Use Safe Recovery to let Windows attempt a solution.
  - Disable any devices just installed.
  - Undo any receive configuration changes.
  - Run ScanDisk and Defrag.
  - For Windows 98, run System File Checker, Automatic Skip Driver Agent, System Configuration Utility.

OBJECTIVES ON THE JOB

Understanding and using Safe Mode and the other options on the Windows 9x Startup menu or the Windows 2000 Advanced Options Menu are important skills to have when troubleshooting problems with the OS.

PRACTICE TEST QUESTIONS

1. **What is the source of the error message "MS-DOS compatibility mode"?**
   a. Windows is using real mode device drivers to access the hard drive.
   b. You are using DOS mode. To load Windows, type WIN at the DOS prompt.
   c. Windows has booted into Safe Mode.
   d. Windows is running a DOS application.

ANSWER

2. **What is the source of the error message "Invalid VxD dynamic link call from IFSMGR" and what do you do to solve the problem?**
   a. The registry is corrupted. Restore the registry files from backup.
   b. MSDOS.SYS is corrupted. Restore the file from a backup.
   c. The boot sector is corrupted. Format the hard drive and reinstall Windows 95.
   d. The partition table is corrupted. Use FDISK to create a new table.

ANSWER

3. **What is one of the first things you should do after booting into Safe Mode?**
   a. Run antivirus software
   b. Reinstall Windows
   c. Use RECOVER to restore the system files
   d. Use SYS C: to restore the system files

ANSWER

4. **What happens if the Win.com file is missing from the Windows 9x load?**
   a. Windows will create a new Win.com file and continue to load.
   b. An error message displays and Windows 9x continues to load.
   c. Windows will automatically boot into Safe Mode.
   d. An error message displays and the load stops.

ANSWER

5. **What might be a cause of the error message "Invalid system disk" under Windows 9x?**
   a. A virus has corrupted system files.
   b. IO.SYS is missing or corrupt.
   c. The registry is corrupted.
   d. either a or b

ANSWER

6. **Which statement about booting Windows 9x into Safe Mode is not true?**
   a. A minimum configuration is used so that the problem is not masked by a complex load.
   b. The registry is rebuilt at the beginning of loading in Safe Mode.
   c. Entries in the registry, CONFIG.SYS, AUTOEXEC.BAT, and most of SYSTEM.INI are not executed.
   d. Standard VGA drivers are loaded.

ANSWER

7. **What is one way to access Safe Mode under Windows 2000?**
   a. Press F1 during startup
   b. Press F8 and select Safe Mode from the Advanced Options Menu
   c. Press F3 during startup
   d. Select Safe Mode from the taskbar tray

ANSWER

3.1
cont. Recognize and interpret the meaning of common error codes and startup messages from the boot sequence, and identify steps to correct the problems

ERROR IN CONFIG.SYS LINE XX • HIMEM.SYS NOT LOADED • MISSING OR CORRUPT HIMEM.SYS

UNDERSTANDING THE OBJECTIVE

Errors when loading Windows 9x can be caused by missing or corrupt program files, errors in command lines stored in AUTOEXEC.BAT and CONFIG.SYS, wrong program files present, or wrong paths to these program files.

WHAT YOU **REALLY** NEED TO KNOW

◆ Press Shift+F8 at startup to step through commands in CONFIG.SYS and AUTOEXEC.BAT.

◆ HIMEM.SYS is loaded from CONFIG.SYS with the DEVICE= command under DOS.

◆ HIMEM.SYS is automatically loaded by Windows 9x and is a required component.

◆ Errors in CONFIG.SYS can be caused by missing or corrupt device drivers or errors in the command line to load a driver.

OBJECTIVES ON THE JOB

When troubleshooting problems with loading an OS, the problem might be with the command being executed, the program file it refers to, or the path or location of the program file. A PC technician should know how to interpret associated error messages, investigate and research the problem, and arrive at a solution.

Error	Meaning of Error Message and What to Do
Bad sector errors	Bad sectors on the hard drive are encountered when trying to load the OS.
	Boot from a floppy and run ScanDisk.
Incorrect DOS version	You are attempting to use a DOS command file that belongs to a different version of DOS than the one now running. Use the DOS software from the same version you are running.
Invalid drive specification	The PC is unable to find a hard drive or a floppy drive that setup tells it to expect.
	The hard drive may have a corrupted partition table.
Invalid or missing COMMAND.COM	This may be caused by a nonbooting disk in drive A, or a deleted COMMAND.COM on drive C. Remove the disk and boot from the hard drive.
Non-system disk or disk error	COMMAND.COM or one of two DOS hidden files is missing from the disk or the hard drive. Remove the disk and boot from the hard drive.
Not ready reading drive A:	The disk in drive A is missing, unformatted, or corrupted. Try another disk. Abort, Retry, Fail?

PRACTICE TEST QUESTIONS

1. Which file is required for Windows 98 to load?

    a. Config.sys

    b. Explorer.exe

    c. Himem.sys

    d. Apps.inf

2. TSR stands for:

    a. Terminal Stay Ready

    b. Terminate and State Receiving

    c. Terminate and Stay Resident

    d. Transmit, Send, Receive

3. Which command line belongs in CONFIG.SYS?

    a. Prompt pg

    b. Device=mouse.sys

    c. Path C:\;C:\Windows

    d. Command.com

4. Pressing Shift+F8 during booting causes:

    a. Step-by-step confirmation

    b. The system to boot into Safe Mode

    c. Config.sys and Autoexec.bat to be skipped

    d. Display the Startup menu

5. What is the result of the command DEVICEHIGH=HIMEM.SYS?

    a. HIMEM.SYS is loaded into upper memory.

    b. Upper memory blocks are created for device drivers.

    c. HIMEM.SYS is loaded into extended memory.

    d. An error results; HIMEM.SYS cannot load into memory above 640K.

6. What is true of device drivers loaded from CONFIG.SYS?

    a. The drivers are 32-bit VXD drivers.

    b. The drivers run in real mode.

    c. The drivers are 16-bit drivers.

    d. both b and c

7. What is the cause of the error "Bad sector"?

    a. A program file is missing.

    b. Windows did not load properly.

    c. A sector on the hard drive is corrupted.

    d. all of the above

3.1
cont.
Recognize and interpret the meaning of common error codes and startup messages from the boot sequence, and identify steps to correct the problems

NO OPERATING SYSTEM FOUND • BAD OR MISSING COMMAND.COM • A DEVICE REFERENCED IN SYSTEM.INI, WIN.INI, REGISTRY COULD NOT BE FOUND • FAILURE TO START GUI

UNDERSTANDING THE OBJECTIVE

Errors can be caused by missing or corrupted system files, including the swap file, or by missing and corrupt device drivers referenced in System.ini, Win.ini, or the registry.

WHAT YOU **REALLY** NEED TO KNOW

◆ For DOS, use the SYS command to restore system files, including IO.SYS, MSDOS.SYS, and COMMAND.COM.

◆ SYSTEM.INI can be used to load device drivers in Windows 9x. In troubleshooting, use a semicolon to disable a command line in SYSTEM.INI or WIN.INI.

◆ The error message "Bad or missing command interpreter" or "Bad or missing Command.com" is caused by COMMAND.COM that is missing, corrupted, or in the wrong directory.

◆ A VxD (virtual device driver) is used by Windows 9x to manage a device.

◆ In Windows 9x, VxDs can be loaded from VMM32.VXD, the Registry, and SYSTEM.INI.

◆ During the installation of Windows 9x, the VxDs needed by the specific computer are combined to create VMM32.VXD, which executes each time Windows 9x starts and loads these VxDs.

◆ Use System Configuration (MSConfig) to disable the loading of entries in System.ini, Win.ini, Config.sys and Autoexec.bat.

◆ When attempting to load Windows 9x from the command prompt, if the normal WIN command does not work, try the following switches:

- WIN /D:F   Turns off 32-bit disk access. Use this option if there appears to be a problem with hard drive access.

- WIN /D:M   Starts the OS in Safe Mode

- WIN /D:S   Instructs Windows to not use memory address F000:0 as a break point.

- WIN /D:V   Instructs Windows that system BIOS should be used to access the hard drive.

- WIN /D:X   Excludes all upper memory addresses from real mode drivers.

OBJECTIVES ON THE JOB

A PC technician is expected to recognize, understand, and solve problems that present themselves as error messages during the process of loading an operating system.

PRACTICE TEST QUESTIONS

1. **What is the purpose of the Windows 98 command WIN.COM /D:F?**
   a. to cause Windows 98 to boot from a floppy disk
   b. to load Windows 98 without 32-bit disk access
   c. to load Windows 98 and create a new BOOTLOG.TXT file
   d. to load Windows 98 into Safe Mode

2. **When does Windows 98 create the Bootlog.txt file?**
   a. During the Windows 98 installation process
   b. When loading Windows from the command prompt using the Win.com/B switch
   c. When booting into Safe Mode
   d. all of the above

3. **Which statement about VxDs is true?**
   a. A static VxD is loaded when a device needs it and unloads when the device is no longer being used.
   b. A dynamic VxD is loaded when a device needs it and unloads when the device is no longer being used.
   c. Dynamic VxDs are loaded from SYSTEM.INI.
   d. Plug and Play uses only static VxDs.

4. **To temporarily disable a command in CONFIG.SYS, you should:**
   a. delete the command line from the CONFIG.SYS file
   b. put a semicolon at the beginning of the command line
   c. put REM at the beginning of the command line
   d. rename CONFIG.SYS

5. **Using Windows 9x, from where can device drivers be loaded?**
   a. System.ini, Win.ini, the registry, and VMM32.vxd
   b. Only from the registry
   c. Config.sys, the registry, System.ini, Vmm32.vxd
   d. Only from Vmm32.vxd

6. **How can you load Windows 98 bypassing entries in System.ini and Win.ini?**
   a. Press F8 during the load process
   b. Disable these files using MSCONFIG
   c. Disable these files using the System icon in Control Panel
   d. Make an entry at the beginning of each file saying the file is to be skipped

7. **Which of the following Windows 9x files is built specifically for the current system?**
   a. Vmm32.vxd
   b. Himem.sys
   c. Win.com
   d. Command.com

3.1
cont.

Recognize and interpret the meaning of common error codes and startup messages from the boot sequence, and identify steps to correct the problems

SCSI • DR. WATSON • WINDOWS PROTECTION ERROR • SWAP FILE

UNDERSTANDING THE OBJECTIVE

Errors loading Windows 9x can be caused by missing or corrupted system files, including the swap file, or by not enough space on the hard drive for the swap file or temporary files. Dr. Watson is one Windows 9x tool that can help solve problems with applications.

WHAT YOU **REALLY** NEED TO KNOW

- ◆ To change the location of the swap file, from the Control Panel, use the System icon. Select the Performance tab and click Virtual Memory.
- ◆ It is recommended that you allow Windows to manage the virtual memory automatically and not make manual settings.
- ◆ Use Dr. Watson to solve problems with applications. Start Dr. Watson, reproduce the error, and then look in the log files created by Dr. Watson for information about the error.
- ◆ To start Dr. Watson, click Start, Programs, Accessories, System Tools, System Information. In the System Information window, click Tools, and click Dr. Watson.
- ◆ Log files created by Dr. Watson are named \Windows\Drwatson\WatsonXX.wlg where XX is an incrementing number.
- ◆ If an application fails to start, try deleting all files and folders under \Windows\Temp.
- ◆ If a SCSI device fails to function after upgrading from DOS to Windows 9x, try using real-mode device drivers loaded from Config.sys. If these work, then suspect the device was not recognized correctly by Windows. Check the Properties window of the device in Device Manager.
- ◆ Before installing the drivers for a SCSI drive that uses removable media such as a CD-ROM drive, insert the media in the drive first.
- ◆ Be certain that both ends of the SCSI chain are terminated correctly.
- ◆ Windows creates an Ios.log file when a protected mode driver cannot be loaded correctly either because the driver is missing or corrupted or a legacy driver is controlling the device. Look for errors in the log file.
- ◆ If the first line of the Ios.log file mentions Mbrint13.sys, suspect a virus.

OBJECTIVES ON THE JOB

A PC technician is expected to recognize, understand, and solve problems related to applications and software used to support hardware devices.

PRACTICE TEST QUESTIONS

1. **Which of the following statements about a Windows 9x swap file is not true?**

    a. The swap file can be stored on a D drive.

    b. The swap file can be stored in any folder on the hard drive.

    c. The size of the swap file can be limited.

    d. The swap file can be stored on a Zip drive.

2. **Where are the log files created by Dr. Watson stored?**

    a. In the root directory of the hard drive

    b. In the \Windows\System folder

    c. In the \Windows\Drwatson folder

    d. In the \Windows\Temp folder

3. **How do you start Dr Watson?**

    a. Click Start, Programs, Accessories, System Tools, System Information

    b. Click Start, Programs, Accessories, Dr Watson

    c. Click Start, Settings, Control Panel, Dr. Watson

    d. Click Start, Programs, Dr. Watson

4. **If an application fails to start, try deleting all the files in this folder:**

    a. \Windows\System32

    b. \Windows\Temp

    c. \Windows\System\Temp

    d. \Windows

5. **What type of information about errors is stored in the Ios.log file?**

    a. Information about protected mode drivers

    b. Information about the Windows setup process

    c. Information about applications that give General Protection Faults

    d. Information about Dr. Watson

6. **What is the recommended approach to managing Windows 9x virtual memory?**

    a. Allow Windows to manage virtual memory automatically

    b. Set virtual memory configuration according to user preferences

    c. Never change the location of the swap file

    d. Set the maximum size of the swap file to 10 MB.

7. **What are the steps to change the location of the Windows 98 swap file?**

    a. From Control Panel, use the System icon, Performance tab. Click Virtual Memory.

    b. From Control Panel, use the Memory icon. Click Virtual Memory.

    c. Click Start, Programs, Accessories, System Tools, System Information, Virtual Memory.

    d. Click Start, Settings, Memory, Virtual Memory.

ANSWER

ANSWER

ANSWER

ANSWER

ANSWER

ANSWER

ANSWER

3.1
cont. Recognize and interpret the meaning of common error codes and startup messages from the boot sequence, and identify steps to correct the problems

NT BOOT ISSUES • EVENT VIEWER – EVENT LOG IS FULL

UNDERSTANDING THE OBJECTIVE

Troubleshooting problems with Windows NT and Windows 2000 require knowing how Windows records problems with booting and problems after the boot. The Event Viewer is one of the more important tools to use when troubleshooting because all failed events are recorded there. These events include users logging on, security violations, application and hardware errors, and so forth. When troubleshooting the Windows NT and Windows 2000 boot process, follow established procedures based on the severity of the problem.

WHAT YOU **REALLY** NEED TO KNOW

◆ After a successful boot, Windows NT saves a copy of the hardware configuration from the registry, which is called the Last Known Good Configuration.

◆ If a problem occurs while booting, a menu appears. Select Last Known Good Configuration to revert to the last time the system booted successfully.

◆ The Last Known Good Configuration is saved after a logon has occurred. If you are having a problem with the boot, don't log on as you might erase a good version of the Last Known Good Configuration.

◆ Use the three Windows NT boot disks to boot the system when it fails to boot from the hard drive.

◆ The Windows NT Emergency Repair Disk (ERD) contains information specific to the system including a copy of the registry. Keep the disk current.

◆ Boot from the three Windows NT boot disks and, from the setup menu that appears, select the option to repair a damaged installation.

◆ Event Viewer is a log of failed events. Using Windows NT, to access it, click Start, Programs, Administrative Tools, Event Viewer. Icons in the event list are: I (event completed successfully), Exclamation point (possible future problem), and Stop Sign (failed event).

◆ In Windows NT, use the Log menu to save Event View information to a log file, open a previously-saved log file, and clear all events from the current log.

◆ Using Windows 2000, to access the Event Viewer, from the Control Panel, select the Administrative Tools icon and then select Event Viewer.

◆ Windows 2000 uses the Action menu for the same functions as the Log menu in the Windows NT Event Viewer.

◆ Tools to use when solving booting problems with Windows 2000 include the Advanced Options Menu, which offers the Last Known Good Configuration and Safe Mode, the Recovery Console, and the Emergency Boot Process.

OBJECTIVES ON THE JOB

A PC technician is expected to recognize, understand, and solve problems that present themselves as error messages during the process of loading an operating system. Windows 2000 and Windows NT offer several utilities designed to help in solving boot and application problems. A technician is expected to be familiar with all these utilities and know how to use them to solve problems.

PRACTICE TEST QUESTIONS

1. **In Windows NT, when is the Last Known Good Configuration saved?**
   a. After the user has logged on
   b. After the first Windows NT screen displays
   c. When the system is shut down
   d. When the first application loads

2. **Which statement is true about the Windows NT ERD?**
   a. The ERD contains enough of the operating system to boot the system.
   b. The ERD contains a compressed copy of the registry.
   c. The ERD contains a full log of all events recorded by Event Viewer.
   d. The ERD contains the DOS operating system and is bootable to DOS.

3. **Using Windows 2000, what menu contains the option to clear the Event Viewer of all events?**
   a. the Log menu
   b. the Action menu
   c. the File menu
   d. the Exit menu

4. **Which statement is true about the Windows 2000 ERD?**
   a. The ERD contains enough of the operating system to boot the system.
   b. The ERD contains a compressed copy of the registry.
   c. The ERD requires you first boot using the four startup disks or the Windows 2000 CD.
   d. The ERD contains the DOS operating system and is bootable to DOS.

5. **Which of the following is required before you can use the Windows 2000 Recovery Console?**
   a. you must know Visual Basic in order to understand the setup screen for the Recovery Console
   b. you must first have booted using the four Windows 2000 startup disks
   c. you must have an ERD inserted in the floppy disk drive
   d. you must know the Administrator password

6. **How do you access the Windows 2000 Event Viewer?**
   a. Click Start, Programs, Administrative Tools, Event Viewer.
   b. Click Start, Programs, Accessories, Administrative Tools, Event Viewer.
   c. From the Control Panel, select the Administrative Tools icon and select Event Viewer.
   d. From the Control Panel, select the Event Viewer icon.

7. **On which menu do you find the Windows 2000 Last Known Good Configuration option?**
   a. the Startup menu
   b. the Advanced Options menu
   c. the Recovery Console menu
   d. the Windows 2000 Repair Options menu

ELICITING PROBLEM SYMPTOMS FROM CUSTOMERS • HAVING CUSTOMER REPRODUCE ERROR AS PART OF THE DIAGNOSTIC PROCESS • IDENTIFYING RECENT CHANGES TO THE COMPUTER ENVIRONMENT FROM THE USER

UNDERSTANDING THE OBJECTIVE

Whether you support PCs on the phone, on-site, or in a shop, you need a plan to follow when you approach a service call. One mistake PC technicians often make is assuming they already understand what the problem is without thoroughly interviewing the customer. Know how to approach a customer, to communicate, and to ask questions to investigate the source of the problem before you turn your attention to the computer system.

WHAT YOU **REALLY** NEED TO KNOW

◆ Let the customer explain the problem in his or her own way. Take notes, and then interview the customer about the problem so you understand it thoroughly.

◆ Have the customer reproduce the problem and carefully note each step taken and its results. This process gives you clues about the problem and about the technical proficiency of the customer, which helps you know how to communicate with the customer.

◆ When interacting with a customer, display confidence that you are competent and can solve the problem. Keep a professional and confident attitude. Don't talk down to the customer or disparage the customer's choice of hardware or software. If you have made a mistake or must pass the problem on to someone with more expertise, be honest.

◆ Protect the confidentiality of the customer's data on the PC.

◆ Here are some helpful questions to ask the user when trying to discover the source of the problem:
  - When did the problem start?
  - Were there any error messages or unusual displays on the screen?
  - What programs or software were you using?
  - Did you move your computer system recently?
  - Has there been a recent thunderstorm or electrical problem?
  - Have you made any hardware changes?
  - Did you recently install any new software?
  - Did you recently change any software configuration setups?
  - Has someone else been using your computer recently?
  - When was the last time you ran antivirus software?

OBJECTIVES ON THE JOB

A PC technician is expected to be able to give good service. Part of providing good service is being a good communicator. By effectively interviewing the customer before you begin work on a PC, you can quickly discover valuable information that can save you hours of time that might have been required without the customer's assistance.

PRACTICE TEST QUESTIONS

1. **What is something you can do to promote good communication?**
   a. Be silent until the customer is finished describing the problem
   b. Take notes as the customer describes the problem
   c. Begin work while the customer is talking
   d. both a and b

2. **What is something you should do while talking with a customer?**
   a. Ask the customer when the problem began
   b. Ask the customer to reproduce the problem
   c. Never admit you have made a mistake
   d. both a and b

3. **What is one question to ask a customer?**
   a. Why did you buy this brand of PC anyway?
   b. Did you recently install any new software?
   c. Why can't you even understand my question?
   d. How much did you pay for this equipment?

4. **What are some things you need to know from the customer?**
   a. Is the PC still under warranty?
   b. Has the PC been moved recently?
   c. Has there been a lightning storm recently?
   d. all of the above

5. **What is the first thing you should do when you arrive at a customer's site?**
   a. Shut the PC down and perform a cold start
   b. Fill out the necessary paperwork about the visit
   c. Interview the customer
   d. Attempt to reproduce the problem

6. **What do you do if you make a mistake while attempting to repair a PC?**
   a. Hide it from your boss
   b. Be honest where appropriate
   c. Resign from your job
   d. Hide it from the customer

7. **When interviewing a customer, why is it important to know if the PC has been near a lightning storm recently?**
   a. the problem might be caused by electrical damage
   b. there still might be ozone in the atmosphere
   c. the customer needs to know to purchase a line conditioner
   d. you can eliminate the power supply as a source of the problem

TROUBLESHOOTING WINDOWS-SPECIFIC PRINTING PROBLEMS
PRINT SPOOL IS STALLED • INCORRECT/INCOMPATIBLE DRIVER FOR PRINT
• INCORRECT PARAMETER

UNDERSTANDING THE OBJECTIVE

Problems with printing can be caused by the printer, the connection from the printer to the computer, the computer hardware, operating system, application attempting to print, the net–work (for network printers), and the printer parameters. The first step in solving a printer problem is narrowing down the problem to one of these sources. The error messages listed in this objective have to do with problems with the operating system.

WHAT YOU **REALLY** NEED TO KNOW

◆ To remove print jobs from the Windows 9x printer queue (spool), access the Printer dialog box and select Purge Print Documents from the Printer menu. For Windows 2000, the menu option in the Printer menu is Cancel All Documents.

◆ Successfully printing a self-test page using controls on the printer eliminate the printer as the source of a printing problem.

◆ Successfully printing an operating system test page eliminates all but the application attempting to print as a source of a printing problem.

◆ A printer self-test page often shows the amount of memory installed in a printer.

◆ Remove and reinstall a printer that is having problems that appear to be operating-system related. To remove a printer, right-click the printer icon in the Printer window and then click Delete on the shortcut menu.

◆ Verify printer properties. For DOS applications, verify the printer is configured to capture DOS application printing to LPT1.

◆ Try lowering the resolution. In the Printer Properties dialog box, try disabling the Check Port State Before Printing option.

◆ Try disabling printer spooling. In the Printer Properties dialog box, select Print Directly to the Printer.

◆ To eliminate bi-directional communication with the printer, in the Printer Properties dialog box, select the Disable bi-directional support for this printer option.

◆ Using Device Manager, examine the properties of LPT1 (I/O addresses are 0378 – 037B and IRQ is 7) and verify that Device Manager reports "No conflicts."

OBJECTIVES ON THE JOB

A PC technician is expected to be able to narrow down the source of a printing problem and, once the source is identified, use a variety of techniques and procedures to solve the problem.

PRACTICE TEST QUESTIONS

1. **If you can print a test page from the Windows 98 Print window, what is the most likely source of a user's continuing print problem?**
   a. the printer cable
   b. the printer
   c. the printer device driver
   d. the application

2. **You cannot print from an application or the Windows 98 Print window. What do you do first?**
   a. Exchange the printer for one you know is working.
   b. Uninstall and reinstall the printer drivers.
   c. Check that the printer is turned on and is online.
   d. Disable the parallel port in CMOS setup.

3. **You are unable to print and several jobs are in the print queue. How do you clear the queue?**
   a. Turn the printer off and back on.
   b. In the Printer window, select Printer on the menu bar, and then select Purge Print Documents.
   c. In the Printer window, select Printer on the menu bar, and then select Empty Printer Queue.
   d. From Device Manager, disable and then enable the printer.

4. **How do you uninstall a printer's device drivers?**
   a. From Device Manager, select the printer and then click Delete.
   b. From Device Manager, right-click the printer and select Uninstall.
   c. In the Printer window, right-click the printer and select Delete.
   d. In the Control Panel window, select Printer on the menu bar, and then select Delete.

5. **What is one source of a problem that would prevent Windows 98 from printing?**
   a. An application is not installed correctly.
   b. The hard drive does not have enough available space.
   c. COMMAND.COM is missing or corrupted.
   d. either b or c

6. **If you can print from a DOS prompt, but cannot print from Windows, what is the next thing you should do?**
   a. uninstall and reinstall the Windows printer drivers
   b. disable Windows printer spooling
   c. replace the printer cable
   d. tell the user to only print from a DOS prompt

7. **Which file extension is used for a bitmap file?**
   a. TIF
   b. BMP
   c. PCX
   d. DOC

OTHER COMMON PROBLEMS: GENERAL PROTECTION FAULTS • ILLEGAL OPERATION • INVALID WORKING DIRECTORY • SYSTEM LOCK UP • OPTION (SOUND CARD, MODEM, INPUT DEVICE) WILL NOT FUNCTION • APPLICATION WILL NOT START OR LOAD • TSR (TERMINATE STAY RESIDENT) PROGRAMS AND VIRUS • APPLICATIONS DON'T INSTALL

UNDERSTANDING THE OBJECTIVE

Problems like the ones listed above generally occur after the OS has loaded successfully and when you are loading or using application software. Problems with application software can be caused by the application, by the installation of other applications, or by other applications currently running. GPFs are generally caused by errors in the software or the OS, by a virus, or by two applications attempting to use the same memory space.

WHAT YOU **REALLY** NEED TO KNOW

◆ Under Windows 9x, when an application is installed, it may write .dll files to the Windows\System folder that can overwrite the .dll file of a previously installed application, which can cause a problem with the older application.

◆ Some problems are caused by insufficient memory because an application is using too much of a memory heap. Close some applications and/or install more RAM.

◆ When an application begins to consistently give errors, try uninstalling and reinstalling the application. In the Control Panel window, double-click the Add/Remove Program icon.

◆ The error message, "Bad command or file not found" is the result of the OS not being able to locate the specified program file. The program file may be in a different directory from the one specified in the path portion of the command line or in the list of paths in the last PATH command executed.

◆ If an application continues to give errors after you have reinstalled it, try verifying Windows system files or reinstalling Windows.

◆ Some errors reported by the OS that have to do with applications can be caused by a virus. Run a current version of antivirus software.

◆ When solving problems with applications, run Defrag and ScanDisk and verify that there is enough extra space on the hard drive for an application to store its temporary files while running.

◆ "Illegal operation" errors are often caused by application bugs or a virus.

◆ When an application fails to install correctly, use Dr. Watson to help isolate the problem. Also check the Web site of the application manufacturer for information about the problem.

OBJECTIVES ON THE JOB

Solving problems with application software is an expected and common task for a PC technician. Know that other software, the hardware, the operating system, or the application itself can be the cause of the problem.

PRACTICE TEST QUESTIONS

1. **When an application fails to load, what should you do first?**
   - a. Close all other applications and try again.
   - b. Uninstall and reinstall the application.
   - c. Reboot and try again.
   - d. Add more memory.

2. **How can you change the icon of a shortcut object on the desktop?**
   - a. Right-click the icon, select Properties, select the Shortcut tab, and then click Change Icon.
   - b. Right-click the icon, and then select Change Icon.
   - c. Click the icon, and then select Change Icon.
   - d. Edit the registry entry for this shortcut.

3. **You are running several applications and one of them locks up. What do you do?**
   - a. Reboot the PC.
   - b. Turn off the PC and turn it back on.
   - c. Press Ctrl+Alt+Del and then end the task.
   - d. Click Start on the taskbar, click Shutdown, and then click End Task.

4. **An application cannot access a device. How can you know if the device is installed properly?**
   - a. From Device Manager, select the device and click Properties.
   - b. Look for an X next to the device name in Device Manager.
   - c. Try to use the device using another application.
   - d. all of the above

5. **In implementing Plug and Play, the bus enumerator inventories the resources required by devices on the bus. Which bus does Windows 95 not support?**
   - a. SCSI
   - b. IDE
   - c. MCA
   - d. ISA

6. **How do you create a shortcut using Windows 98?**
   - a. In Windows Explorer, drag the file to the desktop.
   - b. Right-click the desktop, select New, and then select Shortcut.
   - c. Right-click the taskbar and select Shortcut.
   - d. either a or b

7. **An application gives an "illegal operations" error. What is one possible cause?**
   - a. The application has a bug.
   - b. The application is infected with a virus.
   - c. Windows has corrupted system files.
   - d. all of the above

CANNOT LOG ON TO NETWORK (OPTION – NIC NOT FUNCTIONING) • NETWORK CONNECTION

UNDERSTANDING THE OBJECTIVE

Problems logging onto a network or establishing a network connection can have a variety of sources. Begin with the easy to check and work your way up to the more difficult problems and resolutions. Many times a simple reboot is all that is required to reestablish a failed network connection.

WHAT YOU **REALLY** NEED TO KNOW

◆ Approach problems connecting to a TCP/IP network systematically. Try these things:
  - Verify the user name and password. Try using the Administrator logon.
  - Verify that the PC has a physical connection to the hub by looking for a light on the network card.
  - Try to ping another PC on the LAN.
  - Verify the PC has received an IP address from the DHCP server.
  - Check Network Neighborhood for Windows 9x or My Network Places for Windows 2000 to verify the PC can view resources on the network.
  - Uninstall and reinstall TCP/IP and then reboot.
  - Check physical connections.
  - Try a cold reboot.
  - Scan for viruses.
  - Suspect corrupted NIC drivers. Uninstall and reinstall the drivers.
  - Verify that other computers on the LAN can access the network.
  - Determine what does work. Can you connect successfully through a different port on the hub?
  - Replace the network cable.
  - Replace the NIC.

OBJECTIVES ON THE JOB

Solving problems with network requires patience and perseverance. Many times what didn't work will begin to work after a few retries with no apparent changes. Try several reboots. Go over the same things several times. Don't overlook that the problem can be a failed NIC, network cable or hub port.

PRACTICE TEST QUESTIONS

1. **How can you know a PC has a physical connection to an Ethernet hub?**
   a. Look for resources listed in Network Neighborhood
   b. Look for a light on the NIC
   c. Look for a light on the hub
   d. Either b or c

2. **How can you verify using Windows 2000 that a PC has good communication over the network?**
   a. Look for network resources listed in My Network Places
   b. Look for network resources listed in Network Neighborhood
   c. Check for a blinking light on the back of the network card
   d. Attempt to print to a network printer

3. **How can you verify that your computer can communicate with another computer on the TCP/IP network?**
   a. Use the Ping utility
   b. Use the Winipcfg utility
   c. Use the Router utility
   d. Reinstall TCP/IP

4. **What is a possible cause of a failure to connect to the network?**
   a. A virus
   b. A failed network card
   c. Corrupted Windows system files
   d. all of the above

5. **You cannot connect to a network even after a reboot. What is the next thing to do?**
   a. Replace the NIC
   b. Move the PC to another network port off the hub
   c. Verify network settings
   d. Replace the network cable

6. **You can print to a network printer but cannot see another host on the network that should be listed in Network Neighborhood. What might be the cause?**
   a. The network card has failed
   b. TCP/IP is not installed correctly
   c. The other PC is not online
   d. File and print sharing is not enabled

7. **How do you share a folder on the network?**
   a. Using Windows Explorer, right-click the folder name and select Sharing
   b. Using Windows Explorer, select the folder and click Sharing on the Explorer menu
   c. Drag and drop the folder into Network Neighborhood
   d. Open Network Neighborhood, select the folder and click Sharing on the menu

VIRUSES AND VIRUS TYPES: WHAT THEY ARE • SOURCES (FLOPPY, E-MAILS, ETC.) • HOW TO DETERMINE PRESENCE

UNDERSTANDING THE OBJECTIVE

Viruses are common with today's computer systems. Computer infestations are generally classified as viruses, worms, or Trojan horses. The best line of defense against infestations is to use common sense to not expose the system to a virus, to back up important data in the event of a failure caused by a virus, and to use antivirus software to detect and remove viruses.

WHAT YOU **REALLY** NEED TO KNOW

◆ A **boot sector virus** hides in the boot sector program on a hard drive or diskette. A **file virus** hides in a program file. A **multipartite virus** can hide in either a boot sector program or a program file.

◆ A **macro virus** hides in a **macro** that is part of a word processing document, spreadsheet, or similar file.

◆ A virus cannot hide in text or regular data files that don't contain macros.

◆ Symptoms of a virus include system performance slows, disk access is excessive, unusual error messages appear, files mysteriously disappear and appear, unusual reduction in disk space, the system locks up, devices are not available, number of bad sectors on a hard drive continue to increase, and strange graphics appear.

◆ Use **antivirus software** to detect and remove viruses. Keep the software current as new viruses are discovered daily.

◆ **Polymorphic**, **encrypting**, and **stealth viruses** have different methods of cloaking themselves from detection by antivirus software.

◆ A virus hoax is a letter or e-mail warning about a nonexistent virus that is itself a pest because it overloads network traffic.

◆ The BIOS in some computer systems has antivirus protection that can be enabled in CMOS setup. This protection prevents the partition-table master boot program (MBR) from being altered.

◆ Know the symptoms of a virus and have antivirus software available and use it during a troubleshooting session.

◆ Always scan your bootable disks for a virus before using them on a customer's system.

◆ More viruses are received through e-mail attachments than by any other single means. Never open an e-mail attachment from someone you don't trust without first scanning the file for a virus.

◆ Antivirus software includes Norton AntiVirus, Dr. Solomon's Software, McAfee VirusScan, eSafe, F-PROT, and Command AntiVirus.

◆ Keep antivirus software current by downloading data files about viruses and upgrades to the antivirus software from the antivirus software Web site.

OBJECTIVES ON THE JOB

Be proactive when protecting your own and your customers' systems against viruses. Use antivirus software regularly. If a system supports it, set up a scheduled task so that the OS executes the software automatically at certain times, such as when the PC boots.

PRACTICE TEST QUESTIONS

1. **How does a boot sector virus differ from a file virus?**
   a. the payload they deliver
   b. where they hide
   c. how long they can stay in memory
   d. how many times they can replicate

   ANSWER

2. **How does a virus typically spread over e-mail?**
   a. in the software that provides the e-mail service
   b. in the software downloaded from the ISP
   c. in the boot sector of floppy disks used to attach files to e-mail messages
   d. in files attached to e-mail messages

   ANSWER

3. **What is a macro virus?**
   a. a virus that replicates itself multiple times before unloading from memory
   b. a virus that destroys the hard drive
   c. a virus that hides in scripts or other short programs embedded in document files
   d. a virus that uses two different ways to hide: in files and in boot sectors of the hard drive

   ANSWER

4. **What can you do to protect against a virus?**
   a. Use antivirus software.
   b. Never use pirated software.
   c. Make regular backups.
   d. all of the above

   ANSWER

5. **What is one thing that a virus cannot do?**
   a. erase all data on a hard drive
   b. damage the partition table
   c. damage the boot strap loader program
   d. damage the controller card of the hard drive

   ANSWER

6. **What is the purpose of virus protection in CMOS setup?**
   a. It prevents someone from accidentally making changes to CMOS setup.
   b. It prevents the partition table from being altered.
   c. It prevents someone from uninstalling antivirus software.
   d. It prevents macro files from entering a system.

   ANSWER

7. **What is a symptom of a virus being present or having done damage?**
   a. The PC will not boot.
   b. You cannot access the CD-ROM drive.
   c. The system performance is slow.
   d. all of the above

   ANSWER

4.1 Identify the networking capabilities of Windows including procedures for connecting to the network

PROTOCOLS • IPCONFIG.EXE • WINIPCFG.EXE • INSTALLING AND CONFIGURING BROWSERS • CONFIGURE OS FOR NETWORK CONNECTION

UNDERSTANDING THE OBJECTIVE

Windows 9x and Windows 2000 support several network protocols. The most popular is the protocol used by the Internet—TCP/IP. With TCP/IP, every host or device on the network is assigned an Internet Protocol address (IP address). Ipconfig.exe and Winipcfg.exe are utilities used to diagnose problems with a TCP/IP network. Other network protocols supported by Windows include NetBEUI, IPX/SPX, and DLC protocols.

WHAT YOU **REALLY** NEED TO KNOW

◆ NetBIOS and Windows Sockets are programming interfaces for applications that use a network. Windows Sockets uses a TCP/IP network.

◆ NetBIOS can use a NetBEUI (NetBIOS Extended User Interface) network or use a TCP/IP network if it has the NetBT (NetBIOS over TCP/IP) layer between it and the TCP/IP protocol.

◆ The NetBEUI protocol is a proprietary Microsoft protocol used only by Windows and limited to a LAN because it does not support routing to other networks.

◆ DLC protocol is often used to connect to IBM mainframes and HP network printers.

◆ Winipcfg.exe is a Windows 9x utility that reports the configuration information about the current TCP/IP connection for a device. To access Winipcfg.exe, click Start, Run, and enter winipcfg.exe in the Run dialog box.

◆ Ipconfig.exe is a Windows NT and Windows 2000 utility that reports similar information as Winipcfg.exe about the current TCP/IP connection to a network. To access Ipconfig.exe, enter Ipconfig.exe from a Command prompt window.

◆ To configure an OS for a network connection, first install the network protocol. For Windows 9x, from Control Panel, use the Network icon. From the Network windows, select the Configuration tab. Click Add, Protocol, Microsoft. Select the protocol to install and click OK. The protocol binds itself to any installed network device.

◆ To configure the binding, from Control Panel, access the Network window, select the binding, and click Properties. For TCP/IP, enter an IP address or specify to obtain an IP address automatically. Enter a default gateway to connect to the Internet.

◆ To configure a browser, for Microsoft Internet Explorer, use the Internet Options icon in Control Panel. Set the size of the browser cache, what type of connection to use, and whether or not to use a proxy server to connect to the Internet. IE will automatically sense these settings in some instances.

OBJECTIVES ON THE JOB

A PC technician depends on a network administrator to know user IDs and passwords, network settings and protocols and procedures for connecting to the Internet. The PC technician is then expected to know how to use this information to connect a new or repaired PC to a network and verify the Internet connection is good. Installing and configuring browsers is a common task for a PC technician.

PRACTICE TEST QUESTIONS

1. **When will a Windows-based PC use the IPX/SPX network protocol?**
   - a. When it is connected to a Netware LAN
   - b. When it is connected to the Internet using a cable modem
   - c. When it is using applications that require the NetBIOS interface
   - d. None of the above; a Windows PC will never use the IPX/SPX network protocol.

2. **When is the DLC network protocol likely to be used?**
   - a. when communicating with an HP network printer
   - b. when communicating with an IBM mainframe
   - c. when communicating with a Novel file server
   - d. either a or b

3. **How do you create a new network connection using Windows 2000?**
   - a. Control Panel, Network and Dial-up Connections, Make New Connection
   - b. Control Panel, Add/Remove Programs, Windows Setup
   - c. Right-click My Network Places, select Properties, Make New Connection
   - d. Either a or c

4. **What is one limitation of the NetBEUI protocol?**
   - a. It does not support routing and therefore is limited to a single LAN
   - b. It is a slow protocol when used to access the Internet
   - c. It is only used by IBM mainframe computers
   - d. It was designed by Microsoft

5. **Which utility is not included with Windows 2000?**
   - a. Ipconfig
   - b. Ping
   - c. Winipcfg
   - d. Tracert

6. **Which statement is not true about the TCP/IP protocol?**
   - a. It will work only if it is the only network protocol installed on a system
   - b. When TCP/IP is installed, it automatically binds itself to an installed NIC
   - c. When TCP/IP is installed, it automatically binds itself to an installed modem
   - d. TCP/IP is the protocol used by the Internet

7. **What is the purpose of NetBT?**
   - a. To support IPX/SPX on a TCP/IP network
   - b. To communicate with an HP network printer
   - c. To support NetBIOS on a TCP/IP network
   - d. Either a or c

4.1
cont. Identify the networking capabilities of Windows including procedures for connecting to the network

SHARING DISK DRIVES • SHARING PRINT AND FILE SERVICES

UNDERSTANDING THE OBJECTIVE

A shared disk drive is seen as a network drive on a PC that accesses the drive of another computer. When a printer is connected to a PC by way of a parallel or serial cable or infrared port in a network environment, that PC can share that printer with others on the network. Shared resources are available to others on the network, and, in Windows 9x, can be viewed in Network Neighborhood, and, in Windows 2000, can be viewed in My Network Places. Files and folders can be shared using Windows Explorer and can be password protected.

WHAT YOU **REALLY** NEED TO KNOW

◆ Using Windows 9x, to install file and printer sharing for Microsoft Networks, in the Control Panel, double-click the Network icon, click the Configuration tab, and then click the File and printer sharing for Microsoft Networks button.

◆ If the Network Neighborhood icon appears on the desktop, then Client for Microsoft Networks is installed. Double-click this icon to view and access resources on the network.

◆ To share a file or folder with others on the network using Windows 9x, right-click the file or folder name in Windows Explorer, and select Sharing from the shortcut menu. You must then give the folder or drive a name that will be used by others on the network to access this resource. Enter a password for added security.

◆ A shared drive or folder is displayed in Windows Explorer with a hand underneath the folder or drive icon.

◆ To map a network drive to a remote computer in Windows Explorer, click Tools on the menu bar, and then click Map Network Drive. Enter the host computer name preceded by two backslashes.

◆ To share a printer to others on the network, right-click the printer name in the Printer window and select Sharing from the shortcut menu. Give the printer a name, which will later appear to other users in the Network Neighborhood window on their desktop.

◆ Windows 9x supports Direct Cable Connection that allows two PCs to connect using a **null modem cable** or a parallel cable.

◆ If Direct Cable Connection or other Windows 9x components don't appear in menus, they may not be installed. To install additional components, click Start on the taskbar, point to Settings, click Control Panel, double-click the Add/Remove Programs icon, and then click the Windows Setup tab.

OBJECTIVES ON THE JOB

In a business environment, it is a common practice to share printers, disk drives on file servers, and files on user's PCs. Most often the network administrator is responsible for configuring a PC to access shared resources or to share its own resources, although sometimes a PC technician is called on to assist. When a PC technician services a PC connected to a network, care must be taken to not alter network settings.

PRACTICE TEST QUESTIONS

1. What is the purpose of Windows 98 Direct Cable Connection?

    a. It allows a PC to connect to the Internet.

    b. It allows a PC to connect to another PC by way of a phone line.

    c. It allows two PCs to connect using a null modem cable or parallel cable.

    d. It allows a PC to use a network interface card (NIC).

2. What connects a null modem cable to a PC?

    a. a serial port

    b. a parallel port

    c. a USB port

    d. a NIC

3. How do you install file and printer sharing for Microsoft Networks?

    a. Control Panel, Network, Configuration, Add, Services

    b. Control Panel, Add/Remove Programs, Windows Setup

    c. Control Panel, Add New Hardware

    d. Control Panel, System Properties, Device Manager

4. How do you share a file or folder with others on the network?

    a. In Explorer, select the object, then use Network on the menu.

    b. In Explorer, right-click the object and select Sharing.

    c. In Network Neighborhood, right-click the object and select Sharing.

    d. Right-click the item displayed on the desktop, point to Properties, and then click Sharing.

5. Using Windows 9x, how do you map a drive letter to a network resource?

    a. In Explorer, select Tools, Map Network Drive.

    b. In Network Neighborhood, right-click the object and select Map Network Drive.

    c. In My Computer, right-click the object and select Map Network Drive.

    d. either a or b

6. When you share a printer with others on the network, what is required?

    a. The shared printer must be given a name.

    b. The shared printer must use a parallel cable rather than a serial cable.

    c. The shared printer must be a special network printer.

    d. The network protocol used must be NetBEUI.

7. When using Windows Explorer, how can you tell that an object is network shared?

    a. There is a blue "N" beside the object.

    b. There is a hand underneath the object.

    c. The object name is written in blue and underlined.

    d. all of the above

4.1
cont. Identify the networking capabilities of Windows including procedures for connecting to the network

NETWORK TYPE AND NETWORK CARD

UNDERSTANDING THE OBJECTIVE

The three most common local area network architectures used today are Ethernet, Token Ring, and FDDI. (Ethernet is by far the most popular of the three.) Each type requires its own network interface card (NIC), which must also match the type of network cabling used. Just as with other hardware devices, the NIC requires that device drivers be installed under the OS.

WHAT YOU REALLY NEED TO KNOW

◆ Windows 95 supports Ethernet, Token Ring, and ARCnet networking cards.

◆ Windows 98 supports ATM, Ethernet, Token Ring, FDDI, IrDA, and ARCnet networking cards.

◆ Windows 2000 supports Ethernet, Token Ring, cable modem, DSL, FDDI, ATM, IrDA, wireless, T1, and Frame Relay.

◆ To view how a NIC is configured by Windows 9x, open the Control Panel, double-click the Network icon, and then click the Configuration tab. Right-click the network card and then click Properties on the shortcut menu.

◆ Windows 9x includes drivers for many network cards from many manufacturers, and you can also install drivers provided by the manufacturer.

◆ Windows 95 supports networks from four manufacturers: Banyan, Microsoft, Novell, and SunSoft.

◆ Windows 98 supports networks from three manufacturers: Banyan, Microsoft, and Novell.

OBJECTIVES ON THE JOB

On the job, when installing device drivers for a network card or installing the software to connect to a network, work under the supervision of the network administrator who is responsible for the overall configuration and security of the network.

Item	Ethernet	Token Ring	FDDI
Logical topology or shape	Bus	Single ring	Dual ring
Physical topology or shape	Star or bus	Ring or star	Ring
Media	Twisted-pair, coaxial, or fiber-optic cable	Twisted-pair, fiber-optic cable	Primarily fiber-optic cable
Standard bandwidth	10 Mbps or 100 Mbps	4 or 16 Mbps	100 Mbps to 200 Mbps
How token is released	Not applicable	After receive	After transmit
Advantages	Of the three networks, Ethernet is the least expensive, simplest, and most popular solution	Token Ring operates more reliably under heavy traffic than does Ethernet, but can be difficult to troubleshoot	FDDI is much faster than Token Ring and regular Ethernet and faster than 100BaseT (fast Ethernet)

PRACTICE TEST QUESTIONS

1. **What type of networks does Windows 95 support?**
    a. Ethernet, Token Ring, and FDDI
    b. Ethernet, Token Ring, and ARCnet
    c. Ethernet, Token Ring, and IrDA
    d. Token Ring, FDDI, and ARCnet

2. **You have a network card that has a port that looks like a large phone jack. What type of NIC is it?**
    a. an Ethernet card using a BNC connection
    b. an Ethernet card using a RJ-45 connection
    c. a Token Ring card
    d. a Banyan card

3. **Which is the most popular network architecture for a LAN?**
    a. FDDI
    b. Token Ring
    c. ATM
    d. Ethernet

4. **What is the most common topology used by Ethernet?**
    a. twisted pair
    b. TCP/IP
    c. star
    d. RJ-45

5. **Which type network is not supported by Windows 98?**
    a. DecNet
    b. IPX/SPX
    c. TCP/IP
    d. NetBEUI

6. **Before data can be sent over a network, what happens to it?**
    a. It is put in packets with a header and trailer.
    b. It is segmented into 64-bit segments.
    c. It is converted into 16-bit bytes that are ready for parallel transmission.
    d. It is converted into ASCII form.

7. **Windows 95 has built-in support for what type of networking?**
    a. ATM
    b. peer-to-peer
    c. wide area
    d. SCSI

4.2 Identify concepts and capabilities relating to the Internet and basic procedures for setting up a system for Internet access

CONCEPTS AND TERMINOLOGY: TCP/IP • NETBEUI • IPX/SPX • PING.EXE • TRACERT.EXE • NSLOOKUP.EXE

UNDERSTANDING THE OBJECTIVE

TCP/IP, NetBEUI, and IPX/SPX are three different network protocols used to control network traffic at the operating system level.

WHAT YOU **REALLY** NEED TO KNOW

- ◆ The two most common groups of protocols used by networks are TCP/IP (Transmission Control Protocol/Internet Protocol) and IPX/SPX (Internetwork Packet Exchange/Sequenced Packet Exchange).
- ◆ IPX/SPX was developed by Netware for Novel networks. Computers running Windows can use the Microsoft IPX/SPX protocol to access these networks.
- ◆ NetBEUI is a proprietary Microsoft protocol used only by Windows-based operating systems, and it is limited to LANs.
- ◆ TCP/IP has a suite of utility programs designed to help troubleshoot problems with network communication. The utility programs that are automatically installed when TCP/IP is installed under Windows 9x are listed below:
  - **ARP** manages the IP-to-Ethernet address translation tables that are used to find MAC addresses of a host and other configuration information.
  - **Ipconfig** displays the IP address of the host and other configuration information.
  - **FTP** transfers files over a network.
  - **Nbtstat** displays current information about TCP/IP and NetBIOS when both are used on the same network.
  - **Netstat** displays information about current TCP/IP connections.
  - **Ping** verifies there is a connection on a network between two hosts.
  - **Route** allows you to manually control network routing tables.
  - **Telnet** provides a console session for a UNIX or Windows 2000 computer so you can remotely control the computer on the network.
  - **Tracert** traces and displays the route from the host to a remote destination.
  - **Winipcfg** displays IP address and other configuration information.
  - Windows 2000 TCP/IP includes those listed above (except Telnet and Winipcfg) and the following utilities:
  - **Finger** displays information about a user on a specified system.
  - **Hostname** displays the name of the current computer.
  - **Lpq** displays status of a print queue.
  - **Lpr** is used to print a file to a computer running an LPD server (print service).
  - **Nslookup** shows information about the Domain Name System (DNS) name server on a network.
  - **Rcp** is used to copy files between a Windows 2000 computer and a UNIX computer.
  - **Rexec** and **Rsh** run commands on remote computers.
  - **Tftp** transfers files between two computers.

OBJECTIVES ON THE JOB

A PC technician is expected to help support PCs on a network and the Internet. A technician should be familiar with all these utilities and be comfortable using the more critical ones including Ping, Winipcfg, Ipconfig, and FTP.

PRACTICE TEST QUESTIONS

1. **What are the most common network protocols that work at the operating system level that are supported by Windows 9x and Windows 2000?**
   a. TCP/IP, Ethernet, and Token Ring
   b. TCP/IP, IPX/SPX, and NetBEUI
   c. HTTP, TCP/IP, and SMTP
   d. NFS, LPR, FTP, and HTTP

2. **What protocol is used by Netware Novell?**
   a. FTP
   b. TCP/IP
   c. IPX/SPX
   d. SMTP

3. **How is the NetBEUI protocol used?**
   a. for e-mail services over the Internet
   b. for terminal emulation over a WAN or MAN
   c. on LANs with Windows-based computers
   d. either a or c

4. **Which TCP/IP utility is used to verify that two computers are connected over a network?**
   a. FTP
   b. Ping
   c. Ipconfig
   d. Winipcfg

5. **Which TCP/IP utility is a part of Windows 9x TCP/IP but is not included with Windows 2000 TCP/IP?**
   a. Winipcfg
   b. Ipconfig
   c. Ping
   d. Route

6. **What is Telnet?**
   a. a service that allows a user to enter UNIX commands in a UNIX window on a personal computer
   b. a service that allows files to be transmitted over the Internet from an FTP server
   c. a service that sends HTML documents over the Internet
   d. a service that allows a user to map a network drive to a network resource shared by someone else on the network

7. **What is the main networking protocol used by the Internet?**
   a. TCP/IP
   b. IPX/SPX
   c. FTP
   d. NetBEUI

4.2 cont. Identify concepts and capabilities relating to the Internet and basic procedures for setting up a system for Internet access

E-MAIL • FTP • DOMAIN NAMES (WEB SITES) • HTML • HTTP://

UNDERSTANDING THE OBJECTIVE

The Internet is a transportation service for many services, each using their own protocols. One of these protocols, **HTTP**, is used to pass documents to Web browsers over the World Wide Web originating from hosts (web sites) on the Web which are identified by IP addresses or domain names. These documents are often written so that text in the document can have an embedded link to other text or other documents. These documents are called hypertext files and are written using the **Hypertext Markup Language** (**HTML**). E-mail and **FTP** (**file transfer protocol**) are two popular network services that use the Internet. FTP is used to transfer files across a network that supports TCP/IP. E-mail sends text messages across a network using SMTP protocol. Files can be attached to these e-mail text messages.

WHAT YOU **REALLY** NEED TO KNOW

◆ The Internet is a group of networks that can be used by network services including Web browsers, chat rooms, e-mail, and FTP.

◆ Protocols at the Application layer of the OSI model, such as HTTP, FTP, POP and SMTP, use **sockets** or **NetBIOS** to establish communication with lower-level protocols. HTTP, FTP, POP and SMTP all use the sockets method.

◆ For FTP to work, FTP software must be running at both the host and the client. The host runs FTP server and the client runs FTP client.

◆ For e-mail, a PC client establishes a session with a server to receive e-mail using the POP protocol and send e-mail using the SMTP protocol.

◆ Web browsers use HTTP protocol.

◆ HTML documents have an HTML file extension, or, for DOS, an HTM file extension.

◆ A virus is spread by e-mail through attached files. When the recipient opens an attached document, a macro in the document (which contains the virus) executes.

◆ A Web site is identified by its **IP address**, but a **domain name** can be substituted for the IP address when addressing the Web site.

◆ The protocol, domain name, and a path or filename are collectively called a **uniform resource locator (URL)**, as in *http://www.course.com/pcrepair*. In this URL, *http* is the protocol used, the domain name is *www.course.com* and *pcrepair* is the name of a file on this Web site.

◆ Internet Corporation for Assigned Names and Numbers (ICANN) oversees the process of assigning IP addresses and domain names. A company that can register IP addresses and domain names is called a registrar.

◆ Valid endings for domain names include .com (commercial use), .edu (education), .gov (government), .org (nonprofit institutions), and .net (Internet provider).

◆ Uniform Naming Convention (UNC) is a system for naming folders and files among computers on a network. A valid name for a computer and folder is \\Computer10\Folder12.

OBJECTIVES ON THE JOB

Supporting PCs connected to the Internet, WANs, and MANs includes supporting browsers, e-mail and FTP services. A PC technician also needs to understand how domain names and URLs are written and used.

PRACTICE TEST QUESTIONS

1. A user shares a folder on his hard drive with others on the network. His computer is named JSMITH and his folder is named JOE. What is the UNC name for this shared resource?
   a. \JSMITH\JOE
   b. \\JSMITH\JOE
   c. //JSMITH/JOE
   d. /JSMITH/JOE

2. When configuring a PC using TCP/IP with static IP addressing to log onto a network, what unique information is needed for this PC?
   a. the IP address and subnet mask
   b. the IP address and amount of RAM installed
   c. the IP address and MAC address
   d. the IP address and domain name

3. What is FTP?
   a. a service that allows a user to enter UNIX commands in a UNIX window on a personal computer
   b. a service that allows files to be transmitted over a network to or from a remote computer
   c. a service that sends HTML documents over the Internet
   d. a service that allows a user to map a network drive to a network resource shared by someone else on the network

4. What organization tracks domain names and IP addresses?
   a. ICANN
   b. Microsoft
   c. IBM
   d. National Science Foundation

5. What is UNC?
   a. a system for accessing e-mail from a remote location
   b. a system for downloading files on the Internet
   c. a system for naming resources on a network
   d. a method of connecting to an Internet Service Provider

6. What type of organization uses domain names that end in .org?
   a. commercial companies
   b. government organizations
   c. political organizations
   d. non-profit organizations

7. What is a domain name?
   a. an easy way to remember an IP address
   b. the name of a UNIX or Windows NT server
   c. the name of an organization that provides Web pages
   d. the name of a service on the Internet

Identify concepts and capabilities relating to the Internet and basic procedures for setting up a system for Internet access

ISP • DIAL-UP NETWORKING

UNDERSTANDING THE OBJECTIVE

An Internet Service Provider (ISP) provides access to the Internet for businesses and personal use. Users can access the ISP by any of several methods, including a dedicated circuit, ISDN line, or regular analog phone line. For personal and small business use, dial-up access using a regular phone line is a common practice. In Windows 9x, the service is Dial-Up Networking and in Windows 2000 it is called Dial-Up Connections.

WHAT YOU **REALLY** NEED TO KNOW

◆ When connecting to an ISP and then to the Internet using dial-up access, data is packaged using TCP/IP for Internet traffic, but is also packaged in a line protocol for travel over phone lines to the ISP.

◆ Two line protocols are **Serial Line Internet Protocol (SLIP)** and **Point-to-Point Protocol (PPP)**. The older SLIP has been replaced by the faster PPP.

◆ Windows 9x supports **dial-up networking (DUN)** so that the modem acts like a network card when calling an ISP or other entry point into a network.

◆ An IP address belongs to one of three classes: A, B, or C.

◆ An IP address can be a static IP address (permanently assigned to a workstation) or a dynamic IP address (changes each time a workstation logs onto the network).

◆ The server that manages dynamically assigned IP addresses is called the **dynamic host configuration protocol (DHCP)** server and provides this DHCP service. Most ISPs use dynamic IP addressing for their dial-up users.

◆ Two services that track relationships between domain names and their corresponding IP addresses are **Domain Name Service (DNS)** and **Windows Internet Naming Service (WINS)**.

OBJECTIVES ON THE JOB

A PC technician needs to understand how IP addresses, domain names, and dial-up networking work, to help a user make a successful dial-up connection to an ISP to access the Internet.

◆ Does the phone line work? Do you have a dial tone? Try dialing the number manually from a phone. Do you hear beeps on the other end? Can you dial another phone number?

◆ Does the modem work? Use the modemlog.txt file to troubleshoot problems with the modem. (For Windows 9x, to log modem events to the modemlog.txt file, double-click Modems in the Control Panel, select the modem, click Properties, Connection, Advanced, and select "Recording to a log file.")

◆ Are all components installed? Check for the Dial-Up Adapter and TCP/IP, and check the configuration of each.

◆ Check the Dial-Up Networking connection icon for errors. Is the phone number correct? Does the number need to include a 9 to access an outside line? Has a 1 been added in front of the number by mistake?

◆ Sometimes older copies of the Windows socket DLL interfere with the current Windows 9x socket DLL. (Windows 9x may be finding and executing the older DLL before it finds the newer one.) Search for and rename any files named WINSOCK.DLL except the one in the Windows\System directory.

PRACTICE TEST QUESTIONS

1. When configuring a PC to use a modem to an ISP to connect to the Internet, what line protocol is used?
   - a. PPP
   - b. SLIP
   - c. TCP/IP
   - d. none of the above

ANSWER

2. Which of the following is not a valid IP address?
   - a. 205.300.40.3
   - b. 3.4.5.6
   - c. 190.40.50.48
   - d. 250.80.10.1

ANSWER

3. What network service keeps track of domain names and their corresponding IP addresses?
   - a. TCP/IP
   - b. DNS
   - c. WINS
   - d. Both b and c

ANSWER

4. When an IP address is assigned to a PC each time it logs onto a network, this is called:
   - a. the Internet
   - b. TCP/IP addressing
   - c. dynamic IP addressing
   - d. static IP addressing

ANSWER

5. What protocol must be installed for a PC using Windows 95 to connect to the Internet?
   - a. DHCP
   - b. NetBEUI
   - c. TCP/IP
   - d. IPX

ANSWER

6. What service does a Windows 95 PC use when it contacts a Windows NT server requesting an IP address at logon to the network?
   - a. WINS
   - b. DNS
   - c. DHCP
   - d. TCP/IP

ANSWER

7. In what class is the IP address 129.80.129.240?
   - a. Class A
   - b. Class B
   - c. Class C
   - d. Class D

ANSWER

SPREAD 1

Objective 1.1	Identify basic terms, concepts, and functions of system modules, including how each module should work during normal operation and during the boot process	System board Ports

Practice Test Questions

1. Which statement about the system board is false?

   Correct answer: d

2. In the drawing, item 6 is a(n):

   Correct answer: a

3. In the drawing, item 15 is a(n):

   Correct answer: c

4. In the drawing, item 3 is a(n):

   Correct answer: c

5. In the drawing, item 11 is a(n):

   Correct answer: c

6. A FRU that is installed on the system board is:

   Correct answer: a

7. Timing on the system board is controlled by the:

   Correct answer: d

SPREAD 2

Objective 1.1 continued	Identify basic terms, concepts, and functions of system modules, including how each module should work during normal operation and during the boot process	Power supply

Practice Test Questions

1. Which power supply provides 3 volts of DC current to a system board?

   Correct answer: c

2. What is the symbol for a diode?

   Correct answer: c

3. What is the unit of measure for the capacitance of a capacitor?

   Correct answer: d

4. Which statement is true about the power from an ATX power supply to a system board?

   Correct answer: b

5. Which statement is true about a power supply?

   Correct answer: a

6. The voltage used by a floppy disk drive is:

Correct answer: c

7. An AT system board uses what voltages?

Correct answer: a

SPREAD 3

Objective 1.1 continued	Identify basic terms, concepts, and functions of system modules, including how each module should work during normal operation and during the boot process	Processor/CPU

Practice Test Questions

1. Running a system board at a higher speed than that suggested by the manufacturer is called:

   Correct answer: b

2. What does the CPU do?

   Correct answer: b

3. Which CPU technology is appropriate to improve performance in a multimedia computer system?

   Correct answer: d

4. If the CPU is running at 300 MHz and the system bus is running at 100 MHz, then the multiplier is:

   Correct answer: c

5. Typical speeds for today's system bus are:

   Correct answer: b

6. RISC stands for:

   Correct answer: a

7. A memory cache stored on the CPU microchip is called:

   Correct answer: a

SPREAD 4

Objective 1.1 continued	Identify basic terms, concepts, and functions of system modules, including how each module should work during normal operation and during the boot process	Memory Monitor

Practice Test Questions

1. Another name for reserved memory is:

   Correct answer: d

2. Which type of monitor provides the highest quality performance?

   Correct answer: c

3. A parity error is most likely caused by what device?

   Correct answer: b

4. Which device is not considered a field-replaceable unit?

   Correct answer: d

5. Which DOS device driver is used to gain access to extended memory?

   Correct answer: b

6. Space on the hard drive that is used as though it is RAM is called:

   Correct answer: d

7. Which memory module is used to hold memory cache on the system board?

   Correct answer: c

SPREAD 5

Objective 1.1 continued	Identify basic terms, concepts, and functions of system modules, including how each module should work during normal operation and during the boot process	Storage devices

Practice Test Questions

1. What is the purpose of ATAPI standards?

   Correct answer: b

2. What is a Jaz drive?

   Correct answer: a

3. Which statement is true about an IDE hard drive and a SCSI hard drive?

   Correct answer: b

4. How can you change the boot priority of a system?

   Correct answer: c

5. What is boot priority?

   Correct answer: b

6. Which statement is true about Zip drives and Jaz drives?

   Correct answer: c

7. Which statement is true about secondary storage?

   Correct answer: b

SPREAD 6

Objective 1.1 continued	Identify basic terms, concepts, and functions of system modules, including how each module should work during normal operation and during the boot process	Storage devices – Hard drives

Practice Test Questions

1. A hard disk is divided into concentric circles called:

   Correct answer: b

2. One sector on most hard drives contains:

   Correct answer: d

3. The program that writes sector and track markings to a hard drive is:

   Correct answer: d

4. Which file is not necessary in order for the DOS operating system to load?

   Correct answer: d

5. If a system has two hard drives and the first drive contains two logical drives, what drive letter will be assigned to the first logical drive on the second hard drive?

   Correct answer: b

6. Which port can be used for an external hard drive?

   Correct answer: c

7. How many partitions on a hard drive can Windows 98 support?

   Correct answer: b

SPREAD 7

Objective 1.1 continued	Identify basic terms, concepts, and functions of system modules, including how each module should work during normal operation and during the boot process	Modem

Practice Test Questions

1. A 33.6 modem should transmit data at _____ bits per second.

   Correct answer: b

2. What does the acronym CTS mean?

   Correct answer: b

3. Which modem command is part of the handshaking process?

   Correct answer: d

4. The command to reset a modem is:

   Correct answer: b

5. An external modem connects to:

   Correct answer: c

6. When data is being sent by a modem, the _____ signal is up.

   Correct answer: b

7. The modem command to hang up the phone is:

   Correct answer: b

SPREAD 8

Objective 1.1 continued	Identify basic terms, concepts, and functions of system modules, including how each module should work during normal operation and during the boot process	Firmware BIOS CMOS

Practice Test Questions

1. When the PC loses setup information each time it is booted, a possible cause of this problem is:

   Correct answer: b

2. The system date and time can be set using:

   Correct answer: d

3. One reason you might flash ROM is to:

   Correct answer: a

4. Plug and Play is a feature of:

   Correct answer: d

5. How do you access CMOS to view settings and make changes?

   Correct answer: a

6. The program to change CMOS can be stored:

   Correct answer: d

7. The type of ROM BIOS that can be changed without exchanging the chip is called:

   Correct answer: c

SPREAD 9

Objective 1.1 continued	Identify basic terms, concepts, and functions of system modules, including how each module should work during normal operation and during the boot process	LCD (portable systems) PDA (Personal Digital Assistant)

Practice Test Questions

1. Which type of LCD panel gives the best quality?

   Correct answer: a

2. One pixel on a LCD panel is created by:

   Correct answer: c

3. What is *not* advisable when supporting a notebook?

   Correct answer: b

4. What operating system is typically used by a PDA?

   Correct answer: d

5. Which statement is *not* true concerning a PDA?

   Correct answer: d

6. Which is true concerning dual scan display?

Correct answer: a

7. Which statement is true concerning using a PDA to access the Internet?

Correct answer: d

SPREAD 10

Objective 1.2	Identify basic procedures for adding and removing field replaceable modules for both desktop and portable systems	System board

Practice Test Questions

1. The purpose of a standoff is to:

Correct answer: a

2. Which of the following devices are considered FRUs?

Correct answer: d

3. Before replacing a dead system board, one thing you should do is:

Correct answer: d

4. What is one thing that might cause damage to a system board as you service a PC?

Correct answer: a

5. When installing AT power supply connections to a system board, what should you remember?

Correct answer: b

6. When installing a system board, which is installed first?

Correct answer: b

7. When exchanging a system board, why is it important to remove other components?

Correct answer: d

SPREAD 11

Objective 1.2 continued	Identify basic procedures for adding and removing field replaceable modules for both desktop and portable systems	Storage device Hard drive

Practice Test Questions

1. If a system has two IDE hard drives that each have primary and extended partitions with one logical drive in each partition, what is the drive letter assigned to the primary partition of the second hard drive?

Correct answer: b

2. After performing a low-level format of a hard drive, what is the next step in the installation process?

Correct answer: b

3. What kind of cable is a 34-pin data cable?

Correct answer: d

4. How many pins does an IDE data cable have?

Correct answer: c

5. When a CD-ROM drive and an IDE hard drive are sharing the same data cable:

Correct answer: a

6. A port on the back of a PC has 50 pins. What type port is it?

Correct answer: b

7. What IRQ does the primary IDE channel use?

Correct answer: c

SPREAD 12

Objective 1.2 continued	Identify basic procedures for adding and removing field replaceable modules for both desktop and portable systems	Power supply Input devices Keyboard Mouse

Practice Test Questions

1. The ESD bracelet is designed to protect:

Correct answer: a

2. What might you need to upgrade after installing a new hard drive in a system?

Correct answer: b

3. Before exchanging a power supply, you should:

Correct answer: d

4. If the cable connector on a keyboard does not fit the keyboard port on the system board, then:

Correct answer: b

5. If the mouse port on a system board does not work, then:

Correct answer: d

6. What ports can a mouse use?

Correct answer: d

7. How does a keyboard get its power?

Correct answer: a

SPREAD 13

Objective 1.2 continued	Identify basic procedures for adding and removing field replaceable modules for both desktop and portable systems	Processor/CPU Memory

Practice Test Questions

1. A system has two SIMMs installed and two SIMM slots are still open. Which of the following statements is correct?

   Correct answer: c

2. A system has four DIMM slots and one DIMM installed. Which statement is correct?

   Correct answer: a

3. Which statement is true about RAM on a system board?

   Correct answer: c

4. After installing memory and booting the system, the memory does not count up correctly. The most likely problem is:

   Correct answer: b

5. How many pins are there on a DIMM?

   Correct answer: d

6. Without the system board documentation, how can you tell if a DIMM is the correct type memory for a system board?

   Correct answer: b

7. Why does a Pentium system require that SIMMs be installed in pairs?

   Correct answer: a

SPREAD 14

Objective 1.2 continued	Identify basic procedures for adding and removing field replaceable modules for both desktop and portable systems	Video board Network Interface Card (NIC)

Practice Test Questions

1. The fastest port used for video boards today is:

   Correct answer: c

2. What is the difference in an AGP slot and an AGP Pro slot on a system board?

   Correct answer: b

3. What is one thing you can do to speed up a sluggish system that is graphic intensive?

   Correct answer: a

4. AGP 4X is defined by the AGP 2.0 specification. The 4x refers to:

   Correct answer: a

5. What bus is no longer found on system boards today?

   Correct answer: d

6. The video system does not work. What is the first thing you check?

   Correct answer: a

7. How can you tell that the network card is connected to and communicating with other network equipment on the network?

   Correct answer: c

SPREAD 15

Objective 1.2 continued	Identify basic procedures for adding and removing field replaceable modules for both desktop and portable systems	Portable system components: AC adapter, digital camera, DC controller, LCD panel, PC card, pointing devices

Practice Test Questions

1. Which operating system uses a feature called Offline Files to synchronize files between a PC and notebook?

   Correct answer: c

2. To download data directly from a digital camera to a notebook, which statement must be true?

   Correct answer: c

3. To hot swap an external storage device, which statement must be true?

   Correct answer: b

4. If a notebook does not have an internal modem included in the hardware, how is a modem typically added to the system?

   Correct answer: c

5. What Windows 98 feature allows you to use two modems to speed up data throughput over phone lines?

   Correct answer: c

6. What is the danger in using the AC adapter too much to power a notebook?

   Correct answer: d

7. What is important to first determine before servicing or upgrading a notebook computer?

   Correct answer: a

SPREAD 16

Objective 1.3	Identify available IRQs, DMAs, and I/O addresses and procedures for device installation and configuration	Standard IRQ settings Modems Floppy drive controllers Hard drive controllers USB ports Infrared ports Hexadecimal/Addresses

Practice Test Questions

1. A disk drive can access primary memory without involving the CPU by using a(n):

   Correct answer: c

2. IRQ 14 is reserved for:

   Correct answer: d

3. A jumper group has three positions on the block. What is the largest hex number that can be represented by this block?

   Correct answer: b

4. The purpose of an IRQ is to:

   Correct answer: b

5. The purpose of an I/O address is to:

   Correct answer: a

6. Which IRQ can a device using an 8-bit ISA bus NOT use?

   Correct answer: d

7. On the 16-bit ISA bus, IRQ 2 is used to cascade to the higher IRQs, so its position on the ISA bus is taken by which IRQ?

   Correct answer: c

SPREAD 17

Objective 1.4	Identify common peripheral ports, associated cabling, and their connectors	Cable types Cable orientation Serial versus parallel Pin connections include DB-9, DB-25, PS2/MINI-DIN, RJ-11, RJ-45, BNC, USB, and IEEE1394

Practice Test Questions

1. A 25-pin female port on the back of your computer is most likely to be a(n):

   Correct answer: a

2. What component controls serial port communication?

   Correct answer: c

3. When connecting a floppy drive data cable to a system board connection, how do you know the correction orientation of the cable to the connection?

   Correct answer: b

4. Which port cannot support a printer?

   Correct answer: d

5. Which port provides the fastest data transmission rate for a printer?

   Correct answer: b

6. Which device can use a DMA channel?

   Correct answer: b

7. Which device uses a 9-pin data cable?

   Correct answer: b

SPREAD 18

Objective 1.5	Identify proper procedures for installing and configuring IDE/EIDE devices	Master/slave Devices per channel Primary/secondary

Practice Test Questions

1. When installing a second IDE device on an IDE channel, you must:

   Correct answer: c

2. How many EIDE devices can be installed in a system?

   Correct answer: c

3. A system has a single IDE device installed on the primary IDE channel, and a new IDE device is installed on the secondary IDE channel. The new device does not work. What might be a cause of the problem?

   Correct answer: c

4. What IRQ does the primary IDE channel use?

   Correct answer: c

5. Two IDE devices share a data cable. Which statement is true?

   Correct answer: c

6. What type of hard drive requires a low-level format as part of the installation process?

   Correct answer: c

7. A CD-ROM drive that uses an IDE interface to the system board is following what specifications?

   Correct answer: b

SPREAD 19

Objective 1.6	Identify proper procedures for installing and configuring SCSI devices	Address/termination conflicts Cabling Internal versus external Expansion slots, EISA, ISA, PCI Jumper block settings (binary equivalents)

Practice Test Questions

1. A SCSI ID is set on a SCSI device using three jumpers. If the ID is set to 6, what will be the jumper settings?

   Correct answer: a

2. Which statement is true about a SCSI configuration?

   Correct answer: d

3. Two SCSI hard drives are installed on the same SCSI bus. Which statement is true?

   Correct answer: c

4. How many devices can be used on a single SCSI bus including the host adapter?

   Correct answer: 8

5. A SCSI CD-ROM drive is installed on an already-existing SCSI bus in a system. Which statement is true?

   Correct answer: a

6. How can a SCSI ID be set on a SCSI device?

   Correct answer: d

7. A SCSI bus has three SCSI devices and a host adapter. Which device(s) can communicate with the CPU?

   Correct answer: a

SPREAD 20

Objective 1.6 continued	Identify proper procedures for installing and configuring SCSI devices	Types (example: regular, wide, ultra–wide)

Practice Test Questions

1. SCSI-2 can support how many devices?
   Correct answer: c

2. The data path of Wide Ultra SCSI is:
   Correct answer: c

3. Which is the fastest SCSI standard?
   Correct answer: d

4. Which of the following is a difference between a single-ended SCSI cable and a differential SCSI cable?

   Correct answer: d

5. What is true about SCSI termination?
   Correct answer: a

6. Which major SCSI standard does not include a standard for 16-bit data transmission?

   Correct answer: a

7. How many pins does a Narrow SCSI data cable have?

   Correct answer: a

SPREAD 21

Objective 1.7	Identify proper procedures for installing and configuring peripheral devices	Monitor/Video Card Modem

Practice Test Questions

1. An external modem will most likely use what port on a PC?

   Correct answer: a

2. Video cards are normally installed in which bus expansion slot?

   Correct answer: d

3. A VESA bus expansion slot:

   Correct answer: b

4. The AGP expansion slot:

   Correct answer: a

5. What IRQ does an external modem use?

   Correct answer: a

6. Which device does not require an IRQ?

   Correct answer: c

7. Describe the port typically used by a monitor on today's systems?

   Correct answer: b

SPREAD 22

Objective 1.7 continued	Identify proper procedures for installing and configuring peripheral devices	USB peripherals and hubs IEEE 1284 IEEE 1384 External storage

Practice Test Questions

1. After physically installing a floppy drive, the next step is to:

   Correct answer: b

2. When does a parallel port require a DMA channel?

   Correct answer: b

3. An IDE Zip drive data cable has how many pins?

   Correct answer: d

4. You install a printer, but the PC cannot communicate with the printer. What is one thing to check?

   Correct answer: d

5. You install a floppy drive and reboot the PC. The drive light on the floppy drive stays lit and the system hangs. What is the most likely source of the problem?

   Correct answer: a

6. You have installed an IDE CD-ROM drive as the only device using the secondary IDE channel, and the drive is not recognized by the system. What is likely to be wrong?

   Correct answer: b

7. You have installed a ZIP drive using a second parallel port in a system, and you cannot get the system to recognize the drive. What is likely to be wrong?

   Correct answer: d

SPREAD 23

Objective 1.7 continued	Identify proper procedures for installing and configuring peripheral devices	Portables: docking stations PC cards Port replicators Infrared devices

Practice Test Questions

1. What specification covers PC Cards?

   Correct answer: d

2. What device can a notebook computer use to make it convenient to connect to a LAN?

   Correct answer: b

3. What notebook component is considered fragile?

   Correct answer: d

4. In Windows 98, how do you activate an infrared transceiver?

   Correct answer: b

5. In CMOS setup, if you enable the option named "UART2 Use Infrared", this setting causes the following to happen:

   Correct answer: a

6. What port on the back of a computer allows you to use a keyboard or other input device without a connecting cord to the computer?

   Correct answer: d

7. What type of PC Card can be used for a hard drive of a notebook computer?

   Correct answer: c

SPREAD 24

Objective 1.8	Identify hardware methods of upgrading system performance, procedures for replacing basic subsystem components, unique components and when to use them	Memory Hard drives CPU

Practice Test Questions

1. Which storage device provides the fastest access time for large multimedia files?

   Correct answer: c

2. Cache memory is usually installed on a system board in increments of:

   Correct answer: b

3. What is a reasonable amount of cache memory on a system board?

   Correct answer: c

4. L2 cache memory can exist in a system in as:

   Correct answer: d

5. What is the purpose of installing additional cache memory?

Correct answer: b

6. Why do newer system boards not have cache memory installed?

Correct answer: a

7. What can result if there is not enough RAM installed in a system?

Correct answer: d

SPREAD 25

Objective 1.8 continued	Identify hardware methods of upgrading system performance, procedures for replacing basic subsystem components, unique components and when to use them	Upgrading BIOS When to upgrade BIOS

Practice Test Questions

1. The major advantage of using Flash ROM is:

Correct answer: a

2. One reason to upgrade BIOS is:

Correct answer: a

3. You can find an upgrade for BIOS in:

Correct answer: c

4. How often does a PC technician perform a BIOS upgrade on a system?

Correct answer: a

5. To identify the BIOS manufacturer and model, look:

Correct answer: a

6. When upgrading the BIOS, the most likely way to get the BIOS upgrade is to:

Correct answer: b

7. When upgrading BIOS, what is an important caution?

Correct answer: c

SPREAD 26

Objective 1.8 continued	Identify hardware methods of upgrading system performance, procedures for replacing basic subsystem components, unique components and when to use them	Portable systems: battery, hard drive, types I, II, III cards, memory

Practice Test Questions

1. What type of memory module is used in a notebook computer?

   Correct answer: c

2. Which PC Card is the thickest?

   Correct answer: d

3. Which type of PC Card is typically used for a modem?

   Correct answer: b

4. Hot swapping refers to:

   Correct answer: a

5. How many pins are on a SO-DIMM?

   Correct answer: a

6. A power-saving feature of a notebook computer that turns the power off after a period of inactivity is:

   Correct answer: b

7. Which bus technology is CardBus based on?

   Correct answer: c

SPREAD 27

Objective 2.1	Identify common symptoms and problems associated with each module and how to troubleshoot and isolate the problems	Processor/memory symptoms POST audible/visual error codes

Practice Test Questions

1. A PC continuously reboots itself. What is the most likely cause of the problem?

   Correct answer: b

2. POST error codes in the 1700 range indicate a problem with:

   Correct answer: a

3. One long continuous beep or steady long beeps most likely indicate a problem with:

   Correct answer: d

4. You want to install a large hard drive on a system whose BIOS does not support large drives and you cannot upgrade the BIOS. What is the best solution?

   Correct answer: b

5. An error message, "Parity error," displays and the system hangs. The source of the problem is:

   Correct answer: a

6. When a PC boots, the screen is blank and you hear a single beep. What is most likely to be the problem?

   Correct answer: c

7. When a PC boots, the screen is blank and you hear several beeps. What is most likely to be the problem?

   Correct answer: d

SPREAD 28

Objective 2.1 continued	Identify common symptoms and problems associated with each module and how to troubleshoot and isolate the problems	Motherboards BIOS CMOS

Practice Test Questions

1. During booting, the purpose of the memory test is to:

   Correct answer: c

2. The process that determines what hardware is present and tests critical hardware components is called:

   Correct answer: b

3. Which component could cause a blank screen during booting?

   Correct answer: d

4. Before video is active, errors during booting are communicated as:

   Correct answer: b

5. When a system repeatedly hangs during booting but finally boots successfully, the most likely cause of the problem is:

   Correct answer: a

6. During booting, hardware devices are assigned:

   Correct answer: a

7. Hardware components are checked:

   Correct answer: d

SPREAD 29

Objective 2.1 continued	Identify common symptoms and problems associated with each module and how to troubleshoot and isolate the problems	Mouse Sound card/audio Monitor/video Modems

Practice Test Questions

1. If nothing is showing on the monitor screen, the first thing to do is:

   Correct answer: a

2. If the LED light on the monitor is lit but the screen is blank, what is NOT a source of the problem?

   Correct answer: d

3. What IRQ does a sound card typically use?

   Correct answer: b

4. Your modem was working fine until you install a sound card, now neither the modem nor the sound card work. What is likely the problem?

   Correct answer: b

5. What IRQ does a monitor use?

Correct answer: d

6. ESD is least likely to cause damage to what device?

Correct answer: b

7. Which of the following is typically an input and output device?

Correct answer: b

SPREAD 30

Objective 2.1 continued	Identify common symptoms and problems associated with each module and how to troubleshoot and isolate the problems	CD-ROM DVD

Practice Test Questions

1. How is a real-mode device driver for a CD-ROM drive loaded?

Correct answer: a

2. The DOS extension that manages a CD-ROM drive is:

Correct answer: b

3. What standard does a CD-ROM drive use that is installed as an IDE device in a system?

Correct answer: a

4. Which operating system(s) provides support for most CD-ROM drives?

Correct answer: d

5. Which provides the fastest data access time?

Correct answer: a

6. What utility manages a CD-ROM drive for DOS?

Correct answer: c

7. Why is MSCDEX.EXE not used with Windows 9x?

Correct answer: b

SPREAD 31

Objective 2.1 continued	Identify common symptoms and problems associated with each module and how to troubleshoot and isolate the problems	Power supply Slot covers

Practice Test Questions

1. The device inside a power supply that retains a charge even after power is disconnected is:

   Correct answer: a

2. Covering empty slots on the back of a PC case with slot covers helps to:

   Correct answer: a

3. A power supply uses which IRQ?

   Correct answer: d

4. The IDE hard drive does not spin up when the PC is turned on. What is most likely to be the problem?

   Correct answer: b

5. A PC repeatedly reboots. You replace the power supply with one you know is good. What do you do next?

   Correct answer: a

6. What beep codes could indicate there is a problem with the power supply?

   Correct answer: c

7. The computer system appears dead, with no lights on the front panel, nothing on the screen, and no beeps. What do you check first?

   Correct answer: c

SPREAD 32

Objective 2.1 continued	Identify common symptoms and problems associated with each module and how to troubleshoot and isolate the problems	Floppy drive Parallel ports USB

Practice Test Questions

1. What could cause the error message, "General failure reading drive A, Abort, Retry Fail?"

   Correct answer: b

2. Possible sources of problems with reading a floppy disk include:

   Correct answer: d

3. What could cause the error message, "Non-system disk or disk error. Replace and strike any key when ready"?

   Correct answer: a

4. How many bits of data are transmitted over a parallel port at one time?

   Correct answer: b

5. An external CD-ROM drive typically uses what interface with the computer?

   Correct answer: c

6. Which IRQ does the parallel port LPT1 typically use?

   Correct answer: b

7. The user reports that a floppy drive reads the first disk inserted into the drive after a reboot but does not read subsequent disks. What might be the problem?

   Correct answer: d

SPREAD 33

Objective 2.1 continued	Identify common symptoms and problems associated with each module and how to troubleshoot and isolate the problems	Hard drives Large LBA, LBA

Practice Test Questions

1. The best protection for data on a hard drive is to:

   Correct answer: b

2. Which of the following is considered an FRU?

   Correct answer: b

3. What is the first thing you do when you get the error, "Non-system disk or disk error"?

   Correct answer: a

4. What is the cause of the error message, "Invalid or missing COMMAND.COM" during booting?

   Correct answer: c

5. When an IDE hard drive gives "Bad sector" errors, what is the first thing you should do?

   Correct answer: c

6. What is the difference between a standard and a thorough Scandisk?

   Correct answer: b

7. A cross-linked cluster is a cluster that:

   Correct answer: a

SPREAD 34

Objective 2.1 continued	Identify common symptoms and problems associated with each module and how to troubleshoot and isolate the problems	Troubleshooting tools, e.g., multimeter

Practice Test Questions

1. What measurement should a DVM be set to test a fuse?

   Correct answer: a

2. At what range do you set a multimeter to measure the voltage output as an unknown source?

   Correct answer: c

3. If you set a multimeter to measure resistance with a range of 20K, what will be the reading (in ohms) of a good fuse?

   Correct answer: a

4. You suspect a problem with a serial port. The best way to test the port is to:

   Correct answer: b

5. When using a multimeter to measure resistance, set the meter to measure:

   Correct answer: b

6. When using a multimeter to measure current, set the meter to measure:

   Correct answer: d

7. Current is measured only:

   Correct answer: b

SPREAD 35

Objective 2.1 continued	Identify common symptoms and problems associated with each module and how to troubleshoot and isolate the problems	NIC Cables Keyboard Peripherals

Practice Test Questions

1. If a light on the back of a NIC is lit solid, what can you conclude?

   Correct answer: b

2. What is one check you can make to be certain a PC is communicating properly on a network?

   Correct answer: a

3. If a keyboard fails intermittently, what might be a source of the problem?

   Correct answer: c

4. Video does not work. What are the things you should replace in the order you should replace them?

   Correct answer: a

5. What standard should a parallel printer cable meet?

   Correct answer: b

6. When a printer does not work, what are some things you can check?

   Correct answer: d

7. You have just installed a NIC, which does not work. What is the first thing you should do?

   Correct answer: c

SPREAD 36

Objective 2.2	Identify basic troubleshooting procedures and how to elicit problem symptoms from customers	Troubleshooting/isolation/problem determination procedures Determine whether hardware or software problem

Practice Test Questions

1. You install a second IDE hard drive in a system using the same IDE primary channel used by the first drive. When you boot up, the first drive works but the system fails to recognize the new drive. What is the most likely cause of the problem?

   Correct answer: c

2. A POST error code in the 6000 range indicates a problem with:

   Correct answer: d

3. POST is done when the computer is:

   Correct answer: c

4. POST is performed:

   Correct answer: a

5. When you use a floppy drive cable with a twist, the order of connections on the data cable supporting two floppy drives is:

   Correct answer: b

6. A system appears dead but you notice that the small green light on the front of the monitor is on. What can you safely assume?

   Correct answer: b

7. You replace a system board because the old board is dead. You turn on the PC. It boots up correctly but almost immediately the PC hangs, dies, and refuses to reboot. You have another dead system. What is most likely the source of the problem?

   Correct answer: b

SPREAD 37

Objective 2.2 continued	Identify basic troubleshooting procedures and how to elicit problem symptoms from customers	Gather information from user regarding: customer environment, symptoms/error codes, situation when the problem occurred

Practice Test Questions

1. What question might you ask a user that would best help you locate a problem?

   Correct answer: d

2. How can the customer help you identify the source of an intermittent problem?

   Correct answer: c

3. Which of the following questions is *not* appropriate to ask the user to help you locate the source of a problem?

   Correct answer: c

4. You are late for an appointment with a customer. What should you do when you arrive?

   Correct answer: a

5. A hard drive has failed but you think you can fix it if you reformat the drive. What should you do first?

   Correct answer: a

6. What should you always do at a customer site?

   Correct answer: c

7. When you first arrive at the customer's site, what is the first thing you should do?

   Correct answer: b

SPREAD 38

Objective 3.1	Identify the purpose of various types of preventive maintenance products and procedures and when to use them	Liquid cleaning compounds Types of materials to clean contacts and connections Non-static vacuums (chassis, power supplies, fans)

Practice Test Questions

1. Which product should be used to clean fingerprints and dirt off a keyboard?

   Correct answer: b

2. Which product should be used to clean a notebook computer's LCD screen?

   Correct answer: d

3. Which of the following is most likely to do damage to data stored on a hard drive or floppy disk?

   Correct answer: d

4. Why is dust inside a computer case considered dangerous?

   Correct answer: c

5. The best way to remove dust from inside a computer case is to:

   Correct answer: b

6. Preventive maintenance on a mouse includes:

   Correct answer: b

7. What should you use to clean a monitor screen?

   Correct answer: d

SPREAD 39

Objective 3.2	Identify issues, procedures and devices for protection within the computing environment, including people, hardware and the surrounding workspace	UPS (uninterruptible power supply) and suppressors Determining the signs of power issues Proper methods of storage of components for future use

Practice Test Questions

1. During a power outage, what should you do before the power is restored?

   Correct answer: a

2. Which device helps prevent power surges to computer equipment?

   Correct answer: b

3. Which device prevents interruptions to power to computer equipment?

   Correct answer: a

4. How can computer equipment be completely protected from damage during an electrical storm?

   Correct answer: c

5. What question do you ask to determine if power is getting to a computer?

   Correct answer: a

6. You're working at your computer and a thunderstorm begins. What do you do?

   Correct answer: d

7. What is a brownout?

   Correct answer: a

SPREAD 40

Objective 3.2 continued	Identify issues, procedures and devices for protection within the computing environment, including people, hardware and the surrounding workspace	Potential hazards and proper safety procedures relating to: Lasers, high-voltage equipment, power supply, CRT

Practice Test Questions

1. If the fan inside a power supply stops working, what should you do?

   Correct answer: b

2. When servicing a laser printer, why is it important to first unplug the printer?

   Correct answer: d

3. Why do you *not* wear an ESD bracelet while servicing a monitor?

   Correct answer: c

4. A device that retains a high charge even after disconnected from power is:

   Correct answer: d

5. The electrical component that retains a charge after the power is turned off is:

   Correct answer: c

6. When troubleshooting a monitor, one task a PC technician who is not trained to work inside the monitor can safely do is:

   Correct answer: d

7. The best way to ground an ESD bracelet when servicing a power supply is to:

   Correct answer: d

Objective 3.2 continued	Identify issues, procedures and devices for protection within the computing environment, including people, hardware and the surrounding workspace	Special disposal procedures that comply with environmental guidelines: batteries, CRT, toner kits/cartridges, chemical solvents and cans, MSDS (Material Safety Data Sheet)

Practice Test Questions

1. Which component is easiest to environmentally recycle?

   Correct answer: c

2. Which component requires that you follow EPA environmental guidelines for disposal?

   Correct answer: b

3. How do you recycle a toner cartridge from a laser printer?

   Correct answer: a

4. To know how to properly dispose of a can of contact cleaner, what do you do?

   Correct answer: b

5. How do you dispose of a CMOS battery?

   Correct answer: d

6. Before disposing of a CRT, what must you do?

   Correct answer: c

7. When disposing of an entire computer system, which components need special attention?

   Correct answer: a

SPREAD 42

Objective 3.2 continued	Identify issues, procedures and devices for protection within the computing environment, including people, hardware and the surrounding workspace	ESD (electrostatic discharge) precautions and procedures: what ESD can do, how it may be apparent, or hidden, common ESD protection devices, situations that could present a danger or hazard

Practice Test Questions

1. Damage from ESD can be caused by:

   Correct answer: d

2. To avoid damage from ESD as you work on a computer, you should:

   Correct answer: b

3. An ESD wrist strap contains a:

   Correct answer: c

4. What is the best ground to use when working on a computer?

   Correct answer: a

5. Which situation poses the worst possible potential danger from ESD?

   Correct answer: c

6. ESD is:

   Correct answer: a

7. A human cannot feel ESD unless it reaches a charge of _____ volts

   Correct answer: b

SPREAD 43

Objective 4.1	Distinguish between the popular CPU chips in terms of their basic characteristics	Popular CPU chips (Intel, AMD, CYRIX) Characteristics Physical size Voltage Speeds On board cache or not Sockets SEC (single edge contact)

Practice Test Questions

1. Which processor is the most powerful?

   Correct answer: a

2. Which processor form factor fits into Socket 370?

   Correct answer: c

3. How wide is the data path of the Pentium CPU?

   Correct answer: 64 bits

4. How much L1 cache is there in a Pentium II CPU?

   Correct answer: b

5. The Pentium II typically uses what clock bus speed?

   Correct answer: b

6. Which slot or socket is *not* used by Intel processors?

   Correct answer: d

7. Which processor does not have L2 cache included inside the processor housing?

   Correct answer: c

Objective 4.2	Identify the categories of RAM (Random Access Memory) terminology, their locations, and physical characteristics	Terminology: EDO RAM (Extended Data Output RAM) DRAM (Dynamic Random Access Memory) SRAM (Static RAM) VRAM (Video RAM) WRAM (Windows Accelerator Card RAM) SDRAM (Synchronous Dynamic RAM) RIMM (Rambus Inline Memory Module 184 pin)

Practice Test Questions

1. Which type memory is faster?

   Correct answer: b

2. Which type of memory runs in sync with the system clock?

   Correct answer: b

3. Which type of memory is especially designed to work on a video card?

   Correct answer: c

4. Which type of memory uses a narrow 16-bit data path?

   Correct answer: a

5. The connection inside a SEC between the CPU and the L2 cache is called the:

   Correct answer: c

6. Why must DRAM be refreshed?

   Correct answer: c

7. The Pentium II backside bus is:

   Correct answer: b

SPREAD 45

Objective 4.2 continued	Identify the categories of RAM (Random Access Memory) terminology, their locations, and physical characteristics	Locations and physical characteristics: Memory bank Memory chips (8-bit, 16-bit, and 32-bit) SIMMS (Single In-line Memory Module) DIMMS (Dual In-line Memory Module) Parity chips versus non-parity chips

Practice Test Questions

1. How many pins does a DIMM have?

   Correct answer: d

2. What is the data path of a SIMM?

   Correct answer: b

3. Which type memory has an error-checking technology that can repair the error when it is detected?

   Correct answer: a

4. Which statement about SIMMs is true?

   Correct answer: b

5. If a system contains 64 MB of RAM in two banks of 2 SIMMs each, how much memory is on one SIMM?

   Correct answer: a

6. Which can hold the most memory?

   Correct answer: b

7. A SIMM is held into its socket by:

   Correct answer: a

SPREAD 46

Objective 4.3	Identify the most popular type of motherboards, their components, and their architecture (for example, bus structures and power supplies)	Types of motherboards: AT (Full and Baby) ATX Basic compatibility guidelines IDE (ATA, ATAPI, Ultra-DMA, EIDE) SCSI(Wide, Fast, Ultra, LVD (low voltage differential))

Practice Test Questions

1. The AT power supply connects to the system board with:

   Correct answer: a

2. The ATX power supply connects to the system board with:

   Correct answer: b

3. The SCSI standard that uses LVD is:

   Correct answer: b

4. What is one advantage that the ATX system board has over the AT system board?

   Correct answer: a

5. Which statement is true concerning style of system board?

   Correct answer: b

6. Which type of system board is required for a 500 MHz Pentium II using Slot 1?

   Correct answer: c

7. Which type of system board measures 22 cm × 33 cm?

   Correct answer: b

SPREAD 47

Objective 4.3 continued	Identify the most popular type of motherboards, their components, and their architecture (for example, bus structures and power supplies)	Components: Communication ports SIMM and DIMM Processor sockets External cache memory (Level 2)

Practice Test Questions

1. What slot or socket does the Intel Pentium III use?

   Correct answer: d

2. How many pins does Socket 7 have?

   Correct answer: a

3. What socket or slot does the Pentium Pro use?

   Correct answer: c

4. Which processor uses 5 volts of power?

   Correct answer: b

5. How do you *not* install RAM on a system board?

   Correct answer: a

6. When is the Super Socket 7 used?

   Correct answer: b

7. What is the difference between a SPGA grid and a PGA grid, as used by a CPU socket?

   Correct answer: c

SPREAD 48

Objective 4.3 continued	Identify the most popular type of motherboards, their components, and their architecture (for example, bus structures and power supplies)	Bus Architecture ISA EISA PCI AGP USB (Universal Serial Bus) VESA local bus (VL–Bus)

Practice Test Questions

1. Which bus is primarily used on notebook computers?

   Correct answer: c

2. Which bus only supports a video card?

   Correct answer: d

3. Which bus is fastest?

   Correct answer: b

4. Which bus is no longer included on new system boards?

   Correct answer: c

5. Which bus can support either an 8-bit or 16-bit data path?

   Correct answer: c

6. Which of the following is the most common width of the data path of the PCI bus?

   Correct answer: c

7. Which bus runs in sync with the CPU?

   Correct answer: d

SPREAD 49

Objective 4.4	Identify the purpose of CMOS (Complementary Metal-Oxide Semiconductor), what it contains and how to change its basic parameters	Example Basic CMOS Settings: Printer parallel port ♦ Uni-, Bi-directional ♦ Disable/enable ♦ ECP, EPP COM/serial port ♦ Memory address ♦ Interrupt request ♦ Disable

6. Boot sequence as set in CMOS is the order:

   Correct answer: c

7. System date and time can be set:

   Correct answer: d

SPREAD 51

Objective 5.1	Identify basic concepts, printer operations and printer components	Paper feeder mechanisms Types of printers: laser, inkjet, dot matrix

Practice Test Questions

1. In laser printing, the step between writing and transferring is:

   Correct answer: c

2. What component on a dot matrix printer forms each character?

   Correct answer: d

3. On an ink jet printer, what causes the ink to form characters and shapes on the paper?

   Correct answer: b

4. In laser printing, which stage in the printing process forms the characters or shapes to be printed?

   Correct answer: a

5. In laser printing, which stage puts the toner on the paper?

   Correct answer: c

6. In laser printing, which is the last step?

   Correct answer: b

7. In laser printing, what is the purpose of the laser beam?

   Correct answer: a

SPREAD 52

Objective 5.1 continued	Identify basic concepts, printer operations and printer components	Parallel Network USB Infrared Serial

Practice Test Questions

1. When troubleshooting a parallel port, you should verify that the port is enabled:

   Correct answer: b

2. Which setting for a parallel port gives the fastest data access time?

   Correct answer: c

3. When a parallel port is set to ECP, what resource is required?

   Correct answer: b

4. If the system is short of DMA channels, one thing you can do to free one up is to:

   Correct answer: c

5. If a serial port is not working, what is one thing you should verify?

   Correct answer: a

6. In CMOS setup, when a serial port is set to use IRQ 4 and I/O address 03F8, the port is configured as:

   Correct answer: a

7. If a parallel port in CMOS setup is configured to use IRQ 5 and I/O address 0278, then the port is configured as:

   Correct answer: b

SPREAD 50

Objective 4.4 continued	Identify the purpose of CMOS (Complementary Metal-Oxide Semiconductor), what it contains and how to change its basic parameters	Floppy drive: enable/disable drive or boot, speed, density Hard drive: size and drive type Memory: parity, non-parity Boot sequence Date/time Passwords Plug & Play BIOS

Practice Test Questions

1. When a PC boots with the incorrect date or time, what is the likely cause?

   Correct answer: b

2. Which hard drive parameter is not set using CMOS setup?

   Correct answer: d

3. Which of the following cannot be damaged by a virus?

   Correct answer: b

4. When installing a 3½-inch floppy drive to replace a 5¼-inch floppy drive, how does the system know to expect the new type drive?

   Correct answer: c

5. Which of the following hard drive parameters is set in CMOS?

   Correct answer: d

Practice Test Questions

1. In what ways can a printer connect to a computer system?

   Correct answer: c

2. If a printer is connected to a computer by way of a parallel cable and the computer is connected to a network, what must be done before others on the network can use this printer?

   Correct answer: a

3. To access file and print sharing in Windows 9x, you should do which of the following?

   Correct answer: b

4. To share a printer over a network, you must:

   Correct answer: a

5. When sharing a printer over a network, you must:

   Correct answer: b

6. To use a shared printer on another PC, you must:

   Correct answer: d

7. When troubleshooting problems with shared printers on a network, what is a good question to ask?

   Correct answer: d

SPREAD 53

Objective 5.2	Identify care and service techniques and common problems with primary printer types	Feed and output Errors (printed or displayed) Paper jam Print quality Safety precautions Preventive maintenance

Practice Test Questions

1. Into what format does Windows 9x convert a print job file before printing?

   Correct answer: c

2. Spooling print jobs:

   Correct answer: d

3. When troubleshooting a print problem, you can:

   Correct answer: d

4. If there is a problem with the printer communicating with the computer, the problem can be solved by:

   Correct answer: c

5. When servicing a dot matrix printer, what device might be hot to the touch?

   Correct answer: b

6. When servicing a laser printer, which component might be hot to the touch?

Correct answer: c

7. When troubleshooting a dot matrix printer, if the head moves back and forth but nothing prints, then suspect a problem with the:

Correct answer: c

SPREAD 54

Objective 6.1	Identify basic networking concepts, including how a network works and the ramifications of repairs on the network	Ways to network a PC Physical network topographies Hardware protocols Full-duplex, half-duplex

Practice Test Questions

1. Which is *not* a type of network?

Correct answer: b

2. Which of the following is not a type of hardware protocol?

Correct answer: a

3. What does FDDI stand for?

Correct answer: b

4. Which is the most popular network architecture?

Correct answer: c

5. What device connects two computers or other components within a network?

Correct answer: a

6. Full-duplex communication is communication in:

Correct answer: b

7. A number permanently assigned to a NIC that uniquely identifies the computer to the network is:

Correct answer: b

SPREAD 55

Objective 6.1 continued	Identify basic networking concepts, including how a network works and the ramifications of repairs on the network	Installing and configuring network cards Network access Cabling: twisted pair, coaxial, fiber optic, RS–232 Infrared

Practice Test Questions

1. What is the shape of a BNC connector?

   Correct answer: b

2. The term 10BaseT refers to what network speed?

   Correct answer: a

3. What is the most common Ethernet technology today?

   Correct answer: d

4. Which connector is typically used in an Ethernet bus topology?

   Correct answer: a

5. Which is the more reliable network cable?

   Correct answer: b

6. Which Ethernet technology uses fiber optic cable?

   Correct answer: c

7. Which Ethernet topology uses a hub?

   Correct answer: a

SPREAD 56

Objective 6.1 continued	Identify basic networking concepts, including how a network works and the ramifications of repairs on the network	Increasing bandwidth Loss of data Network slowdown

Practice Test Questions

1. When servicing a PC on a network, before you turn off the PC, you should:

   Correct answer: b

2. When replacing a NIC in a computer system, it is important to use an identical NIC because:

   Correct answer: c

3. Before connecting a computer back to the network, you should:

   Correct answer: a

4. If you must install a different type NIC than the one currently installed, what must you do?

   Correct answer: d

5. When the light on the back of the NIC is not lit solid, what can be the problem?

   Correct answer: a

6. Which type of network port uses a T-connector?

   Correct answer: c

7. What type of NIC works on an Ethernet network and supports more than one cabling media?

   Correct answer: b

SPREAD 1

Objective 1.1	Identify the operating system's functions, structure, and major system files to navigate the operating system and how to get to needed technical information	Major operating system functions

Practice Test Questions

1. What key combination closes a program window?

   Correct answer: c

2. From a program window, how do you bring focus to or activate the menu bar?

   Correct answer: b

3. In Windows 9x, an application is open on the screen, the mouse does not work, and you want to do an orderly shutdown. What do you do?

   Correct answer: b

4. In Windows 9x, what do you press to move from one loaded application to another?

   Correct answer: a

5. In Windows 2000 Explorer, how do you select several files that are listed consecutively?

   Correct answer: b

6. If you delete a file in Explorer, how can you recover it?

   Correct answer: b

7. What is one way to access Device Manager in Windows 98?

   Correct answer: d

SPREAD 2

Objective 1.1 continued	Identify the operating system's functions, structure, and major system files to navigate the operating system and how to get to needed technical information	Create folders Checking OS version

Practice Test Questions

1. What are the steps to hide the Windows 98 taskbar?

   Correct answer: a

2. What steps can you use to create a shortcut on the Windows 98 desktop?

   Correct answer: d

3. In Windows 2000, how do you add an item to the Start menu?

Correct answer: a

4. Which is not a function of an operating system?

Correct answer: d

5. How do you access Windows Explorer in Windows 2000?

Correct answer: d

6. Which of the following is a function of an operating system?

Correct answer: a

7. How do you discover the version number of the operating system?

Correct answer: d

SPREAD 3

Objective 1.1 continued	Identify the operating system's functions, structure, and major system files to navigate the operating system and how to get to needed technical information	Explorer My Computer Control Panel

Practice Test Questions

1. In Device Manager, a diamond icon with a short line through one side of it stands for?

Correct answer: c

2. A yellow exclamation point through a device in Device Manager indicates:

Correct answer: c

3. Which icon in Windows 2000 Control Panel do you use to configure a modem for a dial-up connection to a network?

Correct answer: a

4. Which icon in Windows 98 Control Panel do you use to change the user's password?

Correct answer: b

5. How do you change a password in Windows 2000?

Correct answer: a

6. How can you determine how much space is available on a hard drive?

Correct answer: d

7. How do you access a command line prompt using Windows 98?

Correct answer: c

SPREAD 4

Objective 1.1 continued	Identify the operating system's functions, structure, and major system files to navigate the operating system and how to get to needed technical information	Contrasts between Windows 9x and Windows 2000

Practice Test Questions

1. Which operating system uses dynamically loaded device drivers?

   Correct answer: d

2. Which operating system does not support Plug and Play?

   Correct answer: c

3. Which operating system provides a feature to allow a user at home to connect a notebook computer to a network at his workplace using a virtual private network?

   Correct answer: a

4. Which operating system does not offer the NTFS file system?

   Correct answer: c

5. How does the Windows 95 Virtual Memory Manager assign memory addresses for applications to use?

   Correct answer: a

6. Why would a user choose to use the NTFS file system on a notebook computer?

   Correct answer: b

7. Which operating system is best designed for small, inexpensive PCs where the user needs to run 16-bit application programs that require a graphical interface?

   Correct answer: a

SPREAD 5

Objective 1.1 continued	Identify the operating system's functions, structure, and major system files to navigate the operating system and how to get to needed technical information	Major system files: what they are, where they are located, how they are used and what they contain

Practice Test Questions

1. Which operating system does not allow an application to directly access system resources?

   Correct answer: d

2. Where does Windows 9x store most configuration information?

   Correct answer: b

3. Which core component of Windows 9x manages printing?

   Correct answer: c

4. Which core component of Windows 95 controls the mouse?

   Correct answer: c

5. Which Windows 95 component is responsible for managing Plug and Play tasks?

   Correct answer: d

6. The Windows 2000 Hardware Abstraction Layer (HAL) operates in what mode?

   Correct answer: b

7. Which service or system operates in the kernel mode under Windows 2000?

   Correct answer: b

SPREAD 6

Objective 1.1 continued	Identify the operating system's functions, structure, and major system files to navigate the operating system and how to get to needed technical information	System, configuration, and user interface files: IO.SYS MSDOS.SYS AUTOEXEC.BAT CONFIG.SYS

Practice Test Questions

1. What file contains the BUFFERS= command line?

   Correct answer: c

2. In which file is the command PROMPT PG located?

   Correct answer: b

3. Which command is executed first during the boot process?

   Correct answer: c

4. What is the purpose of the FILES= command?

   Correct answer: a

5. What software can be used to edit CONFIG.SYS?

   Correct answer: d

6. Which files are hidden system files?

   Correct answer: b

7. Which file is the DOS kernel?

   Correct answer: c

SPREAD 7

Objective 1.1 continued	Identify the operating system's functions, structure, and major system files to navigate the operating system and how to get to needed technical information	System, configuration, and user interface files: IO.SYS BOOT.INI WIN.COM MSDOS.SYS AUTOEXEC.BAT CONFIG.SYS command line prompt

Practice Test Questions

1. Which entry in the Msdos.sys file in Windows 98 controls the function keys during startup?

   Correct answer: b

2. Which program file executes to provide a command line prompt in Windows 95?

   Correct answer: b

3. Which operating system uses the text file Boot.ini to control the boot process?

   Correct answer: c

4. Where is the file located that contains the logo screen that displays when loading Windows 9x?

   Correct answer: c

5. What software can be used to edit the Windows file Msdos.sys?

   Correct answer: d

6. Which Windows 9x system file is responsible for loading the real mode core components of Windows 9x?

   Correct answer: a

7. Where is Boot.ini stored?

   Correct answer: b

SPREAD 8

Objective 1.1 continued	Identify the operating system's functions, structure, and major system files to navigate the operating system and how to get to needed technical information	Memory management: Conventional Extended/upper memory High memory

Practice Test Questions

1. What command do you use to load DOS into the high memory area?

   Correct answer: c

2. What command do you use to load a device driver into an upper memory block?

   Correct answer: b

3. What area of memory is known as extended memory?

   Correct answer: b

4. When running a legacy DOS application, what is an advantage to running the application in MS-DOS mode rather than in a DOS box under Windows?

   Correct answer: c

5. What is true when running a DOS application in a DOS box under Windows 9x?

   Correct answer: a

6. What command can you use to determine if DOS loaded high?

   Correct answer: b

7. What programs can use upper memory addresses without any special memory management software?

   Correct answer: a

SPREAD 9

Objective 1.1 continued	Identify the operating system's functions, structure, and major system files to navigate the operating system and how to get to needed technical information	Memory management: Virtual memory

Practice Test Questions

1. The name of the temporary swap file in Windows 98 is:

   Correct answer: b

2. Which statement about the Windows 95 methods of managing virtual memory is true?

   Correct answer: d

3. What is the purpose of a swap file?

   Correct answer: a

4. Which operating system does not use virtual memory?

   Correct answer: b

5. Conceptually, the opposite of virtual memory is:

   Correct answer: a

6. What is the name of the Windows 2000 swap file?

   Correct answer: d

7. In Windows 95, how can you change the location of the swap file?

   Correct answer: a

SPREAD 10

Objective 1.1 continued	Identify the operating system's functions, structure, and major system files to navigate the operating system and how to get to needed technical information	Memory Management: HIMEM.SYS EMM386.EXE Windows 9x: Command.com Run command Setver.exe Dosstart.bat

Practice Test Questions

1. Which Windows file holds settings for several DOS applications to be run under Windows?

   Correct answer: b

2. The purpose of HIMEM.SYS is:

   Correct answer: a

3. The purpose of EMM386.EXE is:

   Correct answer: d

4. Where in memory are upper memory blocks located?

   Correct answer: a

5. The executable program that accommodates legacy DOS applications that require a specific version of DOS is:

   Correct answer: b

6. What are the steps to access the Run command?

   Correct answer: c

7. The location of the Windows file Apps.inf is:

   Correct answer: c

SPREAD 11

Objective 1.1 continued	Identify the operating system's functions, structure, and major system files to navigate the operating system and how to get to needed technical information	Windows 9x: Io.sys Win.ini Sysedit System.ini Msconfig (98) Smartdrv.exe Drivespace

Practice Test Questions

1. Which of the following Windows 9x system files is a text file?

   Correct answer: c

2. To function properly under Windows 9x, a Plug and Play device requires:

   Correct answer: b

3. If CONFIG.SYS is present when Windows 9x loads:

   Correct answer: c

4. How are device drivers loaded under Windows 9x?

   Correct answer: d

5. What is one thing that Msconfig.exe can do?

   Correct answer: b

6. When is it appropriate to use SmartDrive on a Windows system?

   Correct answer: d

7. What is one limitation of DriveSpace under Windows 9x?

   Correct answer: a

SPREAD 12

Objective 1.1 continued	Identify the operating system's functions, structure, and major system files to navigate the operating system and how to get to needed technical information	Windows 9x: Regedit.exe System.dat User.dat

Practice Test Questions

1. What are the two Windows 9x registry back-up files?

   Correct answer: d

2. What program do you execute when you want to edit the Windows 95 registry?

   Correct answer: c

3. Which registry key stores current information about hardware and installed software?

   Correct answer: c

4. How many major branches or keys are there in the Windows 9x registry?

   Correct answer: d

5. What are the names of the Windows 9x registry files?

   Correct answer: c

6. What is one reason that Windows 9x supports using SYSTEM.INI and WIN.INI during the boot process?

   Correct answer: a

7. Most configuration information for Windows 9x is stored in:

   Correct answer: b

SPREAD 13

Objective 1.1 continued	Identify the operating system's functions, structure, and major system files to navigate the operating system and how to get to needed technical information	Windows 2000: Computer management Regedit32 Regedit

Practice Test Questions

1. What are the files that hold the Windows NT registry called?

   Correct answer: b

2. Which program is the best one to use to edit the Windows NT registry?

   Correct answer: a

3. Which Windows 2000 registry key stores information about hardware and installed software and does not change when a new user logs on?

   Correct answer: c

4. How many major branches or keys are there in the Windows NT registry?

   Correct answer: b

5. Where is the Windows 2000 registry located?

   Correct answer: a

6. What utility do you use to back up the Windows NT registry?

   Correct answer: a

7. How do you back up the Windows 2000 registry?

   Correct answer: a

SPREAD 14

Objective 1.1 continued	Identify the operating system's functions, structure, and major system files to navigate the operating system and how to get to needed technical information	Windows 2000: Boot.ini Run cmd Ntldr Ntdetect.com Ntbootdd.sys

Practice Test Questions

1. Where is the Ntldr file located?

   Correct answer: a

2. Which file is only used in the Windows 2000 boot process when a SCSI boot device is used?

   Correct answer: c

3. Which of the following is a hidden text file?

   Correct answer: b

4. Which Windows 2000 file is responsible for most of the booting process?

   Correct answer: b

5. Which two files are used to create most of the Windows NT kernel?

   Correct answer: d

6. How can you attain a Windows 2000 command line prompt?

   Correct answer: d

7. Which Windows 2000 component is responsible for loading device drivers at startup?

   Correct answer: a

SPREAD 15

Objective 1.1 continued	Identify the operating system's functions, structure, and major system files to navigate the operating system and how to get to needed technical information	Command prompt procedures (command syntax): DIR, ATTRIB, VER, MEM, SCANDISK, DEFRAG, EDIT, XCOPY, COPY, FORMAT, FDISK, MSCDEX, SETVER, SCANREG

Practice Test Questions

1. Which command can make a file a hidden system file?

   Correct answer: b

2. What is the purpose of the /C switch in the MEM command (MEM /C)?

   Correct answer: b

3. What command scans and repairs errors on a hard drive?

   Correct answer: b

4. What is a text editor that can be used to edit a text file?

   Correct answer: d

5. Which command copies files including files in the subdirectories of the current folder?

   Correct answer: d

6. What is the purpose of the SETVER command?

   Correct answer: a

7. Which command lets you access a CD-ROM drive during a DOS session?

   Correct answer: a

SPREAD 16

Objective 1.2	Identify basic concepts and procedures for creating, viewing and managing files, directories and disks. This includes procedures for changing file attributes and the ramifications of those changes (for example, security issues)	File attributes: Read Only, Hidden, System, and Archive attributes

Practice Test Questions

1. What command can make a file read-only?

   Correct answer: b

2. Which of the following is a hidden file?

   Correct answer: c

3. What is the result of the ATTRIB -R MYFILE.TXT command?

   Correct answer: b

4. What is the command to hide AUTOEXEC.BAT?

   Correct answer: a

5. Before you edit the registry files, what must you do?

   Correct answer: a

6. What in Windows 95 performs a function similar to the ATTRIB command in DOS?

   Correct answer: c

7. What file attribute does the DOS BACKUP command use to determine if the file is to be backed up?

   Correct answer: c

SPREAD 17

Objective 1.2 continued	Identify basic concepts and procedures for creating, viewing and managing files, directories and disks. This includes procedures for changing file attributes and the ramifications of those changes (for example, security issues)	File naming conventions (most command extensions) Windows 2000 Compress, Encrypt IDE/SCSI Internal/External Backup/Restore

Practice Test Questions

1. In DOS, what is the combined maximum number of characters a filename and file extension can have?

   Correct answer: c

2. A file named My Long File Document in Windows 95 will be displayed in DOS as:

   Correct answer: a

3. What is a valid file extension for DOS?

   Correct answer: a

4. What is the maximum number of characters allowed in a Windows 95 filename?

   Correct answer: b

5. Which file will be listed using this DIR command: DIR TA*.?

   Correct answer: b

6. In Windows 95, how do you format a floppy disk?

   Correct answer: b

7. In Windows 2000, what is the utility that displays information about encrypted files?

   Correct answer: c

SPREAD 18

Objective 1.2 continued	Identify basic concepts and procedures for creating, viewing and managing files, directories and disks. This includes procedures for changing file attributes and the ramifications of those changes (for example, security issues)	Partitioning/formatting/ file system (FAT, FAT16, FAT32, NTFS4, NTFS5, HPFS)

Practice Test Questions

1. For very large hard drives, which file system provides the smallest cluster size?

   Correct answer: c

2. Where is the boot strap loader located?

   Correct answer: b

3. The master boot program is located at:

   Correct answer: d

4. What are the functions of FDISK?

   Correct answer: d

5. What file system is used by floppy disks?

   Correct answer: b

6. Which file system is not supported by Windows NT?

   Correct answer: b

7. What is the first Microsoft OS to support FAT32?

   Correct answer: d

SPREAD 19

Objective 1.2 continued	Identify basic concepts and procedures for creating, viewing and managing files, directories and disks. This includes procedures for changing file attributes and the ramifications of those changes (for example, security issues)	Windows-based utilities: ScanDisk DEFRAG.EXE FDISK.EXE SCANREG ATTRIB.EXE EXTRACT.EXE EDIT.COM

Practice Test Questions

1. Which programs are used to test a hard drive for errors?

   Correct answer: d

2. Which program rewrites files in contiguous cluster chains?

   Correct answer: a

3. What is a fragmented drive?

   Correct answer: a

4. You have Windows 95 installed on your PC, but you boot from a DOS version 6.22 bootable diskette. From the DOS prompt, you run DEFRAG to defragment your hard drive. What happens to the Windows 95 long filenames?

   Correct answer: c

5. The system repeatedly hangs when applications are running. What is a possible cause of this problem?

   Correct answer: d

6. When is it appropriate to run the Thorough version of ScanDisk?

   Correct answer: a

7. When troubleshooting problems with accessing data on the hard drive, which command sequence do you follow to find the "Disable write-behind caching for all drives" option?

   Correct answer: b

SPREAD 20

Objective 1.2 continued	Identify basic concepts and procedures for creating, viewing and managing files, directories and disks. This includes procedures for changing file attributes and the ramifications of those changes (for example, security issues)	Windows-based utilities: Device Manager SystemManager Computer Manager MSCONFIG.EXE REGEDIT.EXE (View information/Backup registry) REGEDT32.EXE WSCRIPT.EXE HWINFO.EXE ASD.EXE (Automatic Skip Driver) CVT1.EXE (Drive Converter FAT16 to FAT32)

Practice Test Questions

1. In Device Manager, a red X through a device icon indicates:

   Correct answer: d

2. What is the purpose of the file Asd.exe?

   Correct answer: b

3. How do you see a list of the I/O addresses currently used by the system?

   Correct answer: b

4. Which Windows program file can execute a file containing a script?

   Correct answer: a

5. Which icon represents SCSI in Device Manager?

   Correct answer: c

6. What are the steps to access the Windows 98 utility to convert a hard drive from FAT16 to FAT32?

   Correct answer: a

7. When a new hardware device is added to a system, Windows 9x usually detects the device at startup and automatically begins the process of installing the device. What might be a reason that Windows 9x never detects a new hardware device?

   Correct answer: c

SPREAD 21

Objective 2.1	Identify the procedures for installing Windows 9x, and Windows 2000 for bringing the software to a basic operational level	Start up Partition Format drive Loading drivers Run appropriate set up utility

Practice Test Questions

1. What command do you use to eliminate the partition table as the source of a problem with a hard drive?

   Correct answer: c

2. Which Windows setup option should you use when installing Windows 98 on a notebook?

   Correct answer: b

3. What is the command to begin installing Windows 9x?

   Correct answer: b

4. After partitioning the hard drive using FDISK, the next step is to:

   Correct answer: c

5. When the FORMAT program is formatting the drive, how are bad sectors handled?

   Correct answer: c

6. How many partitions can a hard drive have using Windows 9x?

   Correct answer: a

7. How many logical drives can the primary partition contain?

   Correct answer: b

SPREAD 22

Objective 2.2	Identify steps to perform an operating system upgrade	Upgrading Windows 95 to Windows 98 Upgrading from Windows NT Workstation 4.0 to Windows 2000 Replacing Windows 9x with Windows 2000 Dual boot Windows 9x/ Windows NT 4.0/2000

Practice Test Questions

1. During a Windows 98 upgrade, VMM32.VXD is built specifically for this PC. Why is that so?

   Correct answer: c

2. What is the purpose of the Windows 95 Setup option "Portable"?

   Correct answer: b

3. To create a dual boot between Windows 2000 and Windows 98, which file system should be used?

   Correct answer: c

4. The name of the setup program to install Windows NT is:

   Correct answer: c

5. Which operating system requires it be the only OS installed on a partition?

   Correct answer: d

6. What is the purpose of the program MSCDEX.EXE?

   Correct answer: b

7. What are the four options for a Windows NT installation?

   Correct answer: b

SPREAD 23

Objective 2.3	Identify the basic system boot sequences and boot methods, including the steps to create an emergency boot disk with utilities installed for Windows 9x, Windows NT, and Windows 2000	Startup disk Creating Emergency Repair Disk (ERD)

Practice Test Questions

1. To create an emergency startup disk in Windows 95:

   Correct answer: b

2. The purpose of the MORE.COM program on the Windows 95 rescue disk is:

   Correct answer: a

3. The purpose of the FC.EXE program on the Windows 95 rescue disk is:

   Correct answer: b

4. What command is used to manage cabinet files?

   Correct answer: d

5. What is the program used by Windows 2000 to create a set of startup disks?

   Correct answer: b

6. What is the purpose of a cabinet file?

   Correct answer: a

7. In Windows 95, what is the difference between a system disk and an emergency startup disk?

   Correct answer: c

SPREAD 24

Objective 2.3 continued	Identify the basic system boot sequences and boot methods, including the steps to create an emergency boot disk with utilities installed for Windows 9x, Windows NT, and Windows 2000	Files required to boot NTLDR (NT loader), BOOT.INI

Practice Test Questions

1. Which Windows 2000 system file is required to boot only when booting from a SCSI device?

   Correct answer: c

2. What is the correct boot sequence using DOS?

   Correct answer: b

3. Which Windows 9x component is responsible for loading static device drivers?

   Correct answer: b

4. Which Windows 2000 component is part of the kernel?

   Correct answer: c

5. Where can installed device drivers be listed so they are loaded when Windows 98 loads?

   Correct answer: d

6. What are the three core components of Windows 9x?

   Correct answer: b

7. How does Windows 98 use COMMAND.COM?

   Correct answer: a

SPREAD 25

Objective 2.3 continued	Identify the basic system boot sequences and boot methods, including the steps to create an emergency boot disk with utilities installed for Windows 9x, Windows NT, and Windows 2000	Safe Mode

Practice Test Questions

1. Which function key allows you to choose between Normal, Safe Mode, Step-by-Step Confirmation, Command Prompt Only, and Previous Version of MS-DOS when booting Windows 95?

   Correct answer: c

2. Which function key allows you to boot directly into Safe Mode when using Windows 95?

   Correct answer: b

3. Which function key allows you to boot Windows 2000 into Safe Mode?

   Correct answer: d

4. What is the name of the command line interface offered by Windows 2000 to recover from a failed installation?

   Correct answer: c

5. Which statement is not true about Safe Mode in Windows 9x?

   Correct answer: a

6. How many startup disks are required to boot Windows NT from floppy disks?

   Correct answer: c

7. When using Windows 95, if you boot from the Startup menu to Option 6, Command Prompt Only, what command do you use to load Windows?

   Correct answer: c

SPREAD 26

Objective 2.3 continued	Identify the basic system boot sequences and boot methods, including the steps to create an emergency boot disk with utilities installed for Windows 9x, Windows NT, and Windows 2000	MS-DOS mode

Practice Test Questions

1. When Windows 9x executes MS-DOS mode, what happens to Windows 9x?

   Correct answer: c

2. What is the purpose of the SYSTEM-ROOT command issued from the Windows 2000 Recovery Console?

   Correct answer: b

3. If you are running MS-DOS mode, how do you load Windows 9x?

   Correct answer: c

4. From Windows 9x, how do you enter MS-DOS mode?

   Correct answer: b

5. Which of the following is an internal DOS command?

   Correct answer: a

6. You suspect a problem when Windows 9x loads. Where is one place to look for information about the problem?

   Correct answer: a

7. What happens when you double-click COMMAND.COM in Windows Explorer?

   Correct answer: b

SPREAD 27

Objective 2.4	Identify procedures for loading/adding and configuring application device drivers, and the necessary software for certain devices	Windows 9x Plug and Play and Windows 2000

Practice Test Questions

1. Which operating system supports Plug and Play?

   Correct answer: c

2. In order for a system to be fully Plug-and-Play compliant, what must be true?

   Correct answer: a

3. A 16-bit device driver is loaded from:

   Correct answer: a

4. One advantage a 32-bit driver has over a 16-bit driver is that the 32-bit driver:

   Correct answer: c

5. Using Windows 9x, where do you look to find the name of a 32-bit device driver used by a device?

   Correct answer: a

6. Plug and Play requires:

   Correct answer: b

7. The message "Windows 98 Ready" on the packaging of a new hardware device probably means that:

   Correct answer: d

SPREAD 28

Objective 2.4 continued	Identify procedures for loading/adding and configuring application device drivers, and the necessary software for certain devices	Identify the procedures for installing and launching typical Windows and non–Windows applications (*Note:* There is no content related to Windows 3.1)

Practice Test Questions

1. What is the result when the same memory is allocated to more than one application?

   Correct answer: a

2. What is one thing you can do so that more applications can be loaded at the same time?

   Correct answer: a

3. What type of multitasking does Windows 9x support?

   Correct answer: a

4. Where are most DLL files stored under Windows 9x?

   Correct answer: c

5. How do you change the environmental settings for a DOS application running under Windows 2000?

   Correct answer: b

6. What is an example of OLE?

   Correct answer: d

7. What is one way to cause an application under Windows 9x to load at startup?

   Correct answer: c

SPREAD 29

Objective 2.4 continued	Identify procedures for loading/adding and configuring application device drivers, and the necessary software for certain devices	Procedures for set up and configuring Windows printing subsystem: Setting Default printer Installing/Spool setting Network printing (with help of LAN admin)

Practice Test Questions

1. What does EMF stand for?

   Correct answer: b

2. What is EMF printing?

   Correct answer: a

3. What is print spooling?

   Correct answer: a

4. When troubleshooting a problem with printing, what can you check in CMOS setup?

   Correct answer: c

5. What is PostScript?

   Correct answer: b

6. What is raw data?

   Correct answer: c

7. What is one advantage of using print spooling?

   Correct answer: d

SPREAD 30

Objective 3.1	Recognize and interpret the meaning of common error codes and startup messages from the boot sequence, and identify steps to correct the problems	Safe Mode

Practice Test Questions

1. What is the source of the error message "MS-DOS compatibility mode"?

   Correct answer: a

2. What is the source of the error message "Invalid VxD dynamic link call from IFSMGR" and what do you do to solve the problem?

   Correct answer: a

3. What is one of the first things you should do after booting into Safe Mode?

   Correct answer: a

4. What happens if the Win.com file is missing from the Windows 9x load?

   Correct answer: d

5. What might be a cause of the error message "Invalid system disk" under Windows 9x?

   Correct answer: d

6. Which statement about booting Windows 9x into Safe Mode is not true?

   Correct answer: b

7. What is one way to access Safe Mode under Windows 2000?

   Correct answer: b

SPREAD 31

Objective 3.1 continued	Recognize and interpret the meaning of common error codes and startup messages from the boot sequence, and identify steps to correct the problems	Error in CONFIG.SYS line XX HIMEM.SYS not loaded Missing or corrupt HIMEM.SYS

Practice Test Questions

1. Which file is required for Windows 98 to load?

   Correct answer: c

2. TSR stands for:

   Correct answer: c

3. Which command line belongs in Config.sys?

   Correct answer: b

4. Pressing Shift+F8 during booting causes:

   Correct answer: a

5. What is the result of the command DEVICEHIGH=HIMEM.SYS?

   Correct answer: d

6. What is true of device drivers loaded from CONFIG.SYS?

   Correct answer: d

7. What is the cause of the error "Bad sector"?

   Correct answer: c

SPREAD 32

Objective 3.1 continued	Recognize and interpret the meaning of common error codes and startup messages from the boot sequence, and identify steps to correct the problems	No operating system found Bad or missing COMMAND.COM A device referenced in SYSTEM.INI, WIN.INI, Registry could not be found Failure to start GUI

Practice Test Questions

1. What is the purpose of the Windows 98 command WIN.COM /D:F?

   Correct answer: b

2. When does Windows 98 create the Bootlog.txt file?

   Correct answer: d

3. Which statement about VxDs is true?

   Correct answer: b

4. To temporarily disable a command in CONFIG.SYS, you should:

   Correct answer: c

5. Using Windows 9x, from where can device drivers be loaded?

Correct answer: c

6. How can you load Windows 98 bypassing entries in System.ini and Win.ini?

Correct answer: b

7. Which of the following Windows 9x files is built specifically for the current system?

Correct answer: a

SPREAD 33

Objective 3.1 continued	Recognize and interpret the meaning of common error codes and startup messages from the boot sequence, and identify steps to correct the problems	SCSI Dr. Watson Windows Protection Error Swap file

Practice Test Questions

1. Which of the following statements about a Windows 9x swap file is not true?

Correct answer: d

2. Where are the log files created by Dr. Watson stored?

Correct answer: c

3. How do you start Dr Watson?

Correct answer: a

4. If an application fails to start, try deleting all the files in this folder:

Correct answer: b

5. What type of information about errors is stored in the Ios.log file?

Correct answer: a

6. What is the recommended approach to managing Windows 9x virtual memory?

Correct answer: a

7. What are the steps to change the location of the Windows 98 swap file?

Correct answer: a

SPREAD 34

Objective 3.1 continued	Recognize and interpret the meaning of common error codes and startup messages from the boot sequence, and identify steps to correct the problems	NT boot issues Event Viewer – Event Log is Full

Practice Test Questions

1. In Windows NT, when is the Last Known Good Configuration saved?

   Correct answer: a

2. Which statement is true about the Windows NT ERD?

   Correct answer: b

3. Using Windows 2000, what menu contains the option to clear the Event Viewer of all events?

   Correct answer: b

4. Which statement is true about the Windows 2000 ERD?

   Correct answer: c

5. Which of the following is required before you can use the Windows 2000 Recovery Console?

   Correct answer: d

6. How do you access the Windows 2000 Event Viewer?

   Correct answer: c

7. On which menu do you find the Windows 2000 Last Known Good Configuration option?

   Correct answer: b

SPREAD 35

Objective 3.2	Recognize common problems and determine how to resolve them	Eliciting problem symptoms from customers Having customer reproduce error as part of the diagnostic process Identifying recent changes to the computer environment from the user

Practice Test Questions

1. What is something you can do to promote good communication?

   Correct answer: d

2. What is something you should do while talking with a customer?

   Correct answer: d

3. What is one question to ask a customer?

   Correct answer: b

4. What are some things you need to know from the customer?

   Correct answer: d

5. What is the first thing you should do when you arrive at a customer's site?

   Correct answer: c

6. What do you do if you make a mistake while attempting to repair a PC?

   Correct answer: b

7. When interviewing a customer, why is it important to know if the PC has been near a lightning storm recently?

   Correct answer: a

SPREAD 36

Objective 3.2 continued	Recognize common problems and determine how to resolve them	Troubleshooting Windows-specific printing problems: Print spool is stalled Incorrect/incompatible driver for print Incorrect parameter

Practice Test Questions

1. If you can print a test page from the Windows 98 Print window, what is the most likely source of a user's continuing print problem?

   Correct answer: d

2. You cannot print from an application or the Windows 98 Print window. What do you do first?

   Correct answer: c

3. You are unable to print and several jobs are in the print queue. How do you clear the queue?

   Correct answer: b

4. How do you uninstall a printer's device drivers?

   Correct answer: c

5. What is one source of a problem that would prevent Windows 98 from printing?

   Correct answer: d

6. If you can print from a DOS prompt, but cannot print from Windows, what is the next thing you should do?

   Correct answer: a

7. Which file extension is used for a bitmap file?

   Correct answer: b

SPREAD 37

Objective 3.2 continued	Recognize common problems and determine how to resolve them	Other common problems: General Protection Faults Illegal operation Invalid working directory System lock up Option (sound card, modem, input device) will not function Application will not start or load TSR (Terminate Stay Resident) programs and virus Applications don't install

Practice Test Questions

1. When an application fails to load, what should you do first?

   Correct answer: a

2. How can you change the icon of a shortcut object on the desktop?

   Correct answer: a

3. You are running several applications and one of them locks up. What do you do?

   Correct answer: c

4. An application cannot access a device. How can you know if the device is installed properly?

   Correct answer: d

5. In implementing Plug and Play, the bus enumerator inventories the resources required by devices on the bus. Which bus does Windows 95 not support?

   Correct answer: c

6. How do you create a shortcut using Windows 98?

   Correct answer: d

7. An application gives an "illegal operations" error. What is one possible cause?

   Correct answer: d

SPREAD 38

Objective 3.2 continued	Recognize common problems and determine how to resolve them	Cannot log on to network (option – NIC not functioning) Network connection

Practice Test Questions

1. How can you know a PC has a physical connection to an Ethernet hub?

   Correct answer: d

2. How can you verify using Windows 2000 that a PC has good communication over the network?

   Correct answer: a

3. How can you verify that your computer can communicate with another computer on the TCP/IP network?

   Correct answer: a

4. What is a possible cause of a failure to connect to the network?

   Correct answer: d

5. You cannot connect to a network even after a reboot. What is the next thing to do?

   Correct answer: c

6. You can print to a network printer but cannot see another host on the network that should be listed in Network Neighborhood. What might be the cause?

   Correct answer: c

7. How do you share a folder on the network?

   Correct answer: a

SPREAD 39

Objective 3.2 continued	Recognize common problems and determine how to resolve them	Viruses and virus types: What they are Sources (floppy, e-mails, etc.) How to determine presence

Practice Test Questions

1. How does a boot sector virus differ from a file virus?

   Correct answer: b

2. How does a virus typically spread over e-mail?

   Correct answer: d

3. What is a macro virus?

   Correct answer: c

4. What can you do to protect against a virus?

   Correct answer: d

5. What is one thing that a virus cannot do?

   Correct answer: d

6. What is the purpose of virus protection in CMOS setup?

   Correct answer: b

7. What is a symptom of a virus being present or having done damage?

   Correct answer: d

SPREAD 40

Objective 4.1	Identify the networking capabilities of Windows including procedures for connecting to the network	Protocols Ipconfig.exe Winipcfg.exe Installing and configuring browsers Configure OS for network connection

Practice Test Questions

1. When will a Windows-based PC use the IPX/SPX network protocol?

   Correct answer: a

2. When is the DLC network protocol likely to be used?

   Correct answer: d

3. How do you create a new network connection using Windows 2000?

   Correct answer: d

4. What is one limitation of the NetBEUI protocol?

   Correct answer: a

5. Which utility is not included with Windows 2000?

   Correct answer: c

6. Which statement is not true about the TCP/IP protocol?

   Correct answer: a

7. What is the purpose of NetBT?

   Correct answer: c

SPREAD 41

Objective 4.1 continued	Identify the networking capabilities of Windows including procedures for connecting to the network	Sharing disk drives Sharing print and file services

Practice Test Questions

1. What is the purpose of Windows 98 Direct Cable Connection?

   Correct answer: c

2. What connects a null modem cable to a PC?

   Correct answer: a

3. How do you install file and printer sharing for Microsoft Networks?

   Correct answer: a

4. How do you share a file or folder with others on the network?

   Correct answer: b

5. Using Windows 9x, how do you map a drive letter to a network resource?

   Correct answer: d

6. When you share a printer with others on the network, what is required?

   Correct answer: a

7. When using Windows Explorer, how can you tell that an object is network shared?

   Correct answer: b

SPREAD 42

Objective 4.1 continued	Identify the networking capabilities of Windows including procedures for connecting to the network	Network type and network card

Practice Test Questions

1. What type of networks does Windows 95 support?

   Correct answer: b

2. You have a network card that has a port that looks like a large phone jack. What type of NIC is it?

   Correct answer: b

3. Which is the most popular network architecture for a LAN?

   Correct answer: d

4. What is the most common topology used by Ethernet?

   Correct answer: c

5. Which type network is not supported by Windows 98?

   Correct answer: a

6. Before data can be sent over a network, what happens to it?

   Correct answer: a

7. Windows 95 has built-in support for what type of networking?

   Correct answer: b

SPREAD 43

Objective 4.2	Identify concepts and capabilities relating to the Internet and basic procedures for setting up a system for Internet access	Concepts and terminology: TCP/IP NetBEUI IPX/SPX PING.EXE TRACERT.EXE NSLOOKUP.EXE

Practice Test Questions

1. What are the most common network protocols that work at the operating system level that are supported by Windows 9x and Windows 2000?

   Correct answer: b

2. What protocol is used by Netware Novell?

   Correct answer: c

3. How is the NetBEUI protocol used?

   Correct answer: c

4. Which TCP/IP utility is used to verify that two computers are connected over a network?

   Correct answer: b

5. Which TCP/IP utility is a part of Windows 9x TCP/IP but is not included with Windows 2000 TCP/IP?

   Correct answer: a

6. What is Telnet?

   Correct answer: a

7. What is the main networking protocol used by the Internet?

   Correct answer: a

SPREAD 44

Objective 4.2 continued	Identify concepts and capabilities relating to the Internet and basic procedures for setting up a system for Internet access	E-mail FTP Domain Names (Web sites) HTML HTTP://

Practice Test Questions

1. A user shares a folder on his hard drive with others on the network. His computer is named JSMITH and his folder is named JOE. What is the UNC name for this shared resource?

   Correct answer: b

2. When configuring a PC using TCP/IP with static IP addressing to log onto a network, what unique information is needed for this PC?

   Correct answer: a

3. What is FTP?

   Correct answer: b

4. What organization tracks domain names and IP addresses?

   Correct answer: a

5. What is UNC?

   Correct answer: c

6. What type of organization uses domain names that end in .org?

   Correct answer: d

7. What is a domain name?

   Correct answer: a

SPREAD 45

Objective 4.2 continued	Identify concepts and capabilities relating to the Internet and basic procedures for setting up a system for Internet access	ISP Dial-up networking

Practice Test Questions

1. When configuring a PC to use a modem to an ISP to connect to the Internet, what line protocol is used?

   Correct answer: a

2. Which of the following is not a valid IP address?

   Correct answer: a

3. What network service keeps track of domain names and their corresponding IP addresses?

Correct answer: b

4. When an IP address is assigned to a PC each time it logs onto a network, this is called:

Correct answer: c

5. What protocol must be installed for a PC using Windows 95 to connect to the Internet?

Correct answer: c

6. What service does a Windows 95 PC use when it contacts a Windows NT server requesting an IP address at logon to the network?

Correct answer: c

7. In what class is the IP address 129.80.129.240?

Correct answer: b

Accelerated graphics port (AGP) — A slot on a system board for a video card that provides transfer of video data from the CPU that is synchronized with the memory bus.

ACPI (Advanced Configuration and Power Interface) — Specification developed by Intel, Microsoft, and Toshiba to control power on notebooks and other devices. Windows 98 supports ACPI.

Active Directory — A Windows 2000 service that allows for a single point of administration for all shared resources on a network, including files, peripheral devices, databases, Web sites, users, and services.

Adapter address — A 6-byte hex hardware address unique to each NIC and assigned by manufacturers. The address is often printed on the adapter. An example is 00 00 0C 08 2F 35. Also called MAC address.

Adapter card — Also called an interface card. A small circuit board inserted in an expansion slot and used to communicate between the system bus and a peripheral device.

Address Resolution Protocol (ARP) — A method used by TCP/IP that dynamically or automatically translates IP addresses into physical network addresses such as Ethernet IDs or Token Ring MAC addresses.

ADSL (asymmetric digital subscriber line) — A method of data transmission over phone lines that is digital, allows for a direct connection, and is about 50 times faster than ISDN.

Advanced Options Menu — A Windows 2000 menu that appears when you press F8 when Windows starts. The menu can be used to troubleshoot problems when loading Windows 2000.

Advanced SCSI programming interface (ASPI) — A popular device driver that enables operating systems to communicate with a SCSI host adapter. (The "A" originally stood for Adaptec.)

Advanced Transfer Cache (ATC) — A type of L2 cache contained within the Pentium processor housing that is embedded on the same core processor die as the CPU itself.

Alternating current (AC) — Current that cycles back and forth rather than traveling in only one direction. Normally between 110 and 115 AC volts are supplied from a standard wall outlet.

Ammeter — A meter that measures electrical current in amps.

Ampere (A) — A unit of measurement for electrical current. One volt across a resistance of one ohm will produce a flow of one amp.

ANSI (American National Standards Institute) — A nonprofit organization dedicated to creating trade and communications standards.

Antivirus (AV) software — Utility programs that prevent infection, or scan a system to detect and remove viruses. McAfee Associates VirusScan and Norton AntiVirus are two popular AV packages.

Asynchronous SRAM — Static RAM that does not work in step with the CPU clock and is, therefore, slower than synchronous SRAM.

AT command set — A set of commands used by a PC to control a modem. AT is the ATtention command, which alerts a modem to prepare to receive additional commands. For example, ATDT means attention and listen for a dial tone.

ATAPI (Advanced Technology Attachment Packet Interface) — An interface standard that is part of the IDE/ATA standards, which allows tape drives and CD-ROM drives to be treated like an IDE hard drive by the OS.

ATTRIB command — A DOS command that can display file attributes and even lock files so that they are "read-only" and cannot be modified (for example, ATTRIB +R FILENAME).

Auto detection — A feature on newer system BIOS and hard drives that automatically identifies and configures a new hard drive in the CMOS setup.

AUTOEXEC.BAT — One startup file on an MS-DOS computer. It tells the computer what commands or programs to execute automatically after bootup.

Back up, Backup — When used as a verb, to make a duplicate copy of important files or data. When used as a noun, refers to the file created when backing up. Backups can be made by saving a file with a different name or by copying files to a different storage media.

Backbone — A network used to link several networks together. For example, several Token Rings and Ethernet LANS may be connected using a single FDDI backbone.

Backside bus — The bus between the CPU and the L2 cache inside the CPU housing.

Backward compatible — Refers to new hardware and software that is able to support older, existing technologies. This is a common choice of hardware and software manufacturers.

Bandwidth — The range of frequencies that a communication cable or channel can carry. In general use, the term refers to the volume of data that can travel on a bus or over a cable.

Bank — An area on the system board that contains slots for memory modules (typically labeled bank 0, 1, 2, and 3).

Base memory — *See* Conventional memory.

Baseband — Relating to a communications system which carries only a single message at a time over wire. Ethernet uses baseband technology. Compare to broadband.

Batch file — A text file containing a series of DOS instructions to the computer, telling it to perform a specific task (for example, AUTOEXEC.BAT, which contains a series of startup commands).

Baud rate — A measure of line speed between two devices such as a computer and a printer or a modem. This speed is measured in the number of times a signal changes in one second. *See* bps.

Beam detect mirror — Detects the initial presence of a laser printer's laser beam by reflecting the beam to an optical fiber.

Binary number system — The number system used by computers where there are only two numbers, 0 and 1, called binary digits, or bits.

Binding — Associating an OSI layer to a layer above it or below it. For example, associating a protocol type such as TCP/IP to a NIC driver.

BIOS (basic input/output system) — Firmware that controls much of a computer's input/output functions, such as communication with the floppy drive, RAM chips, and the monitor. Also called ROM BIOS.

Bitmap file — A type of graphics file in which the image is written as a series of 0s and 1s. These files have the extension .bmp and can be loaded into paint programs to be edited and printed.

BNC connector — A connector used on an Ethernet 10Base2 (Thinnet) network. A BNC connector looks like a TV cable connector.

Boot loader menu — A startup menu that gives the user the choice between Windows NT Workstation Version 4.0 and another OS, such as Windows 98.

Boot partition — The hard drive partition where the Windows NT OS is stored. The system partition and the boot partition may be different partitions.

Boot record (of hard drives) — The first sector of each logical drive in a partition that contains information about the logical drive. If the boot record is in the active partition, then it is used to boot the OS. Also called OS boot record or volume boot record.

Boot sector virus — An infectious program that can replace the boot program with a modified, infected version of the boot command utilities, often causing boot and data retrieval problems.

Bootable disk — For DOS, a floppy disk that can upload the OS files necessary for computer startup. It must have the two hidden system files IO.SYS and MSDOS.SYS, and also COMMAND.COM.

Booting — The process that a computer goes through when it is first turned on to get the computer ready to receive commands.

Bps (bits per second) — A measure of data transmission speed. (Example: a common modem speed is 56,000 bps or 56 Kbps.)

Bridge — A hardware device or box, coupled with software at the data-link layer, used to connect similar networks and network segments. *See* Router.

Briefcase — A Windows 9x system folder used to synchronize files between two computers. When files are transferred from one computer to another, Briefcase automatically updates files on the original computer to the most recent version.

Broadband — Relating to a communications system such as cable modem or ATM networks that carry multiple messages over wire, each message traveling on its own frequency. Compare to baseband.

Buffer — A temporary memory area where data is kept before being written to a hard drive or sent to a printer, thus reducing the number of writes to the devices.

Burst EDO (BEDO) — A refined version of EDO memory that significantly improved access time over EDO. BEDO is not widely used today because Intel chose not to support it. BEDO memory is stored on 168-pin DIMM modules.

Burst SRAM — Memory that is more expensive and slightly faster than pipelined burst SRAM. Data is sent as a two-step process; the data address is sent, and then the data itself is sent without interruption.

Burst transfer — A means of sending data across the bus, with one packet immediately following the next, without waiting for clock beats and/or addressing of the information being sent.

Bus — Strips of parallel wires or printed circuits used to transmit electronic signals on the system board to other devices. Most Pentium systems use a 32-bit bus.

Bus enumerator — A component of Windows 9x Plug and Play that locates all devices on a particular bus and inventories the resource requirements for these devices.

Bus network architecture — A network design in which nodes are connected in line with one another, with no centralized point of contact.

Bus network topology — A network design in which nodes are connected in line with one another, with no centralized point of contact.

Bus speed — The speed or frequency at which the data on the system board is moving.

Cabinet file — A file that contains one or more compressed files, and is often used to distribute software on disk. The Extract command is used to extract one or more files from the cabinet file.

Cable modem — A method of data transmission over cable TV lines that requires a modem and an Ethernet network interface card to receive the transmission.

Cache memory — A kind of fast RAM that is used to speed up memory access because it does not need to be continuously refreshed.

Capacitor — An electronic device that can maintain an electrical charge for a period of time and is used to smooth out the flow of electrical current.

Cards — Adapter boards or interface cards placed into expansion slots to expand the functions of a computer, allowing it to communicate with external devices such as monitors or speakers.

Carrier — A signal used to activate a phone line to confirm a continuous frequency; used to indicate that two computers are ready to receive or transmit data via modems.

CD or CHDIR command — A DOS command to change directories (for example, CD\WINDOWS changes the directory to the Windows directory, and CD\ returns to the Root directory).

CD-R (recordable CD) — A CD drive that can record or write data to a CD. The drive may or may not be multisession, but the data cannot be erased once it is written.

CD-RW (rewritable CD) — A CD drive that can record or write data to a CD. The data can be erased and overwritten. The drive may or may not be multisession.

Chain — A group of clusters used to hold a single file.

Checksum — A method of error checking transmitted data, whereby the digits are added up and their sum compared to an expected sum.

Child directory — *See* Subdirectory.

Child, parent, grandparent backup method — A plan for backing up and reusing tapes or removable disks by rotating them each week (child), month (parent), and year (grandparent).

Chip set — A group of chips on the system board that relieves the CPU of some of the system's processing tasks, providing careful timing of activities and increasing the overall speed and performance of the system.

CHS (cylinders, heads, sectors) mode — The traditional method by which BIOS reads from and writes to hard drives by addressing the correct cylinder, head, and sector. Also called normal mode.

Circuit boards — Computer components, such as the main system board or an adapter board, that have electronic circuits and chips.

Classless addresses — Class C network addresses that a service provider owns and then subleases to small companies.

Clean installation — A Windows 2000 installation that overwrites all previous installations on the hard drive partition.

Client — In a network, a computer that is connected to another computer and uses programs and/or data stored on the other computer.

Clock speed — The speed or frequency that determines the speed at which devices on the system bus operate, usually expressed in MHz. Different components on a system board operate at different speeds, which are determined by multiplying or dividing a factor by the clock speed. The clock speed is itself determined by a crystal or oscillator located somewhere on the system board.

Clone — Originally, a computer that was compatible with IBM computer hardware and MS-DOS software. Today, the word clone often refers to no-name Intel and Microsoft compatibles.

Cluster — One or more sectors that constitute the smallest unit of space on a disk for storing data (also referred to as a file allocation unit). Files are written to a disk as groups of whole clusters.

Cluster chain — A series of clusters used to hold a single file.

CMOS (complementary metal-oxide semiconductor) — One of two types of technologies used to manufacture microchips (the other type is TTL or transistor-transistor logic chips). CMOS chips require less electricity, hold data longer after the electricity is turned off, are slower, and produce less heat than do TTL chips. The configuration or setup chip is a CMOS chip.

COAST (cache on a stick) — Memory modules that hold memory used as a memory cache. *See* Cache memory.

Cold Boot — *See* Hard boot.

Combo card — An Ethernet card that has more than one port to accommodate different cabling media.

Comment lines — Documentation lines that are ignored by a program. A REM in front of a line will comment out an AUTOEXEC command. A semicolon will turn an .ini file line into a comment.

Common access method (CAM) — A standard adapter driver used by SCSI.

Compressed drive — A drive whose format has been reorganized in order to store more data. A compressed drive is really not a drive at all; it's actually a type of file, typically with a host drive called H.

Configuration data — Also called setup information. Information about the computer's hardware, such as what type of hard drive or floppy drive is present, along with other detailed settings.

Configuration manager — A component of Windows 9x Plug and Play that controls the configuration process of all devices and communicates these configurations to the devices.

Configuration parameter — In Windows NT, another name for the value names and values of the Registry; information in the Windows NT Registry.

Connection protocol — In networking, confirming that a good connection is made before transmitting data to the other end. To accomplish this, most network applications use TCP rather than UDP.

Connectionless protocol — When UDP is used and a connection is not required before sending a packet. Consequently, there is no guarantee that the packet will arrive at its destination. An example of a UDP transmission is a broadcast to all nodes on a network.

Console — An administrative tool contains two or more individual administrative tools. For example, Recovery Console contains a set of commands designed to manage a failed Windows 2000 boot, and Computer Management is a console that contains several tools to monitor and manage hardware and software.

Continuity — A continuous, unbroken path for the flow of electricity. A "continuity test" can determine whether or not internal wiring is still intact.

Control blade — A laser printer component that prevents too much toner from sticking to the cylinder surface.

Conventional memory — Memory addresses between 0 and 640K. Also called base memory.

Cooperative multitasking — A type of pseudomultitasking whereby the CPU switches back and forth between programs loaded at the same time. One program sits in the background waiting for the other to relinquish control. Also called task switching.

Coprocessor — A chip or portion of the CPU that helps the microprocessor perform calculations and speeds up computations and data manipulations dramatically.

COPY command — A command that copies files from one location to another (for example, COPY FILE.EXT A: is used to copy the file named FILE.EXT to the floppy disk in drive A).

Corrupted files — Data and program files that are damaged for any of a variety of reasons, ranging from power spikes to user error.

CPU (central processing unit) — Also called a microprocessor. The heart and brain of the computer, which receives data input, processes information, and executes instructions.

Cross-linked clusters — Errors caused when files appear to share the same disk space, according to the file allocation table.

Crosstalk — The interference that one wire, in a twisted pair, may produce in the other.

CVF (compressed volume file) — The file on the host drive of a compressed drive that holds all compressed data.

Data cartridge — A type of tape medium typically used for back-ups. Full-sized data cartridges are $4 \times 6 \times \frac{5}{8}$ inches in size. A minicartridge is only $3\frac{1}{2} \times 2\frac{1}{2} \times \frac{3}{5}$ inches.

Data communications equipment (DCE) — The hardware, usually a dial-up modem, that provides the connection between a data terminal and a communications line.

Data compression — Reducing the size of files by various techniques such as using a shortcut code to represent repeated data.

Data line protectors — Surge protectors designed to work with the telephone line to a modem.

Data path — The number of bits of data transmitted simultaneously on a bus. The size of a bus, such as a 32-bit-wide data path in a PCI bus.

Data terminal equipment (DTE) — This term refers to both the computer and a remote terminal or other computer to which it is attached.

Datagrams — Packets of data that travel between networks from a sender to a receiver. A datagram typically includes an IP header, address information, a checksum, and data.

DEBUG utility — A DOS utility that shows exactly what is written to a file or memory, using the hexadecimal numbering system to display memory addresses and data.

De facto standard — A standard that does not have an official backing, but is considered a standard because of widespread use and acceptance by the industry.

Default directory — The directory that DOS automatically uses to save and retrieve files.

Default drive — The drive that DOS automatically uses to save and retrieve files.

Default gateway — The main gateway or unit that will send or receive packets addressed to other networks.

Default printer — The printer that Windows software will use unless the user specifies another printer.

Defragment — To "optimize" or rewrite a file to a disk in one contiguous chain of clusters, thus speeding up data retrieval.

DEL command — A command that deletes files (for example, DEL A:FILE.EXT deletes the file named FILE.EXT from drive A).

DELTREE command — A command used to delete a directory, all its subdirectories, and all files within it (for example, DELTREE DIRNAME deletes the directory named DIRNAME and everything in it).

Desktop — The initial screen that is displayed when an OS that has a GUI interface is loaded.

Device driver — A small program stored on the hard drive that tells the computer how to communicate with an input/output device such as a printer or modem.

Diagnostic cards — Adapter cards designed to discover and report computer errors and conflicts at POST time (before the computer boots up), often by displaying a number on the card.

Diagnostic software — Utility programs that help troubleshoot computer systems. Some DOS diagnostic utilities are CHKDSK and SCANDISK. PC-Technician is an example of a third-party diagnostic program.

Dial-Up Networking (DUN) — A Windows application that allows a PC to remotely connect to a network through a phone line. A Dial-Up Network icon can be found under My Computer.

Differential backup — Backs up only files that have changed or have been created since the last full backup. When recovering data, only two backups are needed: the full backup and the last differential backup.

Digital diagnostic disk — A floppy disk that has data written on it that is precisely aligned, which is used to test the alignment of a floppy disk drive.

Digital signal — A signal that has only a finite number of values in the range of possible values. An example is the transmission of data over a serial cable as bits, where there are only two values: 0 and 1.

Digital subscriber line (DSL) — A type of technology that is used by digital telephone lines that direct connect rather than dial-up.

Digital video disc (DVD) — A faster, larger CD-ROM format that can read older CDs, store over 8 gigabytes of data, and hold full-length motion picture videos.

DIMM (dual inline memory module) — A miniature circuit board used in newer computers to hold memory. DIMMs can hold 16, 32, 64, or 128 MB of RAM on a single module.

Diode — An electronic device that allows electricity to flow in only one direction. Used in a rectifier circuit.

DIP (dual in-line package) switch — A switch on a circuit board or other device that can be set on or off to hold configuration or setup information.

Direct current (DC) — Current that travels in only one direction (the type of electricity provided by batteries). Computer power supplies transform AC current to low DC current.

Direct Rambus DRAM — A memory technology by Rambus and Intel that uses a narrow, very fast network-type memory bus. Memory is stored on a RIMM module. Also called RDRAM or Direct RDRAM.

Directory — An OS table that contains file information such as name, size, time and date of last modification, and the cluster number of the file's beginning location.

Discrete L2 cache — A type of L2 cache contained within the Pentium processor housing, but on a different die, with a cache bus between the processor and the cache.

Disk cache — A method whereby recently retrieved data and adjacent data are read into memory in advance, anticipating the next CPU request.

Disk cloning — Making an exact image of a hard drive including partition information, boot sectors, operating system installation and applications software to replicate the hard drive on another system or recover from a hard drive crash. Also called disk imaging.

Disk compression — Compressing data on a hard drive to allow more data to be written to the drive.

Disk duplexing — An improvement of disk mirroring, whereby redundant data is written to two or more drives, and each hard drive has its own adapter card. This provides greater protection than disk mirroring.

Disk imaging — *See* disk cloning.

Disk mirroring — A strategy whereby the same data is written to two hard drives in a computer, to safeguard against hard drive failure. Disk mirroring uses only a single adapter for two drives.

Disk striping — Treating multiple hard drives as a single volume. Data is written across the multiple drives in small segments, in order to increase performance and logical disk volume, and, when parity is also used, to provide fault tolerance. RAID 5 is disk striping with an additional drive for parity.

Disk thrashing — A condition that results when the hard drive is excessively used for virtual memory because RAM is full. It dramatically slows down processing and can cause premature hard drive failure.

DISKCOPY command — A command that copies the entire contents of one disk to another disk of the same type, while formatting the destination disk so that the two will be identical (for example, DISKCOPY A: A: uses drive A to duplicate a disk).

Display adapter — *See* Video controller card.

Display power management signaling (DPMS) — Energy Star standard specifications that allow for the video card and monitor to go into sleep mode simultaneously. *See* Energy Star systems.

DLL (dynamic-link library) — A file with a .dll file extension that contains a library of programming routines used by programs to perform common tasks.

DMA (direct memory access) controller chip — A chip that resides on the system board and provides channels that a device may use to send data directly to memory, bypassing the CPU.

Docking station — A device designed to connect to a portable, or notebook, computer in order to make it easy to connect the notebook to peripheral devices.

Documentation — Manuals, tutorials, and Help files that provide information that a user needs in order to use a computer system or software application.

Domain — In Windows NT, a logical group of networked computers, such as those on a college campus, that share a centralized directory database of user account information and security for the entire domain.

Domain name — A unique, text-based name that identifies an IP (Internet address). Typically, domain names in the United States end in .edu, .gov, .com, .org, or .net. Domain names also include a country code, such as .uk for the United Kingdom.

Domain Name System or Domain Name Service (DNS) — A database on a top-level domain name server that keeps track of assigned domain names and their corresponding IP addresses.

Dot pitch — The distance between the dots that the electronic beam hits on a monitor screen.

Double conversion — The process by which the inline UPS converts the AC power to battery power in DC form and then back to AC power.

Double-data rate SDRAM (DDR SDRAM or SDRAM II) — A type of memory technology used on DIMMs that runs at twice the speed of the system clock.

Doze time — The time before an Energy Star or "Green" system will reduce 80% of its activity.

DriveSpace — A utility that compresses files so that they take up less space on a disk drive, creating a single large file on the disk to hold all the compressed files.

Dual boot — The ability to boot using either of two different OSs, such as Windows NT and Windows 98. Note that programs cannot be easily shared between Windows NT and the other OS.

Dual ported — When the video chip set (input) and the RAM DAC (output) can access video memory at the same time. A special kind of video RAM is required.

Dual voltage CPU — A CPU that requires two different voltages, one for internal processing and the other for I/O processing.

Dynamic drive — In Windows 2000, a hard drive that uses a 1-MB database written at the end of the drive to hold information about volumes on the drive and RAID setup information.

Dynamic Host Configuration Protocol (DHCP) — The protocol of a server that manages dynamically assigned IP addresses. DHCP is supported by both Windows 9x and Windows NT, and Windows 2000.

Dynamic IP address — An assigned IP address that is used for the current session only. When the session is terminated, the IP address is returned to the list of available addresses.

Dynamic RAM (DRAM) — The most commonly used type of system memory, with access speeds ranging from 70 to 50 nanoseconds. It requires refreshing every few milliseconds.

Dynamic routing — Routing tables that are automatically updated as new information about routes becomes known and is shared by one router with another. Compare to Static routing.

Dynamic VxD — A VxD that is loaded and unloaded from memory as needed.

ECC (error checking and correction) — A chip set feature on a system board that checks the integrity of data stored on DIMMs and can correct single-bit errors in a byte. More advanced ECC schemas can detect, but not correct, double-bit errors in a byte.

ECHS (extended CHS) mode — A mode of addressing information on a hard drive by translating cylinder, head, and sector information in order to break the 528 MB hard drive barrier. Another name for large mode.

ECP (extended capabilities port) — A bidirectional parallel port mode that uses a DMA channel to speed up data flow.

EDO (extended data output) memory — A type of RAM that may be 10–20% faster than conventional RAM because it eliminates the delay before it issues the next memory address.

EEPROM (electrically erasable programmable ROM) chip — A type of chip in which higher voltage may be applied to one of the pins to erase its previous memory before a new instruction set is electronically written.

EISA (extended standard industry architecture) bus — A 32-bit bus that can transfer 4 bytes at a time at a speed of about 20 MHz.

Electrostatic discharge (ESD) — Another name for static electricity, which can damage chips and destroy system boards, even though it might not be felt or seen with the naked eye.

Embedded SCSI devices — Devices that contain their own host adapter, with the SCSI interface built into the device.

Emergency Repair Process — A Windows 2000 process that restores the OS to its state at the completion of a successful installation.

Emergency startup disk (ESD) — A Windows 9x system disk that also contains some Windows 9x diagnostic and utility files. The ESD serves Windows 9x as a rescue disk. *Also see* Rescue disk.

EMI (electromagnetic interference) — A magnetic field produced as a side effect from the flow of electricity. EMI can cause corrupted data in data lines that are not properly shielded.

EMM386.EXE — A DOS utility that provides both emulated expanded memory (EMS) and upper memory blocks (UMBs).

Encrypting virus — A type of virus that transforms itself into a nonreplicating program in order to avoid detection. It transforms itself back into a replicating program in order to spread.

Energy Star systems — "Green" systems that satisfy the EPA requirements to decrease the overall consumption of electricity. *See* Green standards.

Enhanced BIOS — A newer BIOS that has been written to accommodate larger-capacity gigabyte drives.

Enhanced IDE technology — A newer drive standard that allows systems to recognize drives larger than 504 MB/528 MB and to handle up to four devices on the same controller.

Enhanced metafile format (EMF) — A format used to print a document that contains embedded print commands. When printing in Windows, EMF information is generated by the GDI portion of the Windows kernel.

Environment — As related to OSs, the overall support that an OS provides to applications software.

Environment subsystems — In Windows NT, a user-mode process in which a subsystem runs an application in its own private memory address space as a virtual machine. (Compare to integral subsystems.)

EPP (enhanced parallel port) — A parallel port that allows data to flow in both directions (bidirectional port) and is faster than original parallel ports on PCs that only allowed communication in one direction.

EPROM (erasable programmable ROM) chip — A type of chip with a special window that allows the current memory contents to be erased with special ultraviolet light so that the chip can be reprogrammed. Many BIOS chips are EPROMs.

ERASE command — Another name for the DEL command.

Error correction — The ability of some modems to identify transmission errors and then automatically request another transmission.

ESCD (extended system configuration data) — A list written to the BIOS chip of what you have done manually to the system configuration that Plug and Play does not do on its own.

ESD (electrostatic discharge) — *See* Electrostatic discharge.

Ethernet — The most popular network topology used today. It uses Carrier Sense Multiple Access with Collision Detection (CSMA/CD) and can be physically configured as a bus or star network.

Event Viewer — In Windows NT, a utility that tracks and logs events as they are performed by the applications, processes, or user actions. Accessed by clicking Start, Programs, Administrative Tools, and then selecting Event Viewer.

Executive services — In Windows NT, a subsystem running in kernel mode that interfaces between the user mode and HAL.

Expanded memory (EMS) — Memory outside of the conventional 640K and the extended 1024K range that is accessed in 16K segments, or pages, by way of a window to upper memory.

Expansion bus — A bus that does not run synchronized with the system clock.

Expansion card — A circuit board inserted into a slot on the system board to enhance the capability of the computer.

Expansion slot — A narrow slot on the system board where an expansion card can be inserted. Expansion slots connect to a bus on the system board.

Extended memory — Memory above the initial 1024 KB, or 1 MB, area.

External cache — Static cache memory, stored on the system board or inside CPU housing, that is not part of the CPU (also called level 2 or L2 cache).

Fatal system error — An error that prevents Windows NT from loading. An example is a damaged Registry.

Fault tolerance — The degree to which a system can tolerate failures. Adding redundant components, such as disk mirroring or disk duplexing, is a way to build in fault tolerance.

FDDI (Fiber Distributed Data Interface) — Pronounced "fiddy." A ring-based network, similar to Token Ring, that does not require a centralized hub. FDDI often uses fiber-optic cabling.

Field replaceable unit — A component in a computer or device that can be replaced with a new component without sending the computer or device back to the manufacturer. Example: a DIMM memory module on a system board.

File — A collection of related records or lines that can be written to disk and assigned a name (for example, a simple letter or a payroll file containing data about employees).

File allocation table (FAT) — A table on a disk that tracks the clusters used to contain a file.

File allocation units — *See* Cluster.

File extension — A three-character portion of the name of a file that is used to identify the file type. The file extension follows the filename under DOS naming conventions.

Filename — The first part of the name assigned to a file. In DOS, the filename can be no more than 8 characters long and is followed by the file extension.

File system — The overall structure that an OS uses to name, store, and organize files on a disk. Examples of files systems are FAT16, FAT32, and NTFS.

File virus — A virus that inserts virus code into an executable program and can spread whenever that program is accessed.

Fire Wire — An expansion bus that can also be configured to work as a local bus. It is expected to replace the SCSI bus, providing an easy method to install and configure fast I/O devices. Also called IEEE 1394.

Firmware — Software that is permanently stored in a chip.

Flash memory — A type of RAM that can electronically hold memory even when the power is off.

Flash ROM — ROM that can be reprogrammed or changed without replacing chips.

Flat panel monitor — A desktop monitor that uses an LCD panel.

Flow control — When using modems, a method of controlling the flow of data from a sending PC by having the receiving PC send a message to the sending device to stop or start data flow. Xon/Xoff is an example of a flow control protocol.

FM (frequency modulation) method — A method of synthesizing sound by making a mathematical approximation of the musical sound wave. MIDI may use FM synthesis or wavetable synthesis.

Folder — A Windows directory for a collection of related files (for instance, a person may find it convenient to create a Mydata directory, or folder, in which to store personal files). For example, ATDT means attention and listen for a dial tone.

Formatting (a floppy disk) — To prepare a new floppy disk for use by placing tracks or cylinders on its surface to store information (for example, FORMAT A:). Old disks can be reformatted, but all data on them will be lost.

FPM (fast page mode) memory — An earlier memory mode used before the introduction of EDO memory.

Fragmentation — The distribution of data files, such that they are stored in noncontiguous clusters.

Fragmented file — A file that has been written to different portions of the disk so that it is not in contiguous clusters.

Frame — A small, standardized packet of data that also includes header and trailer information as well as error-checking codes. *See also* Packets.

Front end — In a client/server environment, the application on the client that makes use of data stored on the server.

Frontside bus — The bus between the CPU and the memory outside the CPU housing.

FTP (File Transfer Protocol) — An Internet standard that provides for the transfer of files from one computer to another. FTP can be used at a command prompt, or with a GUI interface, which is available with FTP software or with a Web browser. When using a Web browser, enter the command "ftp" in the browser URL line instead of the usual "http://" used to locate a Web site.

FTP server or FTP site — A computer that stores files that can be downloaded by FTP.

Full backup — A complete backup, whereby all of the files on the hard drive are backed up each time the backup procedure is performed. It is the safest backup method, but it takes the most time.

Full-duplex — Communication that happens in two directions at the same time.

Gateway — A device or process that connects networks with different protocols. *See* Bridge and Router.

General Protection Fault (GPF) error — A Windows error that occurs when a program attempts to access a memory address that is not available or is no longer assigned to it.

Graphics accelerator — A type of video card that has an on-board processor that can substantially increase speed and boost graphical and video performance.

Green Standards — Standards that mean that a computer or device can go into sleep or doze mode when not in use, thus saving energy and helping the environment.

Ground bracelet — An antistatic wrist strap used to dissipate static electricity. Typically grounded by attaching an alligator clip to the computer chassis or to a nearby ground mat.

Ground mat — An antistatic mat designed for electronic workbenches to dissipate static electricity. It often uses a wire attached to the ground connection in an electrical outlet.

GUI (graphical user interface) — A user interface, such as the Windows interface, that uses graphics or icons on the screen for running programs and entering information.

Half-duplex — Communication between two devices whereby transmission takes place in only one direction at a time.

Half-life — The time it takes for a medium storing data to weaken to half of its strength. Magnetic media, including traditional hard drives and floppy disks, have a half-life of five to seven years.

Handshaking — When two modems begin to communicate, the initial agreement made as to how to send and receive data. It often occurs when you hear the modem making noises as the dial-up is completed.

Hard boot — Restart the computer by turning off the power or by pressing the Reset button. Also called cold boot.

Hard copy — Output from a printer to paper.

Hard drive — The main secondary storage device of a PC, a sealed case that contains magnetic coated platters that rotate at high speed.

Hard drive controller — A set of microchips with programs that control a hard drive. Most hard drive controllers today are located inside the hard drive housing.

Hard drive standby time — The amount of time before a hard drive will shut down to conserve energy.

Hard-disk loading — The illegal practice of installing unauthorized software on computers for sale. Hard-disk loading can typically be identified by the absence of original disks in the original system's shipment.

Hardware — The physical components that constitute the computer system, such as the monitor, the keyboard, the system board, and the printer.

Hardware abstraction layer (HAL) — The low-level part of Windows NT, written specifically for each CPU technology, so that only the HAL must change when platform components change.

Hardware cache — A disk cache that is contained in RAM chips built right on the disk controller.

Hardware compatibility list (HCL) — The list of all computers and peripheral devices that have been tested and are officially supported by Windows NT (See *www.microsoft.com/hwtest*).

Hardware interrupt — An event caused by a hardware device signaling the CPU that it requires service.

Hardware profiles — In windows NT, configuration information about memory, CPU, and OS, for a PC. A PC may have more than one profile. For example, a docking station PC may have two profiles, one with and one without the notebook PC docked.

Hardware tree — A database built each time Windows 9x starts up that contains a list of installed components and the resources they use.

Head — The top or bottom surface of one platter on a hard drive. Each platter has two heads.

Header — Information sent ahead of data being transferred over a network to identify it to receiving protocols. An IP header consists of items such as header and datagram length, flags, checksum, addresses, and so on.

Heap — A memory block set aside for a program's data. If the heap fills up, an "Out of memory" error might occur, even if there is plenty of regular RAM left, especially in 16-bit applications.

Heat sink — A piece of metal, with cooling fins, that can be attached to or mounted on an integrated chip (such as the CPU) to dissipate heat.

Hertz (Hz) — Unit of measurement for frequency, calculated in terms of vibrations, or cycles, per second. For example, a Pentium CPU may have a speed of 233 MHz (megahertz). For 16-bit stereo sound, 44,100 Hz is used.

Hibernation — A power-saving notebook feature. When a computer hibernates, it stores whatever is currently in memory and then shuts down. When it returns from hibernating, it restores everything back to the way it was before the shutdown.

Hidden file — A file that is not displayed in a directory list. To hide or display a file is one of the file's attributes kept by the OS.

High memory area (HMA) — The first 64K of extended memory. The method of storing part of DOS in the high memory area is called loading DOS high.

High-level format — Format performed by the OS that writes a file system to a logical drive. For DOS and Windows 9x, the command used is FORMAT, which writes a FAT and a directory to the drive. Also called OS format.

HIMEM.SYS — A device driver that manages memory above 640K. It is often executed by the line DEVICE = C:\DOS\HIMEM.SYS in a CONFIG.SYS file.

Hive — A physical segment of the windows NT Registry that is stored in a file.

Hop count — The number of routers a packet must pass through in a network in order to reach its destination.

Host adapter — The circuit board that controls a SCSI bus that supports as many as eight or 16 separate devices, one of which is a host adapter that controls communication with the PC.

Host drive — Typically drive H on a compressed drive. *See* Compressed drive.

Hot swapping — The ability of a computer to use a device, such as a PC Card on a notebook, that is inserted while the computer is running without the computer needing to be rebooted.

Hot-pluggable — A characteristic of 1394 devices that let you plug in the device without rebooting your PC and remove the device without receiving an error message.

HTML (Hypertext Markup Language) — The language used to create hypertext documents commonly used on web sites. HTML documents have an .html file extension.

HTTP (Hypertext Transfer Protocol) — The common transfer protocol used by Internet browsers on the World Wide Web.

Hub — A network device or box that provides a central location to connect cables.

Hypertext — Text that contains links to remote points in the document or to other files, documents, or graphics. Hypertext is created using HTML and is commonly distributed from Web sites.

I/O addresses — Numbers that are used by devices and the CPU to manage communication between them.

I/O card — A card that often contains serial, parallel, and game ports on the same adapter board, providing input/output interface with the CPU.

IBM-compatible — A computer that uses an Intel (or compatible) processor and can run DOS and Windows.

IEEE 1284 — A standard for parallel ports developed by the Institute for Electrical and Electronics Engineers and supported by many hardware manufacturers.

IEEE 1394 — *See* Fire Wire.

In-band signaling — In modem communication, the name of the signaling used by software flow control, which pauses transmission by sending a special control character in the same channel (or band) that data is sent in.

Incremental backup — A time-saving backup method that only backs up files changed or newly created since the last full or incremental backup. Multiple incremental backups might be required when recovering lost data.

Infestation — Any unwanted program that is transmitted to a computer without the user's knowledge and that is designed to do varying degrees of damage to data and software. There are a number of different types of infestations, including viruses, Trojan horses, worms, and time bombs, among others.

Initialization files — Configuration information files for Windows. Win.ini and System.ini are the two most important Windows 3.x initialization files.

Instruction set — The set of instructions, on the CPU chip, that the computer can perform directly (such as ADD and MOVE).

Integrated Device Electronics (IDE) — A hard drive whose disk controller is integrated into the drive, eliminating the need for a controller cable and thus increasing speed, as well as reducing price.

Intelligent hubs — Network hubs that can be remotely controlled at a console, using network software. These hubs can monitor a network and report errors or problems.

Intelligent UPS — A UPS connected to a computer by way of a serial cable so that software on the computer can monitor and control the UPS.

Interlace — A display in which the electronic beam of a monitor draws every other line with each pass, which lessens the overall effect of a lower refresh rate.

Interleave — To write data in nonconsecutive sectors around a track, so that time is not wasted waiting for the disk to make a full revolution before the next sector is read.

Internal cache — Memory cache that is faster than external cache, and is contained inside 80486 and Pentium chips (also referred to as primary, Level 1, or L1 cache).

Internal DOS commands — DOS commands whose coding is contained within COMMAND.COM and are, therefore, automatically loaded into memory when COMMAND.COM is loaded.

Internet — The worldwide collection of over a million hosts that can communicate with each other using TCP/IP. The lowercase internet simply means multiple networks connected together.

Internet Control Message Protocol (ICMP) — Part of the IP layer that is used to transmit error messages and other control messages to hosts and routers.

Internet Printing Protocol (IPP) — A protocol used to send print jobs across the Internet. A printer is addressed by its URL (uniform resource locator)—for example, *www.ourdomain.com/printer4*.

Internet service provider (ISP) — A commercial group that provides a user with Internet access for a monthly fee. AOL, Prodigy, GTE, and CompuServe are four large ISPs.

Internetwork — Two or more networks connected together, such as a LAN and a WAN joined together.

Interrupt handler — A program (either BIOS or a device driver), that is used by the CPU to process a hardware interrupt.

Interrupt vector table — A table that stores the memory addresses assigned to interrupt handlers. Also called a vector table.

Intranet — A private internet used by a large company.

IP (Internet Protocol) address — A 32-bit "dotted-decimal" address consisting of four numbers separated by periods, used to uniquely identify a device on a network that uses TCP/IP protocols. The first numbers identify the network; the last numbers identify a host. An example of an IP address is 206.96.103.114.

IPX/SPX — A protocol developed and used by Novell NetWare for LANs. The IPX portion of the protocol works at the network layer, which is responsible for routing, and the SPX portion of the protocol manages error checking at the transport layer.

IRQ (interrupt request number) — A line on a bus that is assigned to a device and is used to signal the CPU for servicing. These lines are assigned a reference number (for example, the normal IRQ for a printer is IRQ 7).

ISA bus — An 8-bit industry standard architecture bus used on the original 8088 PC. Sixteen-bit ISA buses were designed for the 286 AT, and are still used in Pentiums for devices such as modems.

ISDN (Integrated Services Digital Network) — A communications standard that can carry digital data simultaneously over two channels on a single pair of wires, at about five times the speed of regular phone lines.

Isochronous data transfer — A method used by IEEE 1394 to transfer data continuously without breaks.

JPEG (Joint Photographic Experts Group) — A "lossy" graphical compression scheme that allows the user to control the amount of data that is averaged and sacrificed as file size is reduced. It is a common Internet file format. See Lossy compression.

Jumper — Two wires that stick up side by side on the system board that are used to hold configuration information. The jumper is considered closed if a cover is over the wires, and open if the cover is missing.

Kernel — Core portion of an operating system that loads applications and manages files, memory, and other resources.

Kernel mode — A Windows NT "privileged" processing mode that has access to hardware components.

Keyboard — A common input device through which data and instructions may be typed into computer memory.

Keys — In Windows 9x, section names of the Windows 9x Registry.

Land — Microscopic flat areas on the surface of a CD or DVD that separate pits. Lands and pits are used to represent data on the disc.

Laptop computer — See Notebook.

Large mode — A format that supports hard drives that range from 504 MB to 1 GB, mapping the data to conform to the 504-MB barrier before the address information is passed to the operating system.

Legacy — An older device or adapter card that does not support Plug and Play, and might have to be manually configured through jumpers or DIP switches.

Let-through — The maximum voltage allowed through a surge suppressor to the device being protected.

Level 1 cache — See Internal cache.

Level 2 cache — See External cache.

Line conditioners — Devices that regulate, or condition the power, providing continuous voltage during brownouts and spikes.

Line protocol — A protocol used over phone lines to allow a connection to a network. Also called a bridging protocol. The most popular line protocol is PPP (Point-to-Point Protocol).

Line speed — See Modem speed.

Line-interactive UPS — A variation of a standby UPS that shortens switching time by always keeping the inverter that converts AC to DC working, so that there is no charge-up time for the inverter.

Load size — The largest amount of memory that a driver needs to initialize itself and to hold its data. It is almost always a little larger than the size of the program file.

Loading high — The process of loading a driver or TSR into upper memory.

Local bus — A bus that operates at a speed synchronized with the CPU speed.

Local I/O bus — A local bus that provides I/O devices with fast access to the CPU.

Logical block addressing (LBA) — A method in which the operating system views the drive as one long linear list of LBAs, permitting larger drive sizes (LBA 0 is cylinder 0, head 0, and sector 1).

Logical drive — A portion or all of a hard drive partition that is treated by the operating system as though it were a physical drive containing a boot record, FAT, and root directory.

Logical geometry — The number of heads, tracks, and sectors that the BIOS on the hard drive controller presents to the system BIOS and the OS. The logical geometry does not consist of the same values as the physical geometry, although calculations of drive capacity yield the same results.

Logical unit number (LUN) — A number from 0 to 15 (also called the SCSI ID) assigned to each SCSI device attached to a daisy chain.

Lossless compression — A method that substitutes special characters for repeating patterns without image degradation. A substitution table is used to restore the compressed image to its original form.

Lossy compression — A method that drops unnecessary data, but with some image and sound loss. JPEG allows the user to control the amount of loss, which is inversely related to the image size.

Lost allocation units — *See* Lost clusters.

Lost clusters — Lost file fragments that, according to the file allocation table, contain data that does not belong to any file. In DOS, the command CHKDSK/F can free these fragments.

Low insertion force (LIF) — A socket feature that requires the installer to manually apply an even force over the microchip when inserting the chip into the socket.

Low-level format — A process (usually performed at the factory) that electronically creates the hard drive cylinders and tests for bad spots on the disk surface.

MAC (media access control) — An element of data-link layer protocol that provides compatibility with the NIC used by the physical layer. A network card address is often called a MAC address. *See* Adapter address.

Macro — A small sequence of commands, contained within a document, that can be automatically executed when the document is loaded, or executed later by using a predetermined keystroke.

Macro virus — A virus that can hide in the macros of a document file. Typically, viruses do not reside in data or document files.

Main board — *See* System board.

Master boot record (MBR) (of a floppy disk) — The record written near the beginning of a floppy disk, containing information about the disk as well as the startup operating system programs.

Master boot record (MBR) (on a hard drive) — The first sector on a hard drive, which contains the partition table and other information needed by BIOS to access the drive.

Material safety data sheet (MSDS) — A document that provides information about how to properly handle substances such as chemical solvents including physical data, toxicity, health effects, first aid, storage, disposal, and spill procedures.

MCA (micro channel architecture) bus — A proprietary IBM PS/2 bus, seldom seen today, with a width of 16 or 32 bits and multiple master control, which allowed for multitasking.

MD or MKDIR command — A command used to create a directory on a drive (for example, MD C:\MYDATA).

MEM command — A DOS utility used to display how programs and drivers are using conventional, upper, and extended memory (Example: MEM/C/P).

MemMaker — A DOS utility that can increase the amount of conventional memory available to DOS-based software applications, by loading drivers and TRSs into upper memory.

Memory — Physical microchips that can hold data and programming located on the system board or expansion cards.

Memory address — A number that the CPU assigns to physical memory to keep track of the memory that it has access to.

Memory bus — The bus between the CPU and memory on the system board. Also called the system bus or the host bus.

Memory cache — A small amount of faster RAM that stores recently retrieved data, in anticipation of what the CPU will request next, thus speeding up access.

Memory caching — Using a small amount of faster RAM to store recently retrieved data, in anticipation of what the CPU will next request, thus speeding up access.

Memory leak — A problem caused when an application does not release the memory addresses assigned to it when it unloads, causing the memory heaps to have less and less memory for new applications.

Memory management — The process of increasing available conventional memory, required by DOS-based programs, accomplished by loading device drivers and TSRs into upper memory.

Memory mapping — Assigning addresses to both RAM and ROM during the boot process.

Memory paging — In Windows 9x, swapping blocks of RAM memory to an area of the hard drive to serve as virtual memory when RAM memory is low.

Memory-resident virus — A virus that can stay lurking in memory, even after its host program is terminated.

Minicartridge — A tape drive cartridge that is only 3½ × 2½ × ⅗ inches. It is small enough to allow two drives to fit into a standard 5½-inch drive bay of a PC case.

Minifile system — In windows NT, a simplified file system that is started so that Ntldr (NT Loader) can read files from either a FAT16 or an NTFS file system.

MIRROR command — An old DOS command that saves information about deleted files as they are deleted. This information can be used later by the UNDELETE command to recover a deleted file. The command can be used to save the partition table to a floppy disk.

Mixed mode — A Windows 2000 mode for domain controllers used when there is at least one Windows NT domain controller on the network.

MMX (Multimedia Extensions) technology — A variation of the Pentium processor designed to manage and speed up high-volume input/output needed for graphics, motion video, animation, and sound.

Modem — From MOdulate/DEModulate. A device that modulates digital data from a computer to an analog format that can be sent over telephone lines, then demodulates it back into digital form.

Modem eliminator — A technique that allows two data terminal equipment (DTE) devices to communicate by means of a null modem cable in which the transmit and receive wires are cross-connected, and no modems are necessary.

Modem riser card — A small modem card that uses an AMR or CNR slot. Part of the modem logic is contained in a controller on the system board.

Modem speed — The speed a modem can transmit data along a phone line measured in bits per second (bps). Two communicating modems must talk at the same speed for data transmission to be successful. Also called line speed.

Modulation — Converting binary or digital data into an analog signal that can be sent over standard telephone lines.

Monitor — The most commonly used output device for displaying text and graphics on a computer.

Motherboard — *See* System board.

Mouse — A pointing and input device that allows the user to move a cursor around a screen and select programs with the click of a button.

MP3 — A method to compress audio files that uses MPEG level 3. It can reduce sound files as low as a 1:24 ratio without losing sound quality.

MPC (Multimedia Personal Computer) guidelines — The minimum standards created by Microsoft and a consortium of hardware manufacturers for multimedia PCs.

MPEG (Moving Pictures Experts Group) — A processing-intensive standard for data compression for motion pictures that tracks movement from one frame to the next, and only stores the new data that has changed.

MSDOS.SYS — In DOS, a program file that contains part of the DOS kernel and controls much of the boot process. In Windows 9x, a text file that contains settings used by Io.sys during booting.

Multibank DRAM (MDRAM) — A special kind of RAM used on video cards that is able to use a full 128-bit bus path without requiring the full 4MB of RAM.

Multiframe dialog — When a limited token is sent that allows a receiving station to communicate only with the sending station, thus providing continuous communication between the two stations.

Multimedia — A type of computer presentation that combines text, graphics, animation, photos, sound, and/or full-motion video.

Multimeter — Either a voltmeter or an ammeter that can also measure resistance in ohms or as continuity, depending on a switch setting.

Multipartite virus — A combination of a boot sector virus and a file virus. It can hide in either type of program.

Multiplier — On a system board, the factor by which the bus speed or frequency is multiplied to get the CPU clock speed.

Multiscan monitor — A monitor that can work within a range of frequencies, and thus can work with different standards and video cards. If offers a variety of refresh rates.

Multisession — A feature that allows data to be read (or written) on a CD during more than one session. This is important if the disc was only partially filled during the first write.

Multistation access unit (MSAU or MAU) — A centralized device used to connect IBM Token Ring network stations.

Multitasking — When a CPU or an OS supporting multiple CPUs can do more than one thing at a time. The Pentium is a multitasking CPU.

Multithreading — The ability to pass more than one function (thread) to the OS kernel at the same time, such as when one thread is performing a print job while another reads a file.

NetBEUI (NetBIOS Extended User Interface) — A proprietary Microsoft networking protocol used only by Windows-based systems, and limited to LANs because it does not support routing.

NetBT (NetBIOS over TCP/IP) — An alternate Microsoft NetBEUI component designed to interface with TCP/IP networks.

Network interface card (NIC) — A network adapter board that plugs into a computer's system board and provides a port on the back of the card to connect a PC to a network.

Network mask — The portion of an IP address that identifies the network.

Node — Each computer, workstation, or device on a network.

Noise — An extraneous, unwanted signal, often over an analog phone line, that can cause communication interference or transmission errors. Possible sources are fluorescent lighting, radios, TVs, lightning, or bad wiring.

Non-interlace — A type of display in which the electronic beam of a monitor draws every line on the screen with each pass. *See* Interlace.

Non-memory-resident virus — A virus that is terminated when the host program is closed. Compare to memory-resident virus.

Nonparity memory — Slightly less expensive, 8-bit memory without error checking. A SIMM part number with a 32 in it (4×8 bits) is nonparity.

Nonvolatile — Refers to a kind of RAM that is stable and can hold data as long as electricity is powering the memory.

Normal mode — *See* CHS.

North bridge — That portion of the chip set hub that connects faster I/O buses (e.g., AGP bus) to the system bus. Compare to South bridge.

Notebook — A personal computer designed for travel, using less voltage and taking up less space than a regular PC. Also called a laptop computer.

NT Hardware Qualifier (NTHQ) — A utility found on the Windows NT installation CD-ROM that examines your system to determine if all hardware present qualifies for NT.

NT virtual DOS machine (NTVDM) — An emulated environment in which a 16-bit DOS application or a Windows 3.x application resides within Windows NT with its own memory space or WOW (Win 16 application on a Win 32 platform). (*See* WOW.)

Ntldr (NT Loader) — In Windows NT, the OS loader used on Intel systems.

Null modem cable — *See* Modem eliminator.

Object linking — A method where one application can execute a command on an object created by another application.

Octet — A traditional term for each of the four 8-bit numbers that make up an IP address. For example, the IP address 206.96.103.114 has four octets.

Ohms — The standard unit of measurement for electrical resistance. Resistors are rated in ohms.

On-board BIOS — *See* System BIOS.

On-board ports — Ports that are directly on the system board, such as a built-in keyboard port or on-board serial port.

Operating system format — *See* High-level format.

OS format — *See* High-level format.

Out-of-band signaling — The type of signaling used by hardware flow control, which sends a message to pause transmission by using channels (or bands) not used for data.

Overclocking — Running a system board at a speed that is not recommended or guaranteed by CPU or chipset manufacturers.

P-A-S-S — An acronym to help remember how to use a fire extinguisher. (Pull the pin, Aim low at the base of the fire, Squeeze the handle of the extinguisher, and Sweep back and forth across the fire.)

P1 connector — Power connection on an ATX system board.

Packets — Network segments of data that also include header, destination addresses, and trailer information. Also called Frames.

Page — Memory allocated in 4K or 16K segments within a page frame.

Page-in — The process in which the memory manager goes to the hard drive to return the data from a swap file to RAM.

Page-out — The process in which, when RAM is full, the memory manager takes a page and moves it to the swap file.

Page fault — An OS interrupt that occurs when the OS is forced to access the hard drive to satisfy the demands for virtual memory.

Page frame — A 64K upper memory area divided into four equal-sized pages through which the memory manager swaps data.

Parallel port — A female port on the computer that can transmit data in parallel, 8 bits at a time, and is usually used with a printer. The names for parallel ports are LPT1 and LPT2.

Parity — An error-checking scheme in which a ninth, or "parity," bit is added. The value of the parity bit is set to either 0 or 1 to provide an even number of ones for even parity and an odd number of ones for odd parity.

Parity error — An error that occurs when the number of 1s in the byte is not in agreement with the expected number.

Parity memory — Nine-bit memory in which the 9th bit is used for error checking. A SIMM part number with a 36 in it (4 2 9 bits) is parity. Older DOS PCs almost always use parity chips.

Partition — A division of a hard drive that can be used to hold logical drives.

Partition table — A table at the beginning of the hard drive that contains information about each partition on the drive. The partition table is contained in the master boot record.

Path — The drive and list of directories pointing to a file.

PC Card — A credit-card-sized adapter card that can be slid into a slot in the side of many notebook computers and is used for connecting to modems, networks, and CD-ROM drives. Also called PCMCIA Card.

PC Card slot — An expansion slot on a notebook computer, into which a PC Card is inserted. Also called a PCMCIA Card slot.

PCI (peripheral component interconnect) bus — A bus common on Pentium computers that runs at speeds of up to 33 MHz, with a 32-bit-wide data path. It serves as the middle layer between the memory bus and expansion buses.

PCI bus IRQ steering — A feature that makes it possible for PCI devices to share an IRQ. System BIOS and the OS must both support this feature.

PCMCIA (Personal Computer Memory Card International Association) card — *See* PC Card.

PCMCIA Card slot — *See* PC Card slot.

PDA (Personal Digital Assistant) — A handheld computer that has its own operating system and applications. The most popular operating systems for PDAs are Palm for Palm Pilot devices and Windows CE.

Peripheral devices — Devices that communicate with the CPU, but are not located directly on the system board, such as the monitor, floppy drive, printer, and mouse.

Physical geometry — The actual layout of heads, tracks, and sectors on a hard drive. *See* Logical geometry.

Physical layer — The OSI layer responsible for interfacing with the network media (cabling).

PIF (program information file) — A file with a .pif file extension that is used by an OS to store the settings of the environment provided to a DOS application.

Pin grid array (PGA) — A feature of a CPU socket where the pins are aligned in uniform rows around the socket.

Pipelined burst SRAM — A less expensive SRAM that uses more clock cycles per transfer than nonpipelined burst, but does not significantly slow down the process.

Pit — Recessed areas on the surface of a CD or DVD, separating lands, or flat areas. Lands and pits are used to represent data on the disc.

Pixel — Small spots on a fine horizontal scan line that are illuminated to create an image on the monitor.

Plug and Play — A technology in which the operating system and BIOS are designed to automatically configure new hardware devices to eliminate system resource conflicts (such as IRQ and port conflicts).

Plug and Play BIOS — Basic input/output system for Plug and Play devices, which are designed to be automatically recognized by the computer when they are installed.

Polling — A process by which the CPU checks the status of connected devices to determine if they are ready to send or receive data.

Polymorphic virus — A type of virus that changes its distinguishing characteristics as it replicates itself. Mutating in this way makes it more difficult for AV software to recognize the presence of the virus.

Port — A physical connector, usually at the back of a computer, that allows a cable from a peripheral device, such as a printer, mouse, or modem, to be attached.

Port settings — The configuration parameters of communications devices such as COM1, COM2, or COM3, including IRQ settings.

Port speed — The communication speed between a DTE (computer) and a DCE (modem). As a general rule, the port speed should be at least four times as fast as the modem speed.

POST (power-on self test) — A self-diagnostic program used to perform a simple test of the CPU, RAM, and various I/O devices. The POST is performed when the computer is first turned on and is stored in ROM-BIOS.

Power conditioners — Line conditioners that regulate, or condition, the power, providing continuous voltage during brownouts.

Power supply — A box inside the computer case that supplies power to the system board and other installed devices. Power supplies provide 3.3, 5, and 12 volts DC.

Power-on password — *See* Startup password.

PPP (Point-to-Point Protocol) — A common way PCs with modems can connect to an internet. The Windows Dial-Up Networking utility, found under My Computer, uses PPP.

Preemptive multitasking — A type of pseudomultitasking whereby the CPU allows an application a specified period of time and then preempts the processing to give time to another application.

Primary cache — *See* Internal cache.

Printer — A peripheral output device that produces printed output to paper. Different types include dot matrix, ink-jet, and laser printers.

Process — An executing instance of a program together with the program resources. There can be more than one process running for a program at the same time. One process for a program happens each time the program is loaded into memory or executed.

Processor speed — The speed or frequency at which the CPU operates. Usually expressed in MHz.

Program — A set of step-by-step instructions to a computer. Some are burned directly into chips, while others are stored as program files. Programs are written in languages such as BASIC and C++.

Program file — A file that contains instructions designed to be executed by the CPU.

Program jump — An instruction that causes control to be sent to a memory address other than the next sequential address.

Program Information File (PIF) — A file used by Windows to describe the environment for a DOS program to use.

Proprietary — A term for products that a company has exclusive rights to manufacture and/or market. Proprietary computer components are typically more difficult to find and more expensive to buy.

Protected mode — An operating mode that supports multitasking whereby the OS manages memory, programs have more than 1024K of memory addresses, and programs can use a 32-bit data path.

Protocol — A set of preestablished rules for communication. Examples of protocols are modem parity settings and the way in which header and trailer information in a data packet is formatted.

PS/2 compatible mouse — A mouse that uses a round mouse port (called a mini-DIN or PS/2 connector) coming directly off the system board.

Quarter-Inch Committee or quarter-inch cartridge (QIC) — A name of a standardized method used to write data to tape. Backups made with the Windows 9x System Tools Backup utility have a .qic extension.

RAID (redundant array of inexpensive disks or redundant array of independent disks) — Several methods of configuring multiple hard drives to store data to increase logical volume size and improve performance, and to ensure that if one hard drive fails, the data is still available from another hard drive.

RAM (random access memory) — Temporary memory stored on chips, such as SIMMs, inside the computer. Information in RAM disappears when the computer's power is turned off.

RAM drive — A RAM area configured as a virtual hard drive, such as drive D, so that frequently used programs can be accessed faster. It is the opposite of virtual memory.

RD or RMDIR command — A DOS command to remove an unwanted directory (for example, RD C:\OLDDIR). You must delete all files in the directory to be removed, prior to using this command.

Read/write head — A sealed, magnetic coil device that moves across the surface of a disk either reading or writing data to the disk.

Real mode — A single-tasking operating mode whereby a program only has 1024K of memory addresses, has direct access to RAM, and uses a 16-bit data path.

RECOVER command — A command that recovers files that were lost because of a corrupted file allocation table.

Recovery Console — A Windows 2000 command-interface utility that can be used to solve problems when the OS cannot load from the hard drive.

Rectifier — An electrical device that converts AC to DC. A PC power supply contains a rectifier.

Refresh — The process of periodically rewriting the data for instance, on dynamic RAM.

Registry — A database used by Windows to store hardware and software configuration information, user preferences, and setup information. Use Regedit.exe to edit the Registry.

Removable drives — High-capacity drives, such as Zip or Jaz drives, that have disks that can be removed like floppy disks.

Repeater — A device that amplifies weakened signals on a network.

Rescue disk — A floppy disk that can be used to start up a computer when the hard drive fails to boot. *Also see* Emergency startup disk.

Resistance — The degree to which a device opposes or resists the flow of electricity. As the electrical resistance increases, the current decreases. *See* Ohms and Resistor.

Resistor — An electronic device that resists or opposes the flow of electricity. A resistor can be used to reduce the amount of electricity being supplied to an electronic component.

Resolution — The number of spots called pixels on a monitor screen that are addressable by software (example: 1024 2 768 pixels).

Resource arbitrator — A PnP component that decides which resources are assigned to which devices.

Resource management — The process of allocating resources to devices at startup.

RET (resolution enhancement technology) — The term used by Hewlett-Packard to describe the way a laser printer varies the size of the dots used to create an image. This technology partly accounts for the sharp, clear image created by a laser printer.

Retension — A tape maintenance procedure that fast-forwards and then rewinds the tape to eliminate loose spots on the tape.

Reverse Address Resolution Protocol (RARP) — Translates the unique hardware NIC addresses into IP addresses (the reverse of ARP).

RISC (reduced instruction set computer) chips — Chips that incorporate only the most frequently used instructions, so that the computer operates faster (for example, the PowerPC uses RISC chips).

RJ-11 — A phone line connection found on a modem, telephone, and house phone outlet.

RJ-45 connector — A connector used on an Ethernet 10BaseT (twisted-pair cable) network. An RJ-45 port looks similar to a large phone jack.

Roaming users — Users who can move from PC to PC within a network, with their profiles following them.

ROM (read-only memory) — Chips that contain programming code and cannot be erased.

ROM BIOS — *See* BIOS.

Root directory — The main directory created when a hard drive or disk is first formatted.

Route discovery — When a router rebuilds its router tables on the basis of new information.

Router — A device or box that connects networks. A router transfers a packet to other networks when the packet is addressed to a station outside its network. The router can make intelligent decisions as to which network is the best route to use to send data to a distant network. *See* Bridge.

Router table — Tables of network addresses that also include the best possible routes (regarding tick count and hop count) to these networks. *See* Tick count and Hop count.

Run-time configuration — A PnP ongoing process that monitors changes in system devices, such as the removal of a PC Card on a notebook computer or the docking of a notebook computer to a docking station.

Safe mode — The mode in which Windows 9x is loaded with minimum configuration and drivers in order to allow the correction

---

of system errors. To enter safe mode, press F5 or F8 when "Starting Windows 95/98" is displayed.

SAM (security accounts manager) — A portion of the Windows NT Registry that manages the account database that contains accounts, policies, and other pertinent information about the domain.

SCAM (SCSI configuration automatically) — A method that follows the Plug and Play standard, to make installations of SCSI devices much easier, assuming that the device is SCAM-compatible.

Scanning mirror — A component of a laser printer. An octagonal mirror that can be directed in a sweeping motion to cover the entire length of a laser printer drum.

SCSI (small computer system interface) — A faster system-level interface with a host adapter and a bus that can daisy-chain as many as seven or 15 other devices.

SCSI ID — *See* Logical unit number.

SCSI bus — A bus standard used for peripheral devices tied together in a daisy chain.

SCSI bus adapter chip — The chip mounted on the logic board of a hard drive that allows the drive to be a part of a SCSI bus system.

SC330 (Slot Connector 330) — A 330-pin system board connector used to contain the Pentium III Xeon. Also called Slot 2.

SECC (Single Edge Contact Cartridge) — A type of cartridge that houses the Pentium III processor.

Secondary storage — Storage that is remote to the CPU and permanently holds data, even when the PC is turned off.

Sector — On a disk surface, one segment of a track, which almost always contains 512 bytes of data. Sometimes a single wedge of the disk surface is also called a sector.

Segmentation — To split a large Ethernet into smaller segments that are connected to each other by bridges or routers. This is done to prevent congestion as the number of nodes increases.

Sequential access — A method of data access used by tape drives whereby data is written or read sequentially from the beginning to the end of the tape or until the desired data is found.

Serial mouse — A mouse that uses a serial port and has a female 9-pin DB-9 connector.

Serial ports — Male ports on the computer used for transmitting data serially, one bit at a time. They are called COM1, COM2, COM3 and COM4.

Server — A microcomputer or minicomputer that stores programs and data to be used remotely by other computers.

SGRAM (synchronous graphics RAM) — Memory designed especially for video card processing that can synchronize itself with the CPU bus clock. They are commonly used for modems and mice, and in DOS are called COM1 or COM2.

Shadow RAM or shadowing ROM — The process of copying ROM programming code into RAM to speed up the system operation, because of the faster access speed of RAM.

Signal-regenerating repeater — A repeater that "reads" the signal on the network and then creates an exact duplicate of the signal, thus amplifying the signal without also amplifying unwanted noise that is mixed with the signal.

SIMM (single inline memory module) — A miniature circuit board used in a computer to hold RAM. SIMMs hold 8, 16, 32, or 64 MB on a single module.

Single voltage CPU — A CPU that requires one voltage for both internal and I/O operations.

Single-instruction, multiple-data (SIMD) — An MMX process that allows the CPU to execute a single instruction simultaneously on multiple pieces of data rather than by repetitive looping.

Slack — Wasted space on a hard drive caused by not using all available space at the end of clusters.

Sleep mode — A mode used in many "Green" systems that allows them to be configured through CMOS to suspend the monitor or even the drive, if the keyboard and/or CPU have been inactive for a set number of minutes. *See* Green standards.

SLIP (Serial Line Internet Protocol) — An early version of line protocol designed for home users connecting to the Internet. SLIP lacks reliable error checking and has mostly been replaced by PPP.

SMARTDrive — A hard drive cache program that comes with Windows 3.x and DOS that can be executed as a TSR from the AUTOEXEC.BAT file (for example, DEVICE=SMARTDRV.SYS 2048).

SMTP (Simple Mail Transfer Protocol) — A common protocol used to send e-mail across a network.

Snap-in — An administrative tool that is contained within a console. For example, Event Viewer is a snap-in in the Computer Management console.

Socket — A virtual connection from one computer to another such as that between a client and a server. Higher-level protocols such as HTTP use a socket to pass data between two computers. A socket is assigned a number for the current session, which is used by the high-level protocol.

SO-DIMM (small outline DIMM) — A small memory module designed for notebooks that has 72 pins and supports 32-bit data transfers.

Soft boot — To restart a PC by pressing three keys at the same time (Ctrl, Alt, and Del). Also called warm boot.

Software — Computer programs, or instructions to perform a specific task. Software may be BIOS, OSs, or applications software such as a word-processing or spreadsheet program.

Software cache — Cache controlled by software whereby the cache is stored in RAM.

Software interrupt — An event caused by a program currently being executed by the CPU signaling the CPU that it requires the use of a hardware device.

South bridge — That portion of the chip set hub that connects slower I/O buses (e.g., ISA bus) to the system bus. Compare to North bridge.

Spanned volumes — Windows 2000 method of linking several volumes across multiple hard drives into a single logical drive.

Spooling — Placing print jobs in a print queue so that an application can be released from the printing process before printing is completed. Spooling is an acronym for simultaneous peripheral operations online.

SSE (streaming SIMD extension) — A technology used by the Intel Pentium III designed to improve performance of multimedia software.

Staggered pin grid array (SPGA) — A feature of a CPU socket where the pins are staggered over the socket in order to squeeze more pins into a small space.

Standby time — The time before a "Green" system will reduce 92% of its activity. *See* Green standards.

Standby UPS — A UPS that quickly switches from an AC power source to a battery-powered source during a brownout or power outage.

Standoffs — Small plastic or metal spacers placed on the bottom of the main system board, to raise it off the chassis, so that its components will not short out on the metal case.

Star network architecture — A network design in which nodes are connected at a centralized location.

Star topology — A network design in which nodes are connected at a centralized location.

Start bit — A bit that is used to signal the approach of data. *See* Stop bit.

Startup BIOS — Part of system BIOS that is responsible for controlling the PC when it is first turned on. Startup BIOS gives control over to the OS once it is loaded.

Startup password — A password that a computer requires during the boot process used to gain access to the PC. Also called power-on password.

Static electricity — *See* Electrostatic discharge.

Static IP addresses —IP addresses permanently assigned to a workstation. In Windows 9x, this can be done under Dial-Up Networking, Server Type, TCP/IP settings. Specify an IP address.

Static RAM (SRAM) — RAM chips that retain information without the need for refreshing, as long as the computer's power is on. They are more expensive than traditional DRAM.

Static routing — When routing tables do not automatically change and must be manually edited. Windows NT and Windows 95 support only static routing. Compare to Dynamic routing.

Static VxD — A VxD that is loaded into memory at startup and remains there for the entire OS session.

Stealth virus — A virus that actively conceals itself by temporarily removing itself from an infected file that is about to be examined, and then hiding a copy of itself elsewhere on the drive.

Stop bit — A bit that is used to signal the end of a block of data.

Streaming audio — Downloading audio data from the Internet in a continuous stream of data without first downloading an entire audio file.

Subdirectory — In DOS, a directory that is contained within another directory. Also called a child directory.

Subnet mask — Defines which portion of the host address within an IP address is being borrowed to define separate subnets within a network. A 1 in the mask indicates that the bit is part of the network address, and a 0 indicates that the bit is part of the host address. For example, the subnet mask 255.255.192.0, in binary, is 11111111.11111111.11000000.00000000. Therefore, the network address is the first two octets and the subnet address is the first two bits of the third octet. The rest of the IP address refers to the host.

Subnetworks or subnets — Divisions of a large network, consisting of smaller separate networks (to prevent congestion). Each subnetwork is assigned a logical network IP name.

Subtree — One of five main keys that make up the Windows NT Registry. Examples are HKEY_CURRENT_USER and HKEY_LOCAL_MACHINE.

Suite — As applies to software, a collection of applications software sold as a bundle, whose components are designed to be compatible with one another. An example is Microsoft Office.

Surge suppressor or surge protector — A device or power strip designed to protect electronic equipment from power surges and spikes.

Suspend time — The time before a green system will reduce 99% of its activity. After this time, the system needs a warmup time so that the CPU, monitor, and hard drive can reach full activity.

Swap file — A file on the hard drive that is used by the OS for virtual memory.

Swapping — A method of freeing some memory by moving a "page" of data temporarily to a swap file on the hard drive; it can later be copied from disk back into memory.

Switch — A device that is used to break a large network into two smaller networks in order to reduce traffic congestion. A switch uses MAC addresses to determine which network to send a packet.

Synchronous DRAM (SDRAM) — A type of memory stored on DIMMs that run in sync with the system clock, running at the same speed as the system board. Currently, the fastest memory used on PCs.

Synchronous SRAM — SRAM that is faster and more expensive than asynchronous SRAM. It requires a clock signal to validate its control signals, enabling the cache to run in step with the CPU.

System BIOS — Basic input/output system chip(s) residing on the system board that control(s) normal I/O to such areas as system memory and floppy drives. Also called on-board BIOS.

System board — The main board in the computer, also called the motherboard. The CPU, ROM chips, SIMMs, DIMMs, and interface cards are plugged into the system board.

System-board mouse — A mouse that plugs into a round mouse port on the system board. Sometimes called a PS/2 mouse.

System bus — Today the system bus usually means the memory bus. However, sometimes it is used to refer to other buses on the system board. *See* memory bus.

System clock — A line on a bus that is dedicated to timing the activities of components connected to it. The system clock provides a continuous pulse that other devices use to time themselves.

System disk — A floppy disk containing enough of an operating system to boot.

System File Checker — System File Checker is part of the new Windows 2000 utility to protect system files, called Windows File Protection (WFP).

System partition — The active partition of the hard drive containing the boot record and the specific files required to load Windows NT.

System State data — All files that Windows 2000 requires to load and perform successfully. The System State data is backed up using the Backup utility.

System variable — A variable that has been given a name and a value; it is available to the operating system and applications software programs.

Task switching — *See* Cooperative multitasking.

TCP/IP (Transmission Control Protocol/Internet Protocol) — The suite of protocols developed to support the Internet. TCP is responsible for error checking, and IP is responsible for routing.

Technical documentation — The technical reference manuals, included with software packages and peripherals, that provide directions for installation, usage, and troubleshooting.

Telephony — A term describing the technology of converting sound to signals that can travel over telephone lines.

Telephony Application Programming Interface (TAPI) — A standard developed by Intel and Microsoft that can be used by 32-bit Windows 9x communications programs for communicating over phone lines.

Temp directory — A location to which inactive applications and data can be moved as a swap file, while Windows continues to process current active applications. (Avoid deleting Temp swap while Windows is running.)

Temporary file — A file that is created by Windows applications, to save temporary data, and may or may not be deleted when the application is unloaded.

Terminating resistor — The resistor added at the end of a SCSI chain to dampen the voltage at the end of the chain. *See* Termination.

Termination — A process necessary to prevent an echo effect of power at the end of a SCSI chain resulting in interference with the data transmission. *See* Terminating resistor.

Thread — A single task that is part of a larger task or program.

Tick count — The time required for a packet to reach its destination. One tick equals 1/18 of a second.

Token — A small frame on a Token Ring network that constantly travels around the ring in only one direction. When a station seizes the token, it controls the channel until its message is sent.

Token ring — A network that is logically a ring, but stations are connected to a centralized multistation access unit (MAU) in a star formation. Network communication is controlled by a token.

Toner cavity — A container filled with toner in a laser printer. The black resin toner is used to form the printed image on paper.

Trace — A wire on a circuit board that connects two components or devices together.

Track — The disk surface is divided into many concentric circles, each called a track.

Trailer — The part of a packet that follows the data and contains information used by some protocols for error checking.

Training — *See* Handshaking.

Transceiver — The bidirectional (transmitter and receiver) component on a NIC that is responsible for signal conversion and monitors for data collision.

Transformer — A device that changes the ratio of current to voltage. A computer power supply is basically a transformer and a rectifier.

Transistor — An electronic device that can regulate electricity and act as a logical gate or switch for an electrical signal.

Translation — A technique used by system BIOS and hard drive controller BIOS to break the 504 MB hard drive barrier, whereby a different set of drive parameters are communicated to the OS and other software than that used by the hard drive controller BIOS.

TREE command — A DOS command that shows the disk directories in a graphical layout similar to a family tree (for example, TREE/F shows every filename in all branches of the TREE).

Trojan horse — A type of infestation that hides or disguises itself as a useful program, yet is designed to cause damage at a later time.

TSR (terminate-and-stay-resident) — A program that is loaded into memory but is not immediately executed, such as a screen saver or a memory-resident antivirus program.

UART (universal asynchronous receiver/transmitter) chip — A chip that controls serial ports. It sets protocol and converts parallel data bits received from the system bus into serial bits.

Unattended installation — A Windows 2000 installation that is done by storing the answers to installation questions in a text file or script that Windows 2000 calls an answer file so that the answers do not have to be typed in during the installation.

UNDELETE command — A command that resets a deleted file's directory entry to normal, provided the clusters occupied by the file have not been overwritten and the file entry is still in the directory list.

UNFORMAT command — A DOS command that performs recovery from an accidental FORMAT, and may also repair a damaged partition table if the partition table was previously saved with MIRROR/PARTN.

Universal serial bus (USB) — A bus that is expected to eventually replace serial and parallel ports, designed to make installation and configuration of I/O devices easy, providing room for as many as 127 devices daisy-chained together. The USB uses only a single set of resources for all devices on the bus.

Upgrade installation — A Windows 2000 installation that carries forward all previous operating system settings and applications installed under the previous operating system.

Upper memory — The memory addresses from 640K up to 1024K, originally reserved for BIOS, device drivers, and TSRs.

Upper memory block (UMB) — A group of consecutive memory addresses in RAM from 640K to 1 MB that can be used by device drivers and TSRs.

UPS (uninterruptible power supply) — A device designed to provide a backup power supply during a power failure. Basically, a UPS is a battery backup system with an ultrafast sensing device.

URL (Uniform Resource Locator) — A unique address that identifies the domain name, path, or filename of a World Wide Web site. Microsoft's URL address is: *http://www.microsoft.com/*

User account — The information, stored in the SAM database, that defines a Windows NT user, including user name, password, memberships, and rights.

User Datagram Protocol (UDP) — A connectionless protocol that does not require a connection to send a packet and does not guarantee that the packet arrives at its destination. (A data packet was once called a datagram.)

User documentation — Manuals, online documentation, instructions, and tutorials designed specifically for the user.

User mode — Provides an interface between an application and an OS, and only has access to hardware resources through the code running in kernel mode.

User profile — A personal profile about the user, kept in the Windows NT Registry, which enables the user's desktop settings and other operating parameters to be retained from one session to another.

Utility software — Software packages, such as Nuts & Bolts or Norton Utilities, that provide the means for data recovery and repair, virus detection, and the creation of backups.

V.34 standard — A communications standard that transmits at 28,800 bps and/or 33,600 bps.

V.90 — A standard for data transmission over phone lines that can attain a speed of 56 Kbps. It replaces K56flex and x2 standards.

Value data — In Windows 9x, the name and value of a setting in the registry.

VCACHE — A built-in Windows 9x 32-bit software cache that doesn't take up conventional memory space or upper memory space, as SmartDrive does.

Vector table — *See* Interrupt vector table.

VESA (Video Electronics Standards Association) VL bus — A local bus used on 80486 computers for connecting 32-bit adapters directly to the local processor bus.

Video card — An interface card installed in the computer to control visual output on a monitor.

Video controller card — An interface card that controls the monitor. Also called video card or display adapter.

Video driver — A program that tells the computer how to effectively communicate with the video adapter card and monitor. It is often found on a floppy disk or CD that is shipped with the card.

Video RAM or VRAM — RAM on video cards that holds the data that is being passed from the computer to the monitor and can be accessed by two devices simultaneously. Higher resolutions often require more video memory.

Virtual device driver (VDD) or **VxD driver** — A 32-bit device driver running in protected mode.

Virtual file allocation table (VFAT) — A variation of the original DOS 16-bit FAT that allows for long filenames and 32-bit disk access.

Virtual machines (VM) — Multiple logical machines created within one physical machine by Windows, allowing applications to make serious errors within one logical machine without disturbing other programs and parts of the system.

Virtual memory manager — A Windows 9x program that controls the page table, swapping 4K pages in and out of physical RAM to and from the hard drive.

Virtual memory — A method whereby the OS uses the hard drive as though it were RAM.

Virtual real mode — An operating mode in which an OS provides an environment to a 16-bit program that acts like real mode.

Virus — A program that often has an incubation period, is infectious, and is intended to cause damage. A virus program might destroy data and programs or damage a disk drive's boot sector.

Virus signature — The distinguishing characteristics or patterns of a particular virus. Typically, AV signature updates for new viruses can be downloaded monthly from the Internet.

Voice — A group of samples for a musical instrument stored in a wavetable.

Volatile — Refers to a kind of RAM that is temporary, cannot hold data very long, and must be frequently refreshed.

Volt — A measure of electrical pressure differential. A computer ATX power supply usually provides five separate voltages: +12V, –12V, +5V, –5V, and +3V.

Voltage — Electrical differential that causes current to flow, measured in volts. *See* Volts.

Voltmeter — A device for measuring electrical voltage.

Volumes — In Windows 2000, a partition on a hard drive that is formatted as a dynamic drive.

Wait state — A clock tick in which nothing happens, used to ensure that the microprocessor isn't getting ahead of slower components. A 0-wait state is preferable to a 1-wait state. Too many wait states can slow a system down.

Warm boot — *See* Soft boot.

Wattage — Electrical power measured in watts.

Watts — The unit used to measure power. A typical computer may use a power supply that provides 200 watts.

Window RAM (WRAM) — Dual-ported video RAM that is faster and less expensive than VRAM. It has its own internal bus on the chip, with a data path that is 256 bits wide.

Windows Custom Setup — A setup feature that allows user customization of such things as directory locations, wallpaper settings, font selections, and many other features.

Windows Express Setup — A setup feature that automatically installs Windows in the most commonly used fashion.

Windows File Protection (WFP) — A Windows 2000 feature that protects system files from being corrupted or erased by applications or users.

Windows Internet Naming Service (WINS) — A Microsoft resolution service with a distributed database that tracks relationships between domain names and IP addresses. Compare to DNS.

Windows NT file system (NTFS) — A file system first introduced with Windows NT that provides improved security, disk storage, file compression, and long filenames.

Windows NT Registry — A database containing all configuration information, including the user profile and hardware settings. The NT Registry is not compatible with the Windows 9x Registry.

Workgroup — In Windows NT, a logical group of computers and users in which administration, resources, and security are distributed throughout the network, without centralized management or security.

Worm — An infestation designed to copy itself repeatedly to memory, on drive space, or on a network until little memory or disk space remains.

WOW (Win 16 on Win 32) — A group of programs provided by Windows NT to create a virtual DOS environment that emulates a 16-bit Windows environment, protecting the rest of the NT OS from 16-bit applications.

Write precompensation — A method whereby data is written faster to the tracks that are near the center of a disk.

XCOPY command — A faster external DOS COPY program that can copy subdirectories (/S) (for example, XCOPY *.* A:/S).

Zero insertion force (ZIF) — A socket feature that uses a small lever to apply even force when installing the microchip into the socket.

Zone bit recording — A method of storing data on a hard drive whereby the drive can have more sectors per track near the outside of the platter.

Windows 2000, 142, 162–163, 182–183
Windows NT, 142
Bootsect.dos, 142
boot sector viruses, 192–193
boot sequence, 10–11, 100–101
boot strap loader, 150–151
bracelets, ESD, 84–85
break codes, 24
bridges, 108
Briefcase, 30
brownouts, 78–79
browsers, 194–195
buck-boost UPS feature, 78
Burst EDO (BEDO), 88–89
busses, 2, 6–7, 88–89, 96–97

C

cabinet files, 160–161
cabling, 34–35
  floppy drives, 35
  hard drives, 36–37
  IDE connections, 20, 22–23, 36–37
  networks, 34, 110–111, 190–191
  null modem cables, 34
  parallel, 34
  printers, 104–105
  SCSI bus system, 38–39, 40–41
  serial, 34
caches, 6–7, 8–9, 48–49
cameras, 120
capacitors, 4–5, 62–63, 81
CD-R drives, 60–61
CD-ROM drives, 10, 23
  command prompt utility, 134
  DOS access to, 145–145
  drivers, 158–159
  IDE connection, 60–61
  MSCDEX.EXE, 60–61
  music CD failure, 58
  SCSI bus system, 38–39
  troubleshooting, 45
  Windows 95 ESD, 60
CD-RW drives, 60–61

Celeron processors, 6, 86
circuit boards, removing, 68
cleaning, 76–77, 82–83
closing windows, 116–117
clusters, 12
CMD.exe, 142–143
CMOS (complementary metal-oxide semiconductor) chips, 2
CMOS setup, 16–17, 98–99
  accessing, keys for, 98–99
  boot sequence, 10–11, 56–57, 100–101
  drive detection, 44
  error messages, 54–55
  floppy drives, 44–45, 100–101
  hard drives, 22, 100–101
  infrared port, 47
  IRQs, reserving, 100–101
  ports, 2, 47, 172–173
  printer port setup, 172–173
  virus protection, 192–193
coaxial cables, 110
cold boots, 56
combo cards, 108, 113
COMMAND.COM, 126, 128–129, 134–135, 176
command line prompt, 120–121, 128–129
  loading Windows 9x from, 178–179
  parameters in, 148–149
  Startup option, 164–165
  Windows 2000, 142
COM ports, 34, 98–99
compression, 148
Computer Management console, 140
Computer Manager, 154
computers, disposal of, 82–83
CONFIG.SYS, 126–128, 136–137, 176–177
Configuration Manager, 124–125, 128
connection problems, 54–55, 76–77

Control Panel, 116–117, 120–121
conventional memory, 8, 130
COPY command, 144
corrosion, 76
CPUs (central processing units), 6–7
  fans for, 2, 26
  form factors, 86–87
  heat sinks, 26
  installing, 26–27
  manufacturers, 86–87
  pins, number of, 94–95
  protected mode, 6
  ratings, 6
  real mode, 6
  slots for, 86–87
  sockets for, 94–95
  system board for, 2–3
  voltage, 2, 94–95
cross-linked clusters, 66–67
CRTs. See monitors
CTS (clear to send), 14–15
customer relations, 74–75, 184–185
CVT.EXE, 154–155
Cyrix CPUs, 86–87

D

data, protecting, 64
data transfer rate, 12
dates, 17, 100–101
date, setting, 17
DCE (data communications equipment) devices, 14
DDR SDRAM, 88
Defrag.exe, 144, 152–153
defragmenting hard drives, 66–67
device drivers, 42
  CD-ROM, 60–61, 158–159
  CONFIG.SYS, 126
  dynamically loaded, 123, 168–169
  HIMEM.SYS, 8–9
  installing, 168–169
  IO.SYS, 126

problems, isolating. *See* troubleshooting, procedure
processors. *See* CPUs (central processing units)
protected mode, 6, 166–167
protocols, network, 194–195

Q

questions for users, 184

R

radio frequency interference. *See* RFI (radio frequency interference)
Rambus RAM. *See* RDRAM (Rambus RAM)
RAM drives, 132
RAM (random access memory), 2, 8–9, 26–27, 48–49, 88–89
raw data printing, 172–173
rcp, 200
RDRAM (Rambus RAM), 88
read-only files, 146–147
real mode, 6, 128–129, 166–167
real-time clocks (RTCs), 100
Recovery Console, 164, 166, 183–184
Recycle Bin, 117
reformatting hard drives, 74–75
refreshing RAM, 88–89
refresh rate, 8
REGEDIT.EXE, 138–141, 154–155
Regedt32.exe, 154–155
registry, 138–141
  editing, 154–155
  keys, 138–141
Registry Checker, 138–139
Regular SCSI, 40–41
removable drives, 10
removing circuit boards, 68
reserved memory, 8–9
resetting modem command, 14–15
resistors, 4
Restart in MS-DOS mode option, 166–167

restoring deleted files, 117
rexec, 200
RFI (radio frequency interference), 84–85
RIMM, 8, 26, 88, 90–91
RISC (reduced instruction set computer), 7
RJ-45 connectors, 34
ROM BIOS. *See* BIOS (basic input output system)
Route, 200–201
routers, 108
RS-232 ports, 34
rsh, 200
RTCs (real-time clocks), 100
Run dialog box, 134–135
running programs, 116–117

S

Safe Mode, 138–139, 164–165, 174–175
safety procedures, 80–81
sags (current), 78
SBAC (SCSI bus adapter chip), 38
ScanDisk, 66–67, 152–153
SCANDISK command, 144–145
scanners, 120
SCANREG command, 145, 152–153
scheduling tasks, 148–149
screen resolutions, 8
SCSI (Small Computer System Interface)
  bus system, 38–41
  hard drives, 10–13
  interfaces on system boards, 92–93
  LVD (low voltage differential), 92–93
  Ntbootdd.sys, 162–163
  system resource use, 32
  upgrades from DOS, 180–181
  Windows 2000 boot file, 142–143

SDRAM (synchronous DRAM), 88–89
SECC (Single Edge Contact Cartridge), 86
secondary caches, 6, 48–49, 88
secondary storage devices. *See* storage devices
sectors, 12–13
seek time, 12
selecting Windows items, 116–117
SEP (Single Edge Processor), 86
serial ports, 34–35, 42–43, 98–99
serial port signals, 14
service call plans, 184–185
Session layer, 200
setup, 156–159
SETVER command, 144–145
Setver.exe, 134–135
SGRAM (synchronous graphics RAM), 88
shares, networks, 194–197
sharing folders, 191
shortcuts, 118–119, 189
shorts, 4
SIMMs, 8, 26–27, 90–91
slack, 150
slave devices, 36–37
SLIP (Serial Line Internet Protocol), 204–205
slot covers, 62–63
SmartDrive, 136–137
SMPT, 202–203
Socket 7, 86, 94–95
Socket 370, 86–87, 94–95
sockets (Internet). *See* Windows Sockets
sockets, system board, 94–95
SO-DIMMs, 46, 52–53
software installation, 170–171
SO-RIMMs, 46
sound cards
  IRQs, 32, 58
  music CD failure, 58
  port identification, 44
spacers, 20